Inside Quatro

UNCOVERING THE EXILE HISTORY OF THE ANC AND SWAPO

PAUL TREWHELA

First published by Jacana Media (Pty) Ltd in 2009
Second and Third impression, 2010

10 Orange Street
Sunnyside
Auckland Park 2092
South Africa
+27 11 628 3200
www.jacana.co.za

ISBN 978-1-77009-776-6

Typesetting system: $\LaTeX\ 2_\varepsilon$
Set in Sumner Stone's Cycles family, 10.5/14.25pt
Job no. 001355
Printed and bound by Ultra Litho (Pty) Limited, Johannesburg

See a complete list of Jacana titles at www.jacana.co.za

With love to Flo and my children,
Paul, Noel, Tania, Siobhan and Karl

The inmates' memories, however, proved harder to erase despite concerted ANC efforts. Prisoners repeatedly testified that as they left Quatro, both prior to 1988 and during the evacuation, they were threatened with death if they ever were to relate to anyone the events that had transpired during their internment. This attempt to prevent reports of the abuses from reaching the public was the first of many times that the ANC would participate in the politics of memory in order to keep the Quatro experience out of the official narrative of the struggle against apartheid.

— Todd Cleveland, '"We still want the truth": The ANC's Angolan detention camps and postapartheid memory' (*Comparative Studies of South Asia, Africa and the Middle East,* Vol. 25, No. 1, Duke University Press, United States, 2005. p 7). Paper first presented to the African Studies Association, Washington, DC, 5–8 December 2002.

Contents

Introduction

Except for one article, all the essays in this book are drawn from over fifty years of published journalism by me relating to South Africa and southern Africa.

Not written by me, though, is the article, 'A Miscarriage of Democracy: The ANC Security Department in the 1984 Mutiny in Umkhonto weSizwe' (pp. 8–45). I secured this first-hand autobiographical narrative for publication in April 1990, and it appeared in July 1990 in a banned exile journal produced in London, *Searchlight South Africa*, of which I was an editor. Because the journal was banned for commercial distribution in South Africa, access to this article in South Africa in print form was very limited (it was distributed later as a pamphlet and in a book, in tiny numbers). It became accessible on the internet about ten years ago. Jacana has now made it possible for this crucial contribution to South African history to become available in bookshops, and so finally overcome the restrictions placed on it by the apartheid regime. Its authors are not responsible for my own views, as their publisher in 1990, in any way. They have no doubt 'moved on' in the 20 years since it was written. Their essay retains its status, however, as a classic account of South African history. President Zuma's commemoration on 21 August at Pango camp in Angola of men killed in the mutiny in the ANC makes it all the more relevant.

I secured it for publication in accordance with a rough, informal division of labour between my co-editor, Baruch Hirson, and me. Baruch, my fellow political prisoner in Local Prison in Pretoria in the 1960s, tended to concentrate on historical writing pre-1960 and on the editorials, whereas with my background in the South African Communist Party and in journalism for Umkhonto weSizwe, I concentrated on more recent and contemporary history, with a principal focus on the African National Congress (ANC), the SACP and the South West Africa People's Organisation (SWAPO). The bulk of this book is made up of essays by me originally published in *Searchlight South Africa*, most of which were also subject to the banning order.

Baruch's and my Pretoria prison colleague, Roman Eisenstein, and I had our first introduction to the reality of SWAPO's terror in its camps in Angola, during a taped interview we conducted in London with Namibian twin sisters, Ndamona and Panduleni Kali, in November 1989. I transferred the interview into writing, and this was published in *SSA* No. 4, February 1990 — see Chapter 11 of this book.

Shortly before publication I was invited to journey to Windhoek to stay with the Kali sisters and to meet other ex-SWAPO detainees, in order to collect material for research and publication. I travelled to Windhoek in my half-term holiday as a schoolteacher in Britain, within days of the release of Nelson Mandela. My ticket was paid for by the single British left-wing group that supported our solidarity work, a breakaway grouping of the trotskyist Workers Revolutionary Party, which had brought the Kali sisters to Britain following a connection made with the WRP in the mid-Eighties by Hewat and Erica Beukes, from Windhoek, while studying in Britain. Hewat's family had a long and honourable history of opposition to colonialist rule in Namibia; Erica's brother, Walter Thiro, had died in one of SWAPO's prison camps.

I spent two weeks in Windhoek and Johannesburg in February 1990, and gathered a good deal of material for subsequent articles in *SSA* on Namibia.

When I set off, I didn't know whether I would be detained by the South African government at Windhoek airport, as I had not tried to secure a visa, despite having left South Africa on an exit permit, which made return a criminal offence, and I carried 40 copies of *SSA* No. 4 for distribution. On the plane from Lusaka to Windhoek, I happened by chance to sit next to Piers Vigne, son of the former Liberal Party leader Randolph Vigne, who had worked for the United Nations High Commissioner for Refugees and had been responsible for returning the survivors of SWAPO's camps in Angola to Namibia, prior to the elections in 1989. Piers agreed to carry half of the *SSA* load through customs, in case my lot was confiscated; and told me that, in his view, the ANC camps in exile had been worse than SWAPO's. (On balance, I doubt this.)

Back in Britain, our tiny *Searchlight South Africa*-based grouping planned a press conference in London on the SWAPO camps issue for mid-April, at which I spoke. On the same day as the conference, a now-defunct British newspaper, the *Sunday Correspondent*, carried a large article by Julian Ozanne about the mutiny in Umkhonto weSizwe in 1984, as well as Quatro prison camp and the crushing of democratic elections in the ANC in Tanzania in December 1989. The first verifiable public account of these previously hidden matters, it was based on interviews with the five authors who shortly afterwards provided the subsequent article in *Searchlight South Africa* No. 5.

The article mentioned that the five were living in the YMCA in Nairobi. I immediately made phone contact with them, with Ozanne and with other journalists in Nairobi. My prison and Umkhonto background enabled trust to be established quickly with the group in the YMCA, and I asked them to send me as quickly as possible a history of their experiences. I did not realise that a very substantial hand-written draft was already in existence, in their hands. This was developed further, photocopied, and sent to me by post. I transcribed it on the computer, subbed it, added very minor editorial corrections and wrote the accompanying unsigned introduction, 'Inside Quadro', passing the disk for final editorial preparation to Baruch. The original text referred to 'Quadro', which is the word for the number four in Spanish. I changed this spelling to 'Quatro' in subsequent texts, when I realised that this was the correct Portuguese for the number 'four', the nickname for The Fort prison in Johannesburg in Sowetan argot, expressed with sardonic humour in the general language spoken in Angola. A few days after Julian Ozanne's major article in the *Sunday Correspondent*, the *Times* in London carried a further article based on an interview with the five authors.

Later in the same month, Roman Eisenstein helped us to secure fax transmission from Nairobi of a letter from the five men addressed to Nelson Mandela, then in London on his first visit since release from prison, calling for a commission of inquiry into human rights abuses within the ANC in exile. The letter, calling for 'a morally clean leadership', was delivered to Mandela at his London hotel, and was probably one of the earliest sources for the future convening of the Truth and Reconciliation Commission.

We succeeded in bringing two of the five authors to London. One of them, Amos Maxongo, confronted Mandela face to face over the issues of Quatro during a press conference in London, but shortly afterwards returned to South Africa. For Bandile Ketelo we managed to secure a place at Ruskin College, Oxford, partly with the aid of a former member of the Umkhonto High Command, David Kitson, who had served twenty years in prison in Pretoria and had taught at Ruskin prior to being expelled by the SACP, a matter I discussed in an article in the final issue of *Searchlight South Africa* — see 'State Espionage and the ANC London Office', pp. 115–126 in this book. (The library at Ruskin College had been named in David's honour.)

Bandile Ketelo acquired university-entrance qualifications through his study at Ruskin, although very sadly the absolute poverty of his family in the Eastern Cape persuaded him to abandon his subsequent study for a degree at the University of Leeds. He then returned to his family in the Eastern Cape, and secured work — the only member of his family in paid employment — in the municipality at Alice.

From this first major article concerning the ANC in exile which we published in *Searchlight South Africa*, others followed. One in particular in the subsequent issue related to the political assassination in South Africa the same year of a colleague of the five authors, Sipho Phungulwa, following a visit to the ANC office in Umtata in the Transkei — see 'A Death in South Africa: The killing of Sipho Phungulwa', pp. 46–62.

The historical importance of the essay by Ketelo et al in *Searchlight South Africa* No. 5 — a classic text of modern South African history, and a magnificent piece of precise, informed, passionate writing in its own right — was recognised in it being cited as a source in the final report of the Truth and Reconciliation Commmission in 1998, eight years later (Volume Two, Chapter 4, paragraph 128). The killers of Sipho Phungulwa were granted amnesty by the TRC in the same year (paragraph 54).

Searchlight South Africa came about because of two very different journeys in the South African political experience, that of Baruch Hirson and myself. The journal could not have been created by either of us on our own, but the dominant contribution was that of Baruch. He willed himself into becoming *the* great historian of the South African left, author of a series of indispensable books, by never forgetting his roots as a physicist. On the one hand, he regarded his ever-growing archive — deposited at his death in 1999 at the Institute of Commonwealth Studies in the University of London — as one of which he was the custodian, not the owner. This was in the sense that it should be available (and it was available) to all who wished to make use of it, provided only that they respected the normal rules of an archive.

On the other hand, Baruch refused admission into his own writing (or any writing we published in *Searchlight South Africa*) of any claim to the status of fact which could not be, and had not been, verified. As a lifelong convinced marxist, and a trotskyist for more than half a century, Baruch never made any attempt to conceal his philosophical orientation; but he had no problem in rejecting any element in the classical heritage of marxism which he felt failed this empirical test. Engels's *Dialectics of Nature* went out of the window, because it failed the criterion of contemporary physics. So too did Trotsky's conception of the Soviet Union under Stalin as a 'deformed workers' state' (how could such a brutal monstrosity, based on the systemic working to death of slave labourers in the Gulag, be considered a means to the liberation of the workers?).

Baruch was open to quiet, thoughtful discussion about whether or not the Bolshevik seizure of power under the direction of Lenin and Trotsky had not after all been ... a putsch, a coup carried out by a despotically-intent minority, and a minority of a minority at that. The young Trotsky's warning in his *Report of the Siberian Delegation* at the founding conference of the Bolshevik tendency — that power would be ceded step by step by this route into the commanding grasp of a single individual — was never far from his mind. He acknowledged that Trotsky's crushing by armed might (and subsequent executions) of the revolt of the Kronstadt sailors in 1921, as with his crushing of the peasant revolt under the anarchist Makhno during the civil war in the Ukraine, had laid seeds for the future horror under Stalin.

So this was a marxist of a very un-South African kind, where narrow partisanship, narrow dogmatism and a fundamental sub-literacy in the texts was, and is, the norm. My own journey proceeded to a more thoroughgoing criticism of marxism from a more absolute stalinism than Baruch had ever accepted. I went from maoism, through the heady wine of the New Left of the 1968 period when Baruch was still in prison — with a particular delight in the writing of Herbert Marcuse — to a non-institutional trotskyism, independent of the rigid, petty, warring sects of the British left of the Seventies and early Eighties. My nine years in Ireland 'in exile from the exile', during which I spent a 48-hour stretch being questioned in the Bridewell Police Station, Dublin, under the Offences Against the State Act, provided me with some understanding of the possible fate of countries claimed by a nationalist movement governed by a practice of revolutionary violence.

One further intellectual strand in the fabric of understanding which informed *Searchlight South Africa* was its notion of the Soviet Union, the prime patron, as global superpower, of the ANC. From the start, when we began planning the journal in 1987, Baruch and I regarded the Soviet Union as doomed. For this understanding, which came to pass as we edited and wrote for the journal, we had the benefit of the first-hand knowledge and study of the Soviet Union of over a quarter of a century of our early editorial colleague, the Capetonian, Hillel Ticktin, whose doctoral thesis written in the Soviet Union in the Sixties had been rejected by his hosts, on the grounds of its incompatibility with their own view. From the early Sixties, Hillel was one of very, very few South Africans of any political hue who could read and speak Russian; and from a trotskyist background in Cape Town in the Fifties, he could think for himself. By the time we began preparing the journal, Hillel had for many years been a senior lecturer in the Department of Soviet and East European Studies at the University of Glasgow, and was lynchpin as editor of the journal *Critique*. He taught Baruch, and through Baruch, me, that the viability of the Soviet Union as a form of state could be summed up in a Russian workers' joke about the sclerotic Party elite which governed them: 'They pretend to pay us, and we pretend to work'.

That joke for us anticipated the downfall of the Soviet Union. As a form of state, economy and society it was an historical aberration, an historical abortion, neither capitalist nor a free socialist society, but instead one which in Marx's sense carried the seeds of its own demise within itself, given the nature of its internal contradictions. With this understanding, *Searchlight South Africa* was in advance of any other journal relating to South Africa. We held the 'theoretical' apparatus of the SACP in very poor regard.

When Baruch and I first came together in the mid-1980s, meeting for the first time since prison at the London reception for our heroic prison colleague Denis Goldberg after his release from a life sentence following the Rivonia Trial, we soon agreed that the petty orthodoxies of the British left and the trench warfare of the South African left allowed no space for our own thinking. Baruch's solution was that we do our own publishing; and since he was by that time in retirement from university teaching (and since I was working full-time as a schoolteacher, responsible for five children in full-time education) by far the greater burden fell on Baruch. All the typesetting was done by Baruch on his computer in the front room of his London house; he made all the arrangements with the printers, arranged all the subscriptions, solicited donations that enabled us to hobble from one issue to another, and dispatched new issues to bookshops and subscribers, as well as maintaining a very wide international correspondence and working on book after book of his own. All this from a man increasingly crippled by a spinal disorder, who never for one moment pleaded for pity.

Nearly all the activist liaison within a very small committee — first called 'Solidarity with ex-SWAPO Detainees', then 'Justice for Southern Africa' — fell within my province. (Baruch's increasing problem with mobility was partly an issue here.) The hero in this solidarity activity was our indefatigable British friend and colleague, Bill McElroy, former Labour councillor in the London borough of Westminster, former Scouser (Liverpudlian) from an Irish-Scots working-class family, former trotskyist, then full-time schoolteacher and permanent welcomer of South Africans from the diaspora to his small flat in working-class Hackney, on the borders of the East End of London. Three of the authors/contributors to 'A Miscarriage of Democracy' stayed in Bill's flat for one time or another during their time in London. Liaison with British left-wing groups (especially the breakaway, more libertarian wing of the trotskyist Workers Revolutionary Party), with the Foreign Office, with Parliament, with university funding agencies and with the national press in London was mainly in Bill's hands, partly in association with me.

This is given warm acknowledgement by Carol Lee in her commemoratory book written in tribute to the young people of the Soweto school students' revolt, *A Child Called Freedom* (Century/Random House, 2006). As Carol writes, I was throughout an 'enthusiastic ally' of this book, which more than any other so far, took further the account in *Searchlight South Africa* of the history of that extraordinary and inspiring generation. Omry Mathabatha Makgoale, the subject of Chapter 18 of Carol's book, 'Where Freedom Lives', shines through from her writing. Under his exile travelling names of Sidwell Moroka and Mhlongo, he is the guiding thread in the article 'A Miscarriage of Democracy' as re-published here. A history of South Africa of the past thirty-odd years is present with this individual, with a focus on the life and character of a single person.

A further chapter in Carol's book, 'Tebello's story', was published very shortly before the death of its subject, Tebello Motapanyane, one of the principal leaders of the events in Soweto on 16 June 1976, whose obituary by me appears in this book in Chapter 10.

A South African friend has written that my article from 1993, 'The ANC Prison Camps: An Audit of Three Years' (pp. 63–90), indicates how isolated *Searchlight South Africa* and Justice for Southern Africa were, at that time, in seeking justice for the detainees. We were totally isolated, bar the single fraction of the Workers Revolutionary Party. At a joint meeting on South Africa held at the London School of Economics, at which *Searchlight South Africa* was one of three contributory groupings, I was told from the platform that I 'deserved a bullet' when I compared the ANC's prison camps with the IRA's bombing campaign of civilian targets. The systemic cruelty of this generality of the trotskyist left in Britain was a great educator to me, at that time, and afterwards, in the pernicious character of Marx's doctrine of the dictatorship of the proletariat; and the degree to which this 'progressive' advocacy of dictatorship among the British intelligentsia was a masked vehicle for personality disorders of all kinds.

A Country Unmasked, the autobiographical history of the Truth and Reconciliation Commission by its deputy-chairman, Alex Boraine (OUP, 2000), makes clear what a sticking point was the issue of 'Quatro' — a metaphor here for the ANC's practice of human rights abuses of its own members — in the contested history of the relation of the ANC's National Executive Committee to the formation and proceedings of the TRC and especially to its final report.

Searchlight South Africa was one of the contributory streams feeding into the TRC, as it was into the convening by the ANC of the Skweyiya (1992) and Motsuenyane (1993) Commissions into human rights abuses in the ANC in exile, before it. The National Party (as it would) included numerous articles from *Searchlight South Africa* (which it had banned, and whose editors it had jailed) in its own submissions to the TRC. So it goes....

Two of the authors of 'A Miscarriage of Democracy', Amos Maxongo and Ronnie Masango, gave evidence to the TRC. Of the individuals mentioned by name in that article, or in subsequent articles in *Searchlight South Africa*, Olefile Samuel Mngqibisa — former batman to the subsequent (disgraced) Minister of Defence, Joe Modise, and a man of truly extraordinary courage — gave uncompromising witness in particular before the Commission. (A further detainee in Quatro, Mwezi Twala, had previously published his own story in *Mbokodo. Inside MK: Mwezi Twala — A Soldier's Story*, written with Ed Bernard, Jonathan Ball, Johannesburg, 1994, including material drawn from 'A Miscarriage of Democracy'.) Generally, the great bulk of the ANC's surviving victims from its suppression of the mutiny in Umkhonto in 1984, and other acts of suppression of opinion, appear to have had little confidence that any good would come from the TRC. In this they were justified, in so far as none of the perpetrators was punished in any way, or relieved of their positions in the state or other institutions. Since the perpetrators, as members of the ANC's Department of Intelligence and Security (iMbokodo, the grindstone), had passed almost without exception into office in the state, their former victims had reason to continue to fear them, and did not believe that a few critical or beneficent phrases from the TRC would make any difference to their own safety. They remain thus a silent generation. A quarter century after the mutiny in Angola, they keep their heads down. This is not yet, for them, the time to speak, although most seem to have regarded the defenestration of Thabo Mbeki and his cabal by the ANC membership at its conference at Polokwane in December 2007 as a good omen. At least this main pillar of their suppression in exile, as they perceived it, had collapsed.

Baruch and I took the view that only good could come from every revelation from this sunless chamber of the South African experience. In this sense we welcomed the TRC, which we felt we had assisted into existence, to some degree, as mid-wives, even while having no illusions as to its ability to banish the reality of South Africa's demons. At the same time, we did not forget the sense of the advice given by one of the Rivonia Trialists and Robben Island lifers, on his return from prison, to the parents of one of the Quatro victims: under no circumstances to make an issue of what had happened, or their son most likely would be killed.

A serious effort has been made to provide a thorough Index, with as complete a set of references as possible to people in southern Africa mentioned in the text. A wide range of names is presented, especially because of the autobiographical character of the essays on the exile experience of the ANC (Chapter 2) and, in interview, SWAPO in exile (Chapter 11).

There were two different kinds of problem in compiling an Index. For members of the ANC in exile, the problem was to align wherever possible the real name of a person with that person's 'travelling' name, or names, used in exile. This was made possible in most cases by the TRC — one of its blessings to the country and to the region as a whole. Submissions by the ANC to the TRC, available online, provide a wealth of information for the historian as well as for surviving individuals, and friends and relatives, about identities and political roles of members of the ANC.

As far as possible, use has been made of this great resource of the TRC in compiling the Index. There are frequently several names recorded for individual ANC members cited in the text. This makes for an unusually long Index; and a number of categories had to be left out for reasons of space. Its advantage is that — perhaps for the first time — this book provides a comparatively inexpensive record available in print of this past but not vanished chapter of the South African historical experience. (Baruch Hirson loved to quote the saying of a character in the work of William Faulkner, the American novelist of the South: 'The past is never dead. It is not even past.')

The problem in relation to SWAPO is in many ways the reverse, to the great disadvantage of Namibians. SWAPO in government convened no Truth and Reconciliation Commission for Namibians. (The Ya Otto Commission convened by SWAPO in 1976 was a scam.) It had too much to hide. The forces that might have compelled it to do so were too weak. While the names of SWAPO's victims given in this book are their real names, those of their persecutors below the level of the Great Men who gave the orders are recorded here only in the form of their 'combat' names. (Although their principal form of combat appears to have been against their fellow members.) As for Zimbabwe — in written terms, even more of the past is a blank, if one were to leave out the exceptional work of the Catholic Commission for Justice and Peace and the Legal Resources Foundation in Harare in uncovering the genocidal massacres by the Mugabe regime in Matabeleland.

To that degree, the principal focus here is not on the great names of recent South African and Namibian history but the nameless ones. This book is in some sense a memorial to the poor bloody infantry of war, the ones with whose lives wars are won and lost.

Paul Trewhela
September 2009

PART A

Inside Quadro & After

1 *Inside Quadro**

END OF AN ERA

The first-hand testimony by former combatants of Umkhonto weSizwe (MK) about the ANC prison regime, together with press reports that began to appear in Britain in March this year, are an event in South African history. Never before has such concentrated factual evidence been presented about the inner nature of the ANC and its *éminence grise*, the South African Communist Party.

If people wish to understand the operation of the ANC/SACP, they must look here. This is the view behind the proscenium arch, behind the scenery, where the machinery that runs the whole show is revealed in its actual workings.

The ANC/SACP did a very good job in preventing public knowledge of its secret history from emerging, and the testimony of the Nairobi five shows how. (Two other South Africans, both women, are with the five in Nairobi at the time of writing, but they have not yet gone public about their experiences.) Those who survived the Gulag system of the ANC/SACP did so knowing that to reveal what they had been through meant re-arrest, renewed tortures, and in all probability, death. They had to sign a form committing them to silence.

As they repeat in this issue, the ex-detainees in Nairobi have revealed that other prisoners, including Leon Madakeni, star of the South African film *Wanaka*, as well as Nonhlanhla Makhuba and another person known as Mark, committed suicide rather than suffer re-arrest at the hands of their KGB-trained guardians. Madakeni drove a tractor up a steep incline in Angola, put it into neutral and died as it somersaulted down the hill (*Sunday Correspondent*, 8 April).

The ex-guerrillas in Nairobi displayed immense courage in speaking out publicly, first through the *Sunday Correspondent* in Britain on April 8 and then in the *Times* on April 11. It was another indicator of the crack-up of stalinism internationally: a snippet of South African *glasnost*.

---

*First published in *Searchlight South Africa* No. 5 (July 1990), pp. 30–34.

Their courage might have contributed to secure the lives of eight colleagues who had fled Tanzania through Malawi hoping to reach South Africa on the principle that better a South African jail than the ANC 'security'. This group, including two leaders of the mutiny in the ANC camps in Angola in 1984, arrived in South Africa in April, was immediately detained at Jan Smuts Airport by the security police for interrogation, and then released three weeks later. The day after their release they gave a press conference in Johannesburg, confirming the account of the mutiny published here.

This regime of terror, extending beyond the gates of the ANC/SACP 'Buchenwald' of Quadro, was a necessary element in the total practice of repression and deception which made the Anti-Apartheid Movement the most successful Popular Front lobby for stalinism anywhere in the world. No international stalinist-run public organization has ever had such an influence and shown such stability, reaching into so many major countries, for so long,

In its thirty years' existence, the AAM put international collaborative organisations of the period of the Spanish Civil War and of the Stalin–Roosevelt–Churchill alliance to shame. Extending to the press, the churches, the bourgeois political parties, the trade unions and the radical, even the 'trotskyist' left, the AAM has been an outstanding success for stalinism, as the review of Victoria Brittain's book in this issue shows. [This review, 'A Question of Truthfulness', written by me, is not included in the present book — PT.]

Vital to its success has been a practice of open and covert censorship now blown wide open, in which individuals such as Ms Brittain have played a sterling part. The ANC's prisoners were its necessary sacrificial victims.

THE KGB IN AFRICA

The prison system to which they were subject goes back to the late 1960s. It was the successor and the complement to the prison system on which blacks in South Africa are weaned with their mothers' milk. In 1969 one of the editors of this journal [Paul Trewhela] met two South Africans in London who said they had fought in the first MK guerrilla operation in mid-1967 — a disastrous fiasco across the Zambezi River into the Wankie area of Rhodesia, along with guerrillas from the Zimbabwe African People's Union (ZAPU), then led by James Chikerema. (The ZAPU president, Joshua Nkomo, was in detention.) The two men described how they had eventually succeeded in escaping from Rhodesia, and how their criticism of the operation had led to their imprisonment in an ANC camp in Tanzania. An article on the theme appeared the same year in the British radical newspaper, *Black Dwarf*, then edited by Tariq Ali.

The revelations by the Nairobi five indicate how little has changed. In his book, *Black Politics in South Africa since 1945* (Ravan, 1987), Tom Lodge writes:

> In 1968 a batch of Umkhonto defectors from camps in Tanzania sought asylum in Kenya, alleging that there was widespread dissatisfaction within the camps. They accused their commanders of extravagant living and ethnic favouritism. The first Rhodesian mission, they alleged, was a suicide mission to eliminate dissenters. In political discussions no challenge to a pro-Soviet position was allowed. (p 300)

From 1968 to 1990, nothing basic altered in the ANC's internal regime in the camps, except that in the high noon of the Brezhnev era it operated para-statal powers under civil war conditions in Angola, where a large Cuban and Soviet presence permitted the ANC security apparatus to 'bestride the narrow world like a Colossus.'

From the account of the ex-mutineers, ANC administrative bodies ruled over its elected bodies, the security department ruled over the administrative organs, and KGB-trained officials — no doubt members of the SACP — ruled over the security apparatus. Umkhonto weSizwe functioned as an extension in Africa of the KGB. Its role in the civil war in Angola was to serve primarily as a surrogate to Soviet foreign policy interests, so that when the ANC rebels proposed that their fight be diverted to South Africa this counted as unpardonable cheek, to be ruthlessly punished. Over its own members, the ANC security apparatus ruled with all the arrogance of a totalitarian power.

There is a direct line of connection between the ANC reign of terror in its prisons — which a UN High Commissioner for Refugees official described as more frightening than SWAPO prisons — and the 'necklace' killings exercised by ANC supporters within South Africa, especially during the period of the 1984-86 township revolt, but now once again revived against oppositional groupings such as AZAPO. (The ANC's 'necklace' politics was also a definite contributory element provoking the carnage in Natal.) Two former ANC prisoners, Similo Boltina and his wife Nosisana, were in fact necklaced on their return to South Africa in 1986, after having been repatriated by the Red Cross (letter from Bandile Ketelo, 9 April 1990).

This is the significance of the 'Winnie issue.' When on 16 February last year, leaders of the Mass Democratic Movement publicly expressed their 'outrage' at Winnie Mandela's 'obvious complicity' in the abduction and assault on 14-year-old Stompie Moeketsi Seipei, leading to his murder, this was in response to very widespread and very well-founded revulsion among Soweto residents — especially ANC supporters such as members of the Federation of Transvaal

Women (FEDTRAW). They were enraged by the jackboot politics of the so-called Mandela United Football Team, whose 'coach' — to the satisfaction of FEDTRAW members — has been convicted of Stompie's murder.

This squad of thugs, based in Mrs Mandela's house, acted within Soweto in the same way that the ANC/SACP security acted abroad, in Angola, Tanzania, Zambia, Mozambique, Ethiopia and Uganda. (According to the ex-detainees, the KGB-apparatus in the ANC even sent its troops to Rhodesia in 1979 to fight against the guerrillas of the Zimbabwe African National Union, ZANU, which was not a Soviet client.)

For this reason, the integration of certain members of MK into the South African army and police — as the MK commander, Joe Modise, a major author of abuses, is seeking — should not present any serious problems. They speak the same language, they are 'all South Africans.' The welcome of Captain Dirk Coetzee, head of the regime's assassination squad, into the arms of the ANC is an indication of the future course of development, as is the decision by the new SWAPO government in Namibia to appoint a number of top South African security policemen, including the former chief of police in the Ovambo region, Derek Brune, to head its secret organs of coercion.

The South African prison system was replicated in the ANC prisons even into everyday terminology, above all at Quadro. This is a name that requires to become common currency in political discourse: it is the Portuguese for 'No. 4' the name used throughout South Africa for the notorious black section of the prison at the Fort. Sneers by warders at soft conditions in 'Five Star Hotels', the common description of punishment cells as *kulukudu* (*Sunday Correspondent*, 8 April) and the whole atmosphere of brutal crassness is quintessentially South African, spiced with the added sadism of the Gulag. The ANC prison system combined the worst of South African and of Russian conditions fused together, and it is this new social type — as a refinement and augmentation of each — that is now offered to the people of South Africa as the symbol of freedom.

BEGINNING OF AN ERA

In returning to South Africa, the ex-ANC detainees have the advantage of the Namibian experience before them. They need an organization of their relatives, along the lines of the Committee of Parents in Namibia, and an organization of former prisoners themselves, such as the Political Consultative Council of ex-SWAPO Detainees (PCC). The ex-detainees who returned to Johannesburg in April have already mentioned that they intend to form an association of 'parents of those who died or were detained in exile' (*Liberation*, 17 May).

These young people — the Nairobi five are aged between 28 and 33 — represent the flower of the generation of the Soweto students' revolt. This was the beginning of their political awakening. The experience of stalinist and nationalist terror at the hands of the ANC/SACP represents a second phase in a cruel journey of consciousness. A third phase is now beginning, in which these young people will be required to discover what further changes in society and thought are needed to bring a richly expressive democracy into being in southern Africa.

Compared with the Namibian experience (see *Searchlight South Africa* No. 4, and this issue — Chapter 11 in this book), South African conditions are both more and less favourable. Unlike in Namibia, the churches in South Africa are not absolutely glued to the torturers. A letter from the group in Nairobi was sympathetically received by the Rev. Frank Chikane, secretary of the South African Council of Churches. Archbishop Desmond Tutu met the ex-detainees when he was in Nairobi early in April and arranged for them to get accommodation at the YMCA there, paid for by the All-African Council of Churches. (Up to that time they had first been in prison in Kenya, since they had arrived absolutely without documents, and had then been living rough.) The Archbishop later took up the mutineers' demand for a commission of inquiry with the National Executive Committee of the ANC. He got no response.

We join with these ex-detainees in demanding that the ANC set up an independent commission of inquiry into the atrocities perpetrated in the Umkhonto weSizwe camps.

Mandela's statement acknowledging that torture had taken place was in any case very different from the ferocious silence of President Nujoma, the chief architect of SWAPO's purges. The ex-detainees' demand for action against top leaders of the ANC, however, goes way beyond what the organization is likely to be able to concede. Therein lies its radical character.

These positive currents, however, are negated by the convergence of very powerful capitalist and stalinist interests which together aim to fix the future with the utmost *Realpolitik*. The leaders of the unions, previously independent and now politically prisoners of the SACP, have become the engineers of the SACP/capitalist fix, and the workers — even when eager for socialism — are disoriented.

It is likely that there will be a very violent period as the ANC's drive for its supposed target of one million members gets under way, through which it aims to wipe the floor with rival groupings that accuse it of sell-out. It is possible that the methods of Quadro will become part of the daily metabolism of South African life. Future capitalist profitability requires in any case that a massive defeat be inflicted on the workers. The Young Upwardly Mobile (Yuppy) stratum of black petty bourgeoisie will ruthlessly attempt to enforce and secure the conditions for its material advance.

Under these conditions, the ex-detainees will need to find the route to the consciousness of the workers, both to win a base of support for their own defence (even survival) and to help speed up the process of political clarification about the nature of the ANC. In the meantime, defensive alliances need urgently to be made: with the left wing of the unions, socialist political groupings of whatever kind, opponents of the new capitalist/ANC autocracy, concerned individuals in the press, the universities and the legal system; and not least, with the ex-SWAPO detainees in Namibia.

As a yeast in which the fermentation of new ideas can develop, the ex-ANC detainees on their return to South Africa will prove one of the most favourable of human resources for a democratic future. They know the future governors of South Africa from the inside. They need the greatest possible international and local support to protect them under very dangerous conditions of life in the townships.

They too will need beware the siren voices of their KGB-trained persecutors, who seek to persuade them that the Brezhnev wolf in Angola has been transformed into a Gorbachev lamb in South Africa. In particular, they will need to inquire whether Joe Slovo, the scourge of Joseph Stalin in 1990, and general secretary of the SACP, is the same Slovo who was chief of staff of MK in the glory days of Quadro. What did he know? When did he know it? And what did he do about it?

Author's note, August 2009: This essay appeared in *Searchlight South Africa* No. 5 (July 1990) as an unsigned introduction by me to the study 'A Miscarriage of Democracy', by five former members of Umkhonto weSizwe, which follows. I regard 'A Miscarriage of Democracy' as the most important and most reliable first-hand historical account of life within the ANC in exile to have emerged so far from within its ranks, covering the ten years prior to its unbanning.

The order of the apartheid government banning *Searchlight South Africa* from being distributed commercially in South Africa remained in force when this issue was published, and for a substantial time afterwards, long after journals published by the ANC, the SACP and other organisations were sold freely. Publication of this history in the present volume is the first time that readers in southern Africa have proper access to this crucial text in print form.

2 *A Miscarriage of Democracy**

The ANC Security Department in the 1984 Mutiny in Umkhonto weSizwe

BANDILE KETELO, AMOS MAXONGO
ZAMXOLO TSHONA, RONNIE MASANGO
and
LUVO MBENGO

PRELUDE TO MUTINY

On 12 January 1984, a strong delegation of ANC National Executive Committee members arrived at Caculama, the main training centre of Umkhonto weSizwe (MK) in the town of Malanje, Angola. In the past, such a visit by the ANC leadership — including its top man, the organization's president, Oliver Tambo — would have been prepared for several days, or even weeks, before their actual arrival. Not so this time. This one was both an emergency and a surprise visit.

It was not difficult to guess the reason for such a visit. For several days, sounds of gunfire had been filling the air almost every hour of the day at Kangandala, near Malanje, and just about 80 kilometres from Caculama, where President Tambo and his entourage were staying. The combatants of MK had refused to go into counter-insurgency operations against the forces of the Union for Total Independence of Angola (UNITA) in the civil war in Angola and defied the security personnel of the ANC. They had decided to make their voice of protest more strongly by shooting randomly into the air. It was pointed out to all the commanding personnel in the area that the shooting was not meant to endanger anybody's life, but was just meant to be a louder call to the ANC leadership to address themselves afresh to the desperate problems facing our organization.

*First published in *Searchlight South Africa* No. 5 (July 1990), pp. 35–68.

Clearly put forward also was that only Tambo, the president of the ANC, Joe Slovo, the chief-of-staff of the army, and Chris Hani, then the army commissar, would be welcome to attend to these issues. An illusory idea still lingered in the minds of the MK combatants that most of the wrong things in our organization happened without the knowledge of Tambo, and that given a clear picture of the situation, he would act to see to their solution.

Joe Slovo, now secretary of the South African Communist Party (SACP), had himself risen to prominence among the new generation as a result of the daring combat operations which MK units had carried out against the racist regime. In 1983 the SACP quarterly, the *African Communist*, had carried an article by Slovo, about J.B. Marks, another of the ANC/SACP leaders, who had died in Moscow in 1972. That article, emphasizing democracy in the liberation struggle, was a fleeting glance into some of the rarely talked-of episodes in the proceedings of the Morogoro Consultative Conference of the ANC, held in Tanzania in 1969. It might have been written for a completely different purpose, but for the guerrillas of MK it was a call for active involvement into the solution of our problems.

[At this point in their narrative, the five authors gave attention for the first time to Chris Hani: the political commissar of Umkhonto in 1984, a member of the ANC National Executive Committee and the future general secretary of the SACP. Following the return of the exiles, he was assassinated in Boksburg, near Johannesburg, on 10 April 1993, three years after this article was written. Despite what follows relating to Hani's role in suppressing the mutiny in Angola, the five authors utterly repudiated his criminal assassination. The editors of *Searchlight South Africa* condemned it as an 'act of terror which we abominate'. (Editorial, 'Chris Hani: Murder most terrible', *SSA* No. 10, April 1993) — Paul Trewhela, August 2009]

The guerrillas in Angola levelled their bitterest criticisms against three men in the NEC of the ANC, men who had had a much more direct involvement in the running of our army. The first was Joe Modise, army commander of the ANC since 1969. He was looked down upon by the majority of combatants as a man responsible for the failures of our army to put up a strong fight against the racist regime, a man who had stifled its growth and expansion. He was above all seen as someone who engaged himself in corrupt money-making ventures, abusing his position in the army.

The second was Mzwandile Piliso, the chief of security. He was then the most notorious, the most feared, soulless ideologue of the suppression of dissent and democracy in the ANC. The last one was Andrew Masondo, freed from Robben Island after twelve years of imprisonment, who had joined the

ANC leadership in exile after the 1976 Soweto uprisings. In 1984 he was the national commissar of the ANC, and was therefore responsible for supervision of the implementation of NEC decisions and political guidance of the ANC personnel. Masondo was to use this responsibility to defend corruption, and was himself involved in abuse of his position to exploit young and ignorant women and girls. He was also a key figure in the running of the notorious ANC prison camp known to the cadres as 'Quadro' (or four, in Portuguese). It was nicknamed Quadro after the Fort, the rough and notorious prison for blacks in Johannesburg, known to everybody as 'No. 4'.

Such was the situation when Chris Hani together with Joe Nhlanhla, then the administrative secretary of the NEC and now chief of security, and Lehlohonolo Moloi, now chief of operations, arrived in Kangandala under instructions from the NEC to silence the ever-sounding guns of the guerrillas. Chris Hani was suddenly thrown into confusion by the effusive behaviour of the combatants as they expressed their grievances, wielding AKs which they vowed never to surrender until their demands were met. What were these demands?

First, the soldiers demanded an immediate end to the war by the MK forces against UNITA and the transfer of all the manpower used in that war to our main theatre of war in South Africa. Secondly, they demanded the immediate suspension of the ANC security apparatus, as well as an investigation of its activities and of the prison camp Quadro, then called 'Buchenwald' after one of the most notorious Nazi concentration camps. Lastly, they demanded that Tambo himself come and address the soldiers on the solution to these problems. All that Chris Hani could do in this situation was to appeal for an end to random shootings in the air, and to appeal to the soldiers to await the decision of the NEC after he had sent it the feedback about his mission.

THE BEGINNINGS OF QUADRO

The demands mentioned above had far-reaching political implications for the ANC, which had managed to win high political prestige as the future government of South Africa. But for anyone to appreciate their seriousness, one must go back to the history of the ANC following the arrival of the youth of the Soweto uprisings to join the ANC. This historical approach to the mutiny of 1984 is more often than not deliberately neglected by the ANC leadership whenever they find themselves having to talk about this event. More than anything else, they fear the historical realities which justify this mutiny and show it to have been inevitable, given the genuine causes behind it.

The mainspring of the 1984 mutiny, known within the ANC as *Mkatashingo,* is the suppression of democracy by the ANC leadership. This suppression of democracy had taken different forms at different times in the development of the ANC, and it had given birth to resistance from the ANC membership at different times, taking forms corresponding to the nature of the suppression mechanisms. We shall confine ourselves to those periods that had become landmarks and turning points in this history.

The first such remarkable events of resistance to the machinations of the ANC leadership were in 1979 at a camp known among South Africans as Fazenda, but whose actual name was Villa Rosa, to the north of Quibaxe, in northern Angola. The majority of the trained personnel of MK had been shifted from Quibaxe in November 1978 to occupy this camp, where they were expected to undergo a survival course to prepare for harsh conditions of rural guerrilla warfare. With the promise that the course would take three months, after which the combatants would be infiltrated back into South Africa to carry out combat missions, everybody took the course in their stride and with high morale. After the first three months and the introduction of a second course, it became crystal clear that we were being fooled, to keep us busy. Voices of discontent began to surface in certain circles of the armed forces. The main cause of discontent was the suppression of our uncontrollable desire to leave Angola and enter into South Africa to supplement the mass political upsurges of the people. Alongside this were also complaints about inefficiency of the front commanders and suspicions that they were treacherously involved in the failure of many missions, leading to the mysterious death of our combatants in South Africa.

Mzwandile Piliso was accused of over-emphasizing the security of our movement against the internal enemy, at the expense of promoting comradely relations among the armed forces. He was promoting unpopular lackeys within the army while suppressing those who fell to his disfavour, branding them as enemy agents who would 'rot in the camps of Angola'. Most of those lackeys defected to the racist South African regime whenever they found it opportune. Such was the case with the most notorious traitors in MK like Thabo Selepe, Jackson, Miki and others, all of whom wormed their way up in the military structures assisted by Piliso.

The late Joe Gqabi [assassinated in Harare in 1981, while ANC representative in Zimbabwe] attended one such explosive meeting and commended the soldiers for their spirit of openness and criticism. Fazenda was getting out of hand, and the feeling of discontent began to spill into certain nearby ANC bases.

Something had to be done to stamp down this resistance. The security organ of the ANC, which till then had just been composed of a few old cadres of the 1960s, began to be reorganized in all of the camps. Young men from our own generation who had recently undergone courses in the Soviet Union and East Germany were spread into all the camps. It was during this time that construction of a prison camp near Quibaxe was speeded up, which later took the form of the dreaded Quadro. ANC general meetings, which were held weekly, and had been platforms for criticism and self-criticism, were now terminated.

The very first occupants of Quadro prison were three men from Fazenda: Ernest Khumalo, Solly Ngungunyana and Drake, who had defiantly left Fazenda to go to Luanda, where they hoped to meet the ANC chief representative, Max Moabi, to demand their own resignation from the ANC. The ANC did not accept resignation of its membership [still the same ten years later, in January this year, after the authors of this document had presented their resignations — PT]. Worse still, this was in Angola, a country where lawlessness reigned. After being beaten in a street in Luanda by ANC and Angolan security, they were bundled into a truck and taken straight to Quadro. Solly was released after two years, Ernest in 1984 and Drake's end is still unknown. The camp remained highly secret within the ANC. Everyone sent to work there as a security guard undoubtedly had to have proved his loyalty to Mzwandile Piliso, and was expected not to disclose anything to anybody. Even among the NEC, the only ones who had access to Quadro were Mzwandile Piliso, Joe Modise and Andrew Masondo.

AN 'INTERNAL–ENEMY–DANGER-PSYCHOSIS'

To completely efface the spirit of resistance in Fazenda, the majority of the MK forces there were taken to Zimbabwe, where they fought alongside guerrillas of the Zimbabwe African People's Union (ZAPU), led by Joshua Nkomo, against the Smith forces as well as the guerrillas of the Zimbabwe African National Union (ZANU), led by Robert Mugabe. Many worthy fighters perished there. Fazenda camp was closed in 1980, and fighters there were distributed among the two main camps of the ANC, Pango and Quibaxe, both to the north of Luanda. The chapter on Fazenda was closed.

But a burning urge to liberate South Africa, with the only language the Boers understood, the gun, could not be trampled on as contemptuously as that. Yet it had become very dangerous to raise even a voice against the leadership. The ANC had become divided into a force of the rank and file and that of the leadership clubbed together with the security apparatus, which had grown to such enormous levels that practically every administration of whatever ANC institution was run by the security personnel, and practically every problem was viewed as a security risk and an 'enemy machination'.

In a bid to strengthen their repressive apparatus, Andrew Masondo created a security crack force in a camp known as Viana, near Luanda. This unit, known as ODP (People's Defence Organisation), was composed mainly of very young men or boys. Its tasks were to guard the ANC leadership when they paid visits to different camps, to enforce discipline and bash up any forms of dissent and 'disloyalty'. By this time, after the Fazenda events, the ANC leaders had begun to whip up an 'internal-enemy-danger-psychosis,' and whenever they visited the camps they had to be heavily guarded. Worse still if it was Tambo who visited: the whole camp would be disarmed, and only the security personnel and those attached to it would be allowed to carry weapons.

The next hot spot for the ANC was in Zambia, where the headquarters of the ANC was based and where most of the leadership was living. This was in 1980. MK cadres, who had been drilled for months in 'communist ideology' of the Soviet-East European type to denounce all luxuries and accept the hazards of the struggle, here came into direct confrontation with the opposite way of life lived by the ANC leaders. It became clear that the financial support extended to the ANC was used to finance the lavish way of life of the ANC leadership. Corruption, involving rackets of car, diamond and drug smuggling, was on a high rise. The security department itself was rocked by internal dissent between those who supported a heavy-handed approach and the predominantly young cadres who opposed it.

There was also the burning problem of the insignificant progress made by our forces in South Africa, at a time when our people were alone locked into bitter mass struggles against the racists. This aspect was further complicated by the decision of the NEC to send back to Angola a batch of MK forces who had survived the war in Zimbabwe and were discovered by the provisional government authorities in the assembly points, disguised as ZAPU guerrillas. These guerrillas, still itching to go to South Africa and aware of the conditions in the camps in Angola, refused point blank the instructions to return to Angola.

Faced with these and many other related problems, a meeting was arranged between the leadership and the representatives of the three detachments, the Luthuli, June 16 and Moncada detachments. Among their representatives, the June 16 Detachment was represented by Sidwell Moroka and Moncada by Timmy Zakhele, both of whom later ended up in Quadro. The June 16 Detachment advanced the proposal to hold a conference of the whole ANC membership where these issues could be settled democratically. This proposal, which had popular backing from the overwhelming majority of the young cadres, was rejected by the ANC leadership, which never accepts any idea that puts in question its competence and credibility to lead.

It was in the process of these discussions that a discovery of a spy network was disclosed and a clampdown on the 'ambitious young men who wanted to overthrow the leadership of Tambo' was put into operation. The ANC security went into full swing, detaining the so-called enemy spies and those who were proponents of the conference. It was said that this spy-ring was not only concentrated in Zambia, but was everywhere that the ANC had its personnel. Many of these young men — Pharoah, Vusi Mayekiso, Kenneth Mahamba, Oshkosh and others — were later known to have died under torture and beatings in Quadro prison camp. Others such as Godfrey Pulu, Sticks and Botiki were released years later, after torture and the failure of the security department to prove their treachery. Men who were bodyguards of President Tambo and were unwilling to continue serving in the notorious security organs were almost all sent to serve punishments in other camps in Angola. Sidwell Moroka, James Nkabinde (executed at Pango in 1984), David Ngwezana, Earl and others were among those men. The guerrillas from Zimbabwe who refused to return to Angola were flogged and beaten and were later smuggled into Angola.

After this clampdown, and with the majority of the membership panic-stricken, a strong entourage of ANC National Executive Committee members, including President Tambo, took the rounds in all ANC camps in Angola in February 1981. Appearing triumphant but with agonizing apprehension, the ANC leadership addressed the cadres about a spy network that had besieged the ANC, and emphasized the need for vigilance. Some awful threats were also thrown at 'enemy agents and provocateurs' by Piliso, who rudely declared in Xhosa: 'I'll hang them by their testicles'.

Soon thereafter, a tape-recorded address by Moses Mabhida, the late general secretary of the SACP, was circulated, criticising dagga-smoking and illicit drinking in ANC camps, and calling for strong disciplinary measures to be taken against the culprits. Commissions to investigate these breaches of discipline were set up in April 1981 in every ANC establishment. They were supervised by camp commanders and security officers in four of the camps, and all those implicated were detained, beaten and tortured to extract information. The issue was treated as a security risk, an enemy manoeuvre to corrupt the culprits' loyalty to the ANC leadership. Most of those arrested were known critics of the ANC leadership and were labelled as anti-authority.

During the whole period of investigation they were tied to trees outside and slept there. In Camalundi camp in Malanje province, Oupa Moloi, who was head of the political department, lost his life during the first day of interrogation. Thami Zulu (the travelling name of Muzi Ngwenya), who was the camp commander, and who himself died in ANC security custody in 1989, addressed the camp detachments about the death of Oupa, threatening to kill even more of these culprits who, at that time, swollen and in excruciating pain, were lined up in front of the detachment. Zulu/Ngwenya died in the ANC security department's hands in 1989 from poisoning.

In Quibaxe, Elik Parasi and Reggie Mthengele were 'finished off' at the instruction of the camp commander, Livingstone Gaza, at a time when they were in severe pain with little hope of survival. Others like Mahlathini (the stage name of Joel Gxekwa), one of the talented artists who was responsible for the composition of many of the first songs of the Amandla Cultural Ensemble, were taken from Pango to Quadro, where they met their death.

It is important to realize that most of these atrocities were carried out in the camps themselves, and not in the secrecy of Quadro, where only a few would know. The operation succeeded in its objectives. Fear was instilled and hatred for the ANC security crystallized. Every cadre of MK took full cover, and the security department was striding, threatening to pounce on any forms of dissent. Camps were literally run by the security personnel. Many underground interrogation houses were set up in all places where the ANC had its personnel, and underground prisons were established in the places known as 'R.C' and Green House in Lusaka and at a place in Tanzania disguised as a farm near the Solomon Mahlangu Freedom College (SOMAFCO) at Mazimbu, the main educational centre of the ANC in exile. In Mozambique a detention camp was set up in Nampula where 'suspects' and those who kept pestering the leadership about armed struggle in South Africa were kept.

MK began to crack into two armies, the latent army of rebels which kept seething beneath the apparent calm and obedience, and the army of the leadership, their loyal forces. The former was struggling for its life, kicking into the future, but all its efforts were confined within the suffocating womb of the latter. Security personnel were first-class members of the ANC. They had the first preference in everything, ranging from military uniforms and boots right up to opportunities for receiving the best military, political and educational training in well-off institutions in Europe.

Face to face with this state of affairs, disappointment and disillusion set in and the cadres began to lose hope in the ANC leadership. The rate of desertion grew in 1982–83. There occurred more suicides and attempted suicides. The political commissars, whose task was to educate the armed forces about the ideological and moral aspects of our army, became despised as the protectors of corruption and autocracy. It became embarrassing to be in such structures. Cases of mental disturbance increased. This was mostly the case with the security guards of Quadro, rumoured by the cadres to be caused by the brutalities they unleashed against the prisoners. It was this worsening state of the cadres that made Tambo issue instructions in September 1982 to all the army units to discuss and bring forward proposals to the leadership about the problems in which the ANC was enmeshed.

A CHANGE OF FORMS

Series of meetings followed and the MK cadres, thirsty to exploit this oasis of democracy which the ANC president had decided to have them taste, levelled bitter criticisms about the state of our organization. Once again the issue of the need for a conference was put forward. Among the questions raised by the paper issued by Tambo was what our response would be if the South African military decided to attack Mozambique. Were we ready to lay down our lives for a common cause with the Mozambican people? This question was treated by the combatants in a simplistic way, for it bore no significance to the nature of the problems we were faced with in the ANC. But the answer to it was right, in that the cadres emphasized the importance of intensifying armed action in South Africa, rather than fighting in foreign territories.

The reasoning behind such an approach by the MK cadres stemmed from their realization of the weakness of our army, both numerically and in relation to the quality of training. This was a time when the heroic PLO guerrillas were locked into bloody battles against the invading Israeli army in Lebanon. One could not but call this to mind eight months later, when the overwhelming majority of our armed forces were mobilized for counter-insurgency operation against UNITA in the Malanje and Kwanza provinces. One could not but note the similarities when Tambo appealed to the MK forces to 'bleed a little in defence of the beleaguered Angolan people,' as he addressed the MK forces in preparation for launching a raid against the UNITA bases across the Kwanza River.

With the discussions over and papers from different camps submitted to the leadership, Masondo took rounds in all the camps expressing the disappointment of President Tambo about papers submitted from Pango camp and Viana. Claiming to be echoing the views of President Tambo, he said the papers were 'unreadable' and that Tambo had not expected that this opportunity would be used for launching attacks against the leadership and military authorities.

In April 1983, some structural changes were announced. The Revolutionary

Council, adopted at the 1969 Morogoro Conference, was abolished by the NEC and a new body was set up, the Political Military Council (PMC). Announcements of personnel to man the Political Council and the Military Council were also made. The mere mention that Joe Modise would remain the army commander demoralized many cadres, who had speculated that he would be sacked as commander after rumours that he had been arrested in Botswana for diamond dealing (some cadres were severely punished for circulating that account) and because of his dismal failure to lead our army into meaningful battles against the South African racist regime.

All the changes announced by the NEC became meaningless and a farce for the armed forces. Meaninglessness stemmed from the fact that the cadres had come to realize that the change of structures was not the main issue: the personnel that manned these positions had to be changed. Their farcical nature derived from realization by the membership that these changes had been advanced to forestall any demands for a democratic conference where the NEC could be subjected to scrutiny. This contempt for the demands and ideas of the grassroots, at a time when the balance of forces was turning in disfavour of the leadership, could only have the result that the ANC would pay dearly for it. To understand this scornful behaviour, one needs to understand the deep-seated stalinist ideological leanings of the ANC leadership. We will consider this later. For now, having briefly set out the general outline of the background to the 1984 mutiny, let us examine the course of events.

THE MUTINY AT VIANA

Having received a dressing down from the rebellious armed forces at Kangandala on 12 January 1984, and having been presented with a package of demands, Chris Hani sped back to Caculama, where he delivered the news to Tambo and his NEC. During his address that afternoon in the camp at Caculama, which was composed overwhelmingly of new trainees, President Tambo felt the need to introduce his NEC to the recruits and to lay stress on certain political issues. Pointing at the NEC members on the rostrum, he said: 'This is the political leadership of the ANC…,' and suddenly turning his eyes to a man next to him, he declared: 'This man founded this army…,' patting him on his shoulder. That man was Joe Modise, the man whom the armed forces, in their majority, were saying should be deposed.

Acclaimed as a man of wisdom, a man no-one could match in the way he had led the ANC, President Tambo saw the need even at that hour to firmly entrench Joe Modise in the MK commanding position. Tambo did not see a need to respond to the calls of the cadres to come and address them, in spite of the fact that he was only an hour's drive away. But, perhaps, nobody knows about armed soldiers, and the life of the most important man must be secured. Tambo and his entourage left Caculama for Luanda that same evening, without having addressed even a message to the mutineers.

No sooner had the NEC left for Luanda than mutiny began to grow to higher levels. The whole of the Eastern Front was engulfed in sounds of gunshots, and there were stronger demands for the closure of the front and the deviation of the whole manpower to a war against Pretoria. A few days later word came from the NEC that the front would be closed and that all the soldiers must prepare themselves to leave Malanje for Luanda, where they would meet with the ANC leadership. The first convoy of a truckload of guerrillas left, followed by a second the following day, all eager for the meeting which they expected to put the ANC on a new footing.

Located at the outskirts of the capital city, Luanda, the ANC transit camp of Viana had been evacuated of all personnel, who had been sent to an ANC area in Luanda to prevent contact with the mutineers. Strict orders were circulated by the ANC security personnel that nobody in the district of Luanda should visit Viana or have any form of contact with the mutineers. Guerrillas from the Malanje Front entered Viana in a gun salute, shooting in the air with all the weapons in hand. Later the security personnel in Viana, under the command of a man known as Pro — a former security guard at Quadro and then also a camp commander at Viana, also very notorious among the mutinying guerrillas — demanded that every soldier surrender his weapons, explaining the danger they posed to the capital. The demand was dismissed summarily with the reason that arms provided security for the mutineers against the reprisals the security department would launch, given that situation. Instead, all the security personnel within the premises of the camp were searched and disarmed, but never even once were they pointed at with weapons. The administration of the camp deserted to other ANC establishments in Luanda.

In one of the metal containers, used for detention, a corpse was found with a bullet hole in the head. It was the corpse of Solly [not to be confused with the earlier named Solly], one of the strong critics of the ANC military leadership. At some stage he had tasted the bitter treatment of the security department and had in the process got his mind slightly disturbed. At the news of the mutiny in Malanje he had become vociferous and fearless, and that was the mistake of a lifetime.

That same day, some crews of guerrillas volunteered to round up ANC establishments in Luanda to explain their cause and to understand the political positions of others. Even though this was a dangerous mission, given the mobility of the ANC security personnel in Luanda and the likely collaboration with them of FAPLA [armed forces of the Angolan state, controlled by the Popular Movement for the Liberation of Angola, MPLA], the task was fulfilled. That very same day again, people from all ANC establishments came streaming to Viana to join and support the mutineers. The efforts of the leadership to isolate the mutineers were shattered and they resorted to force by laying ambushes to attack those who were travelling to Viana with guns. In one such an encounter, Chris Hani with an AK submachine gun made his appearance on the side of the loyalists by chasing and firing at those who wanted to join the mutineers. For the first time since the mutiny began, a series of mass meetings were held in an open ground in Viana. Everybody was allowed to attend, even members of the security department.

THE DEMAND FOR DEMOCRACY

It was in these mass meetings that the political essence of this rebellion began to solidify. A committee was elected by the guerrillas themselves, to take control of the situation and serve as their representative in meetings with the leadership. This body, which became known as the Committee of Ten, was chaired by Zaba Maledza (his travelling name). Zaba was a former black consciousness activist in the South African Students' Organisation (SASO) during the days of Steve Biko, who had joined the ANC in exile during the early Seventies and served as one of the foremost propagandists in the ANC Radio programmes alongside Duma Nokwe. A brother to Curtis Nkondo, one of the leaders of the United Democratic Front (UDF) in South Africa, Zaba had landed in Quadro in 1980 after some disagreements with the ANC military leadership while working for the movement in Swaziland, and was released in 1981. He then rejoined the Radio broadcasting staff of the ANC in Luanda, where his unwavering opposition to men like Piliso and Modise, and his clarity of mind, had earned him the respect of both friends and foes within the ANC, something which even the ANC security begrudgingly appreciated.

Other members of the Committee of Ten, their real names given in brackets, included: 1. Sidwell Moroka (Omry Makgoale), who was formerly Tambo's personal bodyguard and was one of the group of security personnel who were punished by being sent to Angola following a mop-up operation in Lusaka in 1981. At the outbreak of the mutiny he was the district chief of staff in Luanda; 2. Jabu Mofolo, who was at that time the political commissar of the Amandla Cultural Ensemble; 3. Bongani Matwa, formerly a camp commissar in Camalundi; 4. Kate Mhlongo (Nomfanelo Ntlokwana), at that time part of the Radio Propaganda Staff in Luanda; 5. Grace Mofokeng , also attached to the Radio Staff; 6. Moses Thema (Mbulelo Musi), a former student at the Moscow Party School and at that time serving as the head of the political department at Caxito camp; 7. Sipho Mathebula (E. Mndebela), formerly a battalion commander at the Eastern Front; 8. Khotso Morena (Mwezi Twala) and 9. Simon Botha (Sindile Velem).

Also adopted at those meetings was a set of demands addressed to the ANC National Executive Committee. They were:

1. An immediate suspension of the Security Department and establishment of a commission to investigate its all-round activities. Included here was also the investigation of one of the most feared secret camps of the ANC, Quadro.
2. A review of the cadre policy of the ANC to establish the missing links that were a cause for a stagnation that had caught up with our drive to expand the armed struggle.
3. To convene a fully representative democratic conference to review the development of the struggle, draw new strategies and have elections for a new NEC.

The demands were a backhand blow in the face of the ANC leadership. They threatened to explode the whole myth of a 'tried and tested' leadership. No wonder Chris Hani, in one of those tense and emotionally charged meetings, in bewilderment retorted: 'You are pushing us down the cliff. You are stabbing us at the back!' And like a cornered beast they used everything within their reach to destroy their opponents. Election of people to leadership positions was long preached and accepted as unworkable within the ANC. The last conference had been held in 1969 in Morogoro, and it had also come about as a result of a critical situation which threatened to break the ANC, and as a result of pressure from below. The very elevation of Oliver Tambo from the deputy presidency in 1977, something that never received support at Morogoro, was done behind the backs of the entire membership, without even prior discussion or announcement. Not that it did not have the support of the membership, but such decisions in a politically prestigious body such as the ANC needed at least a semblance of democracy, even if a sugar-coating.

The demand for a conference had been deflected in 1981 through the discovery of a 'spy-ring', and all those who talked about it then, feared even the word thereafter. When the same demand had been voiced out in 1982, the ANC leadership came out with its own fully worked-out changes and structures without the participation of the membership, even changing structures adopted at the past conference. And this time, as Joe Modise said later, a group of soldiers thought they could send the ANC leadership to a conference room 'at gunpoint'. Those demands were clearly unacceptable to the leadership.

COMMISSION OF INQUIRY, AND AFTER

In anticipation of a heavy-handed reaction from the ANC leadership, the committee members felt it was necessary to secure protection by the people of South Africa and the world. Placards calling for a political solution and reading 'No to Bloodshed, We Need Only a Conference' were plastered on the walls of Viana camp. Journalists were called, but they were never given the slightest chance to get nearer the mutineers. Two men, Diliza Dumakude and Zanempi Sihlangu, both of them members of the Radio Propaganda Staff, were intercepted by the security personnel and murdered while on their way to the studios of Radio Freedom.

While all this was happening, the presidential brigade of FAPLA (the Angolan army) was being mobilized and prepared to launch an armed raid on Viana. The decision was that the whole mutiny must be drowned in blood. The ANC could not be forced by soldiers to a conference hall 'at gunpoint'. Early the following day, the mutineers were woken up by the noise of military trucks and armoured personnel carriers (APCs) as the forces of FAPLA encircled the camp. An exchange of fire ensued as the guerrillas retaliated to the attack with their arms. Shortly thereafter, shouts of 'Ceasefire' emerged from one of the firing positions and Callaghan Chama (Vusi Shange), one of the commanders of the guerrillas, rose out of a trench beseeching for peace. One MK combatant, Babsey Mlangeni (travelling name), and one FAPLA soldier were already dead and an Angolan APC was on the retreat engulfed in flame.

What followed were negotiations between the national chief of staff of FAPLA, Colonel Ndalo, and the Committee of Ten. An agreement was reached after lengthy discussions with the guerrillas, with the Angolans trying to convince them that there would be no victimizations. Weapons were surrendered to the FAPLA commanders and they promised to provide security for everybody who was in Viana, and that even the ANC security would be disarmed. Two members of the OAU Liberation Committee arrived together with Chris Hani who delivered a boastful address, denouncing the whole mutiny and its demands as an adventure instigated by disgruntled elements. Then the usual political rhetoric followed, that the ANC was an organization of the people of South Africa, and that those mutineers were not even a drop in an ocean and that the ANC could do without them. To demonstrate this, Hani called on all those who were still committed to serve as ANC members to move out of the hall. The hall was left empty. All the mutineers were still committed to the ideals of the ANC, they were committed to ANC policies. Nevertheless, they could discern deviations from the democratic norms proclaimed in those policy documents and declared on public platforms. It was a concern for this that had forced them to use arms in conditions where criticism of the leadership and democratic election of NEC members by the rank and file were branded as counter-revolutionary.

During the period of these events, another rebellion was breaking out in Caculama, the very camp in which President Tambo had delivered his address about the illegitimacy of the mutiny which had then been in progress in Kangandala. Some groups of trained guerrillas and officers, including the staff unit commissar, Bandile Ketelo (MK travelling name Jacky Molefe), moved out of the camp, boarding trucks and trains to join and support the mutineers at Viana. The training programme for the new recruits came to an abrupt stop, and this was another slap in the face of the ANC leadership because Caculama camp was their last hope to counterbalance the popularity of the mutiny. With the support from Caculama, the mutiny acquired a 90 per cent majority among the whole trained forces of MK in Angola, which was then the only country where the ANC had guerrilla camps.

The Angolan government authorities played a very dishonest role thereafter. They began to throttle this popular unrest in collaboration with the ANC security, dishonouring all the agreements they had made with the guerrillas. The security personnel of the ANC were allowed to enter the camp armed, which was defended by the Angolan armed forces with their weapons. Later Joe Modise and Andrew Masondo arrived, together with five men from headquarters in Lusaka. The five men, James Stuart, Sizakele Sigxashe, Tony Mongalo, Aziz Pahad and Mbuyiselo Dywili, were introduced as a commission of inquiry set up on the instructions of Oliver Tambo to examine the whole episode. The following day, 16 February 1994, a group of about thirty guerrillas, including all the members of the Committee of Ten, were shoved with gun barrels of the ANC security into a waiting military vehicle of FAPLA. The tension that had captured the moment was eased when a group of guerrillas inside the closed truck broke out into a song, *Akek' uMandela, usentilongweni, Saze saswel' ikomand' ingenatyala* (Mandela is not here, he is in prison, we have lost a commander). The trucks and some ANC security officers left for the Maximum State Security Prison in Luanda, where the guerrillas were locked up. The rest of the mutineers in Viana were transported to the two camps of the

ANC north of Luanda, Quibaxe and Pango. Once again the Angolan authorities dishonoured the forces of change within the ANC, and added another point in their collaboration to abort a drive to veer the ANC towards democracy.

The mutineers in prison in Luanda were thrown into dark, damp cells with very minimal ventilation. The cells had cement slab beds without mattresses and blanket, and the toilets in the cells were blocked with shit spilling out. The gallery in which the mutineers were held was the one which housed UNITA prisoners, and it had last preference in all prison supplies, including food. Starvation and lack of water were so acute that prisoners were collapsing and dying of hunger and thirst, the only ones surviving being those who were allowed visits from their families and relatives, who even brought them water from their homes.

Several days later, the commission of inquiry arrived at the prison led by James Stuart [Hermanus Loots, an ANC veteran and trade unionist]. Interviews and recording of statements followed. Five questions were asked:

1. What are the causes of the unrest?
2. What role have you played in the mutiny?
3. Why do you want a national conference?
4. What can you say about the role of the enemy in this?
5. What do you think can be done to improve the state of affairs in the army?

In the process of these interviews, those in prison were joined by Vuyisile Maseko (Xolile Siphunzi), who had some head injuries he had received while resisting arrest in one of the ANC centres in Luanda. He had then decided to explode a grenade inside the military vehicle in which he was being transported, which contained also Chris Hani and Joe Modise, who had accompanied a group of security personnel to round up those who had escaped arrest in Viana. Hani and Modise managed to escape unharmed, and in the confusion that ensued Hani issued instructions to the security personnel to shoot Maseko on the spot, but Modise had intervened, saying 'he (Maseko) must go and suffer first'. He had since 'suffered', and was left in prison in Luanda when most of the mutineers were released in December 1988, where he probably still is, if not dead now.

INTERROGATION AND TORTURE IN LUANDA

The James Stuart Commission concluded its work after more than a week. What followed were interrogations conducted by the security department under two of the most notorious security officers, Itumeleng and Morris Seabelo. These interrogations were conducted not in the way the ANC security was used to. This was because, firstly, the armed revolts that had surprisingly engulfed the whole army had been characterized by open denunciation of the ANC leadership and a call to investigate the crimes of the security department and Quadro. It was a great shock to the entire leadership of the ANC to learn about their unpopularity within the army. They therefore had to exercise caution in dealing with those arrested so as not to confirm the allegations of atrocities that they were accused of, and they therefore had to restrain their interrogation teams. Secondly, the Angolan State Security Prison contained a lot of foreigners from different parts of the world, and the Angolan authorities had to make sure that those prisoners did not leave prison confirming the brutalities of the ANC security.

But if you are trained and used to extracting information through beatings and torture, it becomes difficult to sustain a laborious and tedious process of interrogation without falling back to your usual habit. So, here too, they started becoming impatient with this sluggish method, and they resorted to torture and beatings. The prison became more often than not filled with screams from the interrogation rooms as the security personnel began beating up mutineers, hitting them with fists and whipping them with electric cables underneath their feet to avoid traces. Kate Mhlongo, a woman who was a member of the Committee of Ten, had to be hospitalized in the prison wards for injuries sustained under interrogation, followed by Grace Mofokeng, who was also subjected to beatings.

The mutineers decided to take the matter up with the Angolan prison authorities and, in particular, with a Cuban major who was at the top of the prison administration. Promises were made by the prison authorities to stop the torture, but the beatings continued and no action was taken. When Angolan and foreign prisoners began to express their indignation to the authorities about these tortures, beatings and screams, the ANC prisoners decided to take action themselves. In mid-March they embarked on a hunger strike, demanding an immediate end to physical abuses, that they be charged and tried or released immediately, and that President Tambo himself should intervene and understand the political position of the mutineers. The hunger strike was broken up in its second week when the ANC security took away to Quadro about eleven prisoners, including Zaba Maledza (chairman of the Committee of Ten) and Sidwell Moroka.

The ANC security complained that Luanda prison was a 'Five Star Hotel' and felt that we were taking advantage of that. They told us that they would take us to 'ANC prisons' where we would never even think of taking any action to secure our release. The ANC interrogation team was saying that the mutiny was an enemy-orchestrated move to oust the leadership of President Tambo, and they wanted to know who was behind this. They could not accept it as spontaneous, and to confirm that they cited the sudden response of support the mutiny got from all the centres of the ANC in Luanda. Coming out of one of those interrogation sessions in Luanda prison, Zaba Maledza pointed out that the ANC security had decided to frame him up as the one responsible for the whole unrest. They had questioned him about his relationship with [first name?] Mkhize, the chairman of the ANC Youth Section Secretariat, who had paid a visit from Lusaka to Angola shortly before the outbreak. Mkhize had since been deposed from the Youth Secretariat by the NEC.

Later in March while still in Luanda prison, we were joined by Khotso Morena (Mwezi Twala), who had been in military hospital following an incident in which he had been shot from behind in the presence of Joe Modise and Chris Hani during their round-up of other mutineers. A bullet had pierced through his lung and got out through his front, and he was still in a critical condition. Later still, in April, another three men were imprisoned for their role in the mutiny. The conditions in the prison were worsening and almost everyone was sick, their bodies skeletal and emaciated by lack of food and water. Some began to suffer from anaemia. Their bodies were swollen because of the dampness of the cells, which they were not allowed to leave for exercise or to bask in the sun like the other prisoners. To make things worse, the prison itself had no medicines or qualified medical doctors and all our efforts to appeal to the ANC security personnel to grant us medical treatment, which we knew they could afford better than the Angolan government, were ridiculed. They said the mutineers 'chose to leave the camps, and what was there was only for committed ANC members.'

In that 'Five Star Hotel', Selby Mbele and Ben Thibane lost their lives in a very pathetic way. Selby was speeded to an outside military hospital through the pressure of the mutineers themselves when he was already losing his breath and he died the same day in the intensive care wards. Ben Thibane was also speedily admitted into an internal prison hospital on a Saturday evening, again through the pressure of his colleagues, at a time when he could hardly walk. In spite of his critical condition, he did not receive any treatment and he lost his life early the following Monday. Both these deaths happened within a space of ten days of each other. With a clear probability of more deaths to follow, the Angolan prison authorities and the ANC leadership were in a state of panic. It was only then that we were allowed, for the very first time, after nine months in that prison, to go out of the dark cells and do some exercises in the sun. Lawrence, a Cuban-trained ANC security official, who coordinated between ANC security and the Angolan prison authorities, for the first time brought us some medicines and even two ANC doctors, Peter Mfelang and Haggar, to examine us. He also brought some food from ANC centres outside.

In February 1985, we received the first visit in Luanda prison from the leadership of the ANC: from Chris Hani, John Motshabi (who died in 1986 after he was taken out of the NEC at the Kabwe Conference in 1985) and John Redi, the director of ANC security. The meeting, which was held in one of the lounges of the Maximum Security Prison, was never fruitful as the guerrillas for the first time levelled bitter criticisms directly at Chris Hani for the treacherous role he had played in suppressing the mutiny. They further called directly on him to stage a public trial of the mutineers. Hani tried his best to defend his position and announced that the NEC had decided to hold a conference. 'The ANC is committed to justice,' he said, and the mutineers would be given a 'fair trial'. He left the prison ashamed of himself. From that time on, Chris Hani, who had managed to win the support of the armed forces before the outbreak of mutiny through false promises, would never even wish to meet with the mutineers on an open platform, except with them as prisoners.

FROM THE PANGO REVOLT TO PUBLIC EXECUTIONS

It will do at this stage to go back a bit, and have a look at one of the bloodiest episodes in the history of MK. This was in Pango camp in May 1984, three months after the suppression of the mutiny and the arrest of the first group at Viana. After the group considered to be the main instigators and ringleaders of the mutiny had been arrested on 16 February, the remaining soldiers at Viana were transported in military vehicles to two camps of the ANC to the north of Luanda, Pango and Quibaxe. These two were the oldest camps of the ANC in Angola and had been evacuated following a mobilization of the whole army in preparation for the war against UNITA, leaving them with only a few guerrillas to man their defences. On their arrival, the guerrillas from Viana had to go through interviews with the Stuart Commission. With this over and the commission gone, life began to be tough for the mutineers as the authorities of the camp — composed squarely of those who were loyal to the military leadership — started enforcing castigative rules on people whose emotional indignation at the ANC leadership had barely settled.

A course was introduced arrogantly called 'reorientation'. The political motives behind that were not difficult to know. Mutiny had to be understood as the work of enemy provocateurs who had been detained, while others had just been blind followers who had fallen prey to their manipulation. The immediate response of the whole group of guerrillas was negative, arguing that their demand for a conference was not disorientation and that they saw no need for the course. Through intimidation, some of the mutineers conformed to pressure to undertake the course but another group refused to comply. It is worth noting that the only people who had weapons in the camp were those loyal to the leadership, and fear and panic had gripped some of the guerrillas about the possible retaliation of the ANC security. Already by that time the security department was conducting interrogations on soldiers, and had been detaining others secretly and sending them to Quadro. The fate of those still in Luanda prison was becoming a concern of everyone, and a serious state of insecurity had set in. This state of insecurity and harassment reached a peak in Pango after some guerrillas had been beaten, tied to trees and imprisoned by the camp security and administration, following an incident in which the camp authorities pointed weapons at a 'culprit' who was between them and the assembled guerrillas.

That Sunday, 13 May 1984, the guerrillas stormed the ANC armoury in Pango camp, disarmed the guards and shot one who refused to surrender his weapon, injuring him. Having laid their hands on the weapons, gun battles ensued throughout the night between the rebel guerrillas and those loyal to the administration of the camp. Zenzile Pungule, who was the camp commissar and a staunch defender of the status quo, Wilson Sithole, a staff commissar, Duke Maseko (another loyalist) and a security guard who was guarding prisoners in the camp prison were killed during the fighting that night. Cromwell Qwabe was found dead in the bush with bullet holes; Mvula and Norman were missing in combat. The camp commander and other forces loyal to the administration managed to escape and the camp was occupied and run by the mutineers.

The mutineers tried to reach the local authorities of the nearest town to report the matter, but the squad was intercepted by the security forces and after a short battle managed to retreat safely. It became clear then that the ANC commanders had mobilized a crack force of all its loyal cadres in all its camps and establishments in Angola, and they were encircling the guerrilla base. Running battles ensued from five o'clock in the morning the following Friday and continued the whole day as forces under Timothy Mokoena, then a regional commander in Angola and now the army commissar of MK, and Raymond Monageng (then regional chief of staff of MPC, arrested in 1988 by the ANC as an enemy plant) struggled to overcome the camp occupied by the mutineers. At dusk that same day the battle ended. About fourteen guerrillas were down, and a lot more captured from the side of the mutineers.

Some managed to break out of the encirclement and marched through the bushes further up north. Those captured were subjected to beatings and tortures under interrogation, with melting plastic dripped on their naked bodies and private parts, whipped while tied to trees and forced under torture to exhume the bodies of the ANC loyalists who had died several days before and wash them for a heroic burial. A military tribunal was set up shortly thereafter, headed by Sizakele Sigxashe, now head of ANC Intelligence, and composed predominantly of security personnel such as Morris Seabelo, a former commander and commissar at Quadro, and at that time chief of security in the whole of the Angola region of MK. Seven men were summarily sentenced to death by public execution by firing squad. They were James Nkabinde (one of Tambo's former bodyguards), Ronald Msomi, Bullet (Mbumbulu), Thembile Hobo, Mahero, Wandile Ondala and Stopper.

Motivated by a genuine desire to democratize the ANC and push it forward to higher levels of armed confrontation for people's freedom, they demonstrated a bravery and a spirit of sacrifice as they walked tall to the firing squad which shocked even their executioners, not budging an inch from the demand for a national conference and the release of their imprisoned colleagues. Chris Hani, a man who endorsed their execution, was himself forced to comment that 'had this bravery and self-sacrifice been done for the cause of democracy and freedom in South Africa, it would be praiseworthy.' But history teaches us that the jackboot of autocracy knows no limits, and should therefore be opposed limitlessly, starting from wherever you are.

The executed MK soldiers were buried in a mass grave in Pango. Later in the week a group of about 15 who had managed to break through the encirclement of the loyal forces were caught in the province of Uige. After many days marching through the bush, they had decided to stop at one of the Soviet establishments in the region. After explaining their cause, they requested temporary sanctuary and requested the Soviet officials to inform the Angolan government and the ANC president about the matter. To show that they posed no harm to them and to the local population, they surrendered their weapons to the Soviet-FAPLA authorities. The Soviet officials sent the message to the security department of the ANC, whose personnel arrived in a convoy of military vehicles. The men were surprised in their sleep, tied hand and foot, and under whips, lashings and military boots they were thrown into the trucks, and all the way from there to Pango they were tortured and beaten. In Pango, torture and untold brutalities were unleashed against them, and in the process one of the captured mutineers, Jonga Masupa, died. Others like Mgedeza were found dead in the bushes nearby with bullet holes in them.

The mutineers were kept naked with ropes tied on them for three weeks in the prison at Pango, and any security officer or guards (who had been temporarily withdrawn from Quadro) could satisfy their sadistic lusts on the helpless prisoners. The head of the ANC Women's Section, Gertrude Shope, appeared on the scene from Lusaka at that time and was taken aback by what she saw. She ordered an end to executions and tortures, and that the prisoners should be allowed to get clothes, which was done. Eight of those arrested were taken to Quadro and the rest were given punishments which they served in the camp.

The end of the episode at Pango closed the chapter of armed resistance to enemies of democracy within the ANC. Zaba Maledza, the elected chairman of the Committee of Ten, died in Quadro shortly after these events in an isolation cell in which he had been kept since 16 February. The spectre of these young fighters will never stop haunting those who, for fear of democracy and in defence of their selfish interests at the expense of people's strivings for freedom, had nipped their lives at a budding stage.

THE KABWE CONFERENCE... AND QUADRO

Overwhelmed by shock as a result of the great momentum of the forces for change, the ANC National Executive Committee succumbed. Shortly after the events at Pango, it announced that it had decided to hold a National Consultative Conference the following year, in June 1985. Defensively, ANC leaders rushed to deny that they had been forced to comply to the demands of the mutineers, and that it was the political situation in South Africa that had made them take this decision. Equivocally, they declared that the conference would not be the type of conference that the mutineers had demanded. And what did they mean?

In April 1985, two months after Chris Hani's visit to the mutineers in the State Security Prison in Luanda and two months before the National Consultative Conference at Kabwe, in Zambia, thirteen mutineers were released from the Luanda prison and one from a group imprisoned in Quadro. Propaganda was whipped up within the ANC membership that those who had been released were innocent cadres who had been misled, and that those remaining in jail were still to be thoroughly investigated. On 12 April, all the remaining mutineers in prison in Luanda were transported to Quadro in handcuffs under a heavy escort of ANC security personnel. What followed, even as the conference proceeded at Kabwe, was their humiliation and dehumanization in a place talked about in whispered tones within the ANC.

Quadro was best described in a terse statement by Zaba Maledza, when he said: 'When you get in there, forget about human rights.' This was a statement from a man who had lived in Quadro during one of the worst periods in its history, 1980–82. Established in 1979, it was supposed to be a rehabilitation centre of the ANC where enemy agents who had infiltrated the ANC would be 're-educated' and would be made to love the ANC through the opportunity to experience the humane character of its ideals. Regrettably, through a process that still cries for explanation, Quadro became worse than any prison that even the apartheid regime — itself considered a crime against humanity — had ever had. However bitter the above statement, however disagreeable to the fighters against the monstrous apartheid system, it is a truth that needs bold examination by our people, and the whole of the ANC membership. To examine the history of Quadro is to uncover the concealed forces that operate in a political organization such as the ANC.

Quadro, officially known as Camp 32, was renamed after Morris Seabelo (real name Lulamile Dantile), one of its first and trusted commanders. He was a Soviet-trained intelligence officer, a student at the Moscow Party Institution and a publicized young hero of the South African Communist Party. In late 1985 he mysteriously lost his life in an underground ANC residence in Lesotho, where none of those he was with, including Nomkhosi Mini, was spared to relate the story. Located about 15Km from the town of Quibaxe north of Luanda, Quadro was one of the most feared of the secret camps of the ANC to which only a selected few in the ANC leadership (viz., Mzwandile Piliso, Joe Modise, Andrew Masondo and also the then general secretary of the SACP, Moses Mabhida) had access. The administration of the camp was limited to members of the security forces, mostly young members of the underground SACP. Such were most of its administrative staff: for example, Sizwe Mkhonto, also a GDR-Soviet trained intelligence officer and former political student at the Moscow Party Institution, who was camp commander for a long time; Afrika Nkwe, also Soviet intelligence and a politically trained officer, who was a senior commander and commissar at Quadro, with occasional relapses of mental illness; Griffiths Seboni; Cyril Burton, Itumeleng, all falling within the same categories, to name but a few.

The security guards and warders were drawn from the young and politically naive fanatic supporters of the military leadership of Modise and Tambo, who kept to strict warnings about secrecy. They are not allowed to talk to anyone about anything that takes place in an 'ANC rehabilitation centre'. The prisoners themselves are transported blindfolded and lying flat on the floor of the security vehicle taking them there. Upon arrival in the camp they are given new pseudonyms and are strictly limited to know only their cellmates, and cannot peep through the windows. From whatever corner they emerge, or any turn they take within the premises of the prison, they must seek 'permission to pass'. Any breaches of these rules of secrecy, whether intentional or a mistake, are seriously punishable by beatings and floggings. To crown it all, when prisoners are being released they must sign a document committing them never to release any form of information relating to their conditions of stay in the prison camp, and never to disclose their activities there or the forms of punishment meted out to them.

The place has seven communal cells, some of which used to be storerooms for the Portuguese colonisers, and five isolation cells, crowded so much that a mere turn of a sleeping position by a single prisoner would awaken the whole cell. With minimal ventilation, conditions were suffocating, dark and damp even in the dry and hot Angolan climate. Even Tambo was forced to comment, when he visited the place for the first time in August 1987, that the cells were too dark and suffocating. In every cell there is a corner reserved for 5-litre bottle-like plastic containers covered with cardboard, which serves as a toilet where to the eyes of all cellmates you are expected to relieve yourself. With a strong stench coming from the toilet area and lice-infected blanket rags that stay unwashed for months or even years on end, the prison authorities would keep the doors wide open and perhaps light perfumed lucky-sticks before visiting ANC leaders could enter the cells. Outside, the premises of the camp are so clean from the beaten and forced prison labour that again Tambo found himself commenting: 'The camp is very clean and beautiful, but the mood and atmosphere inside the cells is very gloomy.'

IN THE HANDS OF THE SACP

The life activity of the inmates at Quadro is characterized by aggressive physical and psychological humiliation that can only be well documented by the efforts of all the former prisoners and perhaps honest security guards combined. Confronted by questions from the MK combatants before the outbreak of the mutiny, Botiki, one of the former detainees who had lived through camp life in Quadro during its worst period, simply answered: 'What I've seen there is frightening and incredible.' For a long time, Quadro had been a place of interest to many cadres, and it was so difficult to get knowledge of the place from ex-detainees. The ANC security had instilled so much fear in them that they hardly had any hopes that the situation could be changed. The meek behaviour and fear of authority shown by ex-detainees, the intimidating and domineering posture of the security personnel, attempted and successful suicides committed by ex-prisoners such as Leon Madakeni, Mark, and Nonhlanhla Makhuba when faced with the possibility of re-arrest, and the common mental disturbance of the guards and personnel at Quadro, and what they talked about in their deranged state, threw light on what one was likely to expect in this 'rehabilitation centre.'

In Quadro the prisoners were given invective names that were meant to destroy them psychologically, names 'closely reflecting the crimes committed by the prisoners.' Among the mutineers, we had Zaba Maledza named Muzorewa, after a world-known traitor in Zimbabwe; Sidwell Moroka was named Dolinchek, a Yugoslav mercenary involved in a coup attempt in the Seychelles; Maxwell Moroaledi was named *Mgoqozi*, a Zulu name for an instigator; and there were many other extremely rude names that cannot be written here. Otherwise, generally every prisoner was called *umdlwembe*, a political bandit.

The daily routine started at six with the emptying of toilet chambers, during which prisoners would run down to a big pit under whipping from 'commanders' (security guards) who lined the way to the pits. After this, prisoners would be allowed to wash from a single quarter-drum container at incredible speed. The whole prisoner population was washing from a single container, with water unchanged, taking turns as they went out to dispose of the 'chambers.' The last cells out would suffer most, because they would find water very little and very dirty. The very activity of prisoners washing was a very big concession, because before 1985 it was not even considered necessary for the prisoners to wash and they were infested with lice. Each group of prisoners was required to use literally one minute to wash and any delay would lead to serious beatings.

Back to the cell after washing in the open ground, the prisoners of Quadro would be given breakfast which would either be tea or a piece of bread, or sometimes a soup of beans or even tea. They were normally given spoiled food that was rejected by the cadres of the ANC in the camps, and it was normally half-cooked by the beaten, insulted and frightened prisoners. The two other meals, lunch and supper, were usually mealie meal and beans, or rice and beans, sometimes in extremely large quantities, which you were forced to eat. To make certain that you had eaten all, there was an irregular check of toilet chambers to detect a breach of this regulation. Alongside the emaciated prisoners there were security guards who lived extravagantly, drinking beer every week: privileges unknown in other ANC establishments. During periods of extreme shortages of food for the prisoners, those who were working would bank their hopes on the left-overs from the tables of the security officers and guards.

Simultaneously with the taking of breakfast, those who wished to visit the medical point would be allowed out. A clinic at Quadro was one of the most horrible places to visit. Usually manned by half-baked and very brutal personnel, a visit to the clinic usually resulted in beatings of sick people and a very inhuman treatment for the prisoners. Errol, one of the mutineers, who had problems with his swelling leg, was subjected to such inconsiderate treatment and beatings whenever he visited the clinic that he finally lost his life. Some prisoners would be forced to go to work while sick, for fear of revealing their state of health that would land them in the clinic. Even reporting your sickness needed a very careful choice of words. For instance, if you had been injured during beatings by the 'commanders', you were not supposed to say that you had been beaten. In Quadro, the 'commanders' don't beat prisoners, they 'correct' them: this was the way the propaganda went. A prisoner receives a 'corrective measure.'

After the prisoners had shined the boots of the commanders and ironed their uniforms, at eight o'clock the time for labour would begin. In Quadro there are certain cells that are earmarked for hard and hazardous labour. During this period, the cells predominantly containing mutineers were subjected to the hardest tasks. Lighter duties such as cooking and cleaning the surroundings were given to other groups of prisoners, while the mutineers carried out other work such as chopping wood and cutting logs, digging trenches and constructing dug-outs, and — most feared of all — pushing the water tank up a steep and rough road.

A SOUTH AFRICAN LABOUR PROCESS

Every kind of work at Quadro is done with incredible speed. Prisoners are not allowed to walk: they are always expected to be on the double from point to point in the camp. The group that is chopping wood would leave the camp at eight to search for a suitable tree to fell. Everybody had to have an implement, an axe. With work starting after eight, chopping would continue without a break until twelve, and you were not even expected to appear tired. 'A bandit doesn't get tired,' so goes the saying. Whipping with coffee tree sticks, trampling by military boots, blows with fists and claps on your inflated cheeks (known as *ukumpompa*) became part of the labour process. A work quota you are expected to accomplish is so unreasonable and you are liable to a serious punishment for any failure to fulfil it. Many prisoners at Quadro had their ears damaged internally because of *ukumpompa*, which was sometimes done by using canvas shoes or soles of sandals for beating the prisoners. The same situation prevailed in other duties. Unreasonably heavy logs for dug-outs had to be carried up the slopes. Every prisoner was cautious to get a piece of cloth for himself to cushion the heavy logs so as to protect his shoulders, but you would still find prisoners doing these duties with patches of bruises incurred through this labour form.

The most feared duty in Quadro was the pushing of the huge water tank, normally drawn by heavy military trucks, by the prisoners themselves for a distance of about three or four kilometres from the water reservoir to the camp. Like cattle, they would struggle with the tank and the 'commanders' wielding sticks would be around whipping prisoners like slaves whenever they felt like it or when the pace was too slow.

Prisoners in Quadro behaved like frightened zombies who would nervously jump in panic just at the sight of commanders, let alone at a rebuke or a beating, In the process of these beatings during labour time, prisoners who could not cope with the work were sometimes beaten to death. Such was the death of one prisoner who died from blows on the back of his head from Leonard Maweni, one of the security guards. Two others were unable to carry some heavy planks from a place far away from the camp, after the truck that had been carrying them broke down. Upon arrival in the camp they were summoned from their cell, under instructions from Dan Mashigo, who was the camp's chief of staff, and were taken for flogging at a spot near the camp. One never came back to the cell, and the other one died a short while after returning to his cell.

This was in complete conflict with what Dexter Mbona — the security chief in Quadro and later ANC regional chief of security in Angola — told the mutineers when addressing them on their very first day of arrival. On that occasion, he said: 'This camp is not a prison but a rehabilitation centre, and it has changed from what you portrayed it to be during the time of *Mkatashingo* [the mutiny].' Quadro was still a place of daily screams and pleas for mercy from physically abused prisoners. Saturday was the worst. It was a day of strip and cell searches, the 'commanders' would enter each cell with sticks and the search would commence. At the slightest mistake made by a single prisoner as a result of panic, the whole cell would be in for it, and to drown the noise of their screams, other cells would be instructed to sing.

As already hinted, the whole matter about this camp needs to be investigated to establish who were the masterminds behind these gross violations of human rights. Both psychologically and physically, the camp has done a lot of damage to those who unfortunately found themselves imprisoned there.

Some have become psychological wrecks, while other have contracted sicknesses such as epileptic fits: for instance, Mazolani Skhwebu, Hamba Zondi and Mzwandile, three colleagues of the mutineers who were left in Quadro when other members of the group were released in 1988. What is certain is that Andrew Masondo, Mzwandile Piliso and Joe Modise were highly involved in these sinister political machinations. But was the topmost leadership of the ANC unaware? Let justice take its course, and with fairness and honesty let nothing be concealed from the people of South Africa.

FROM QUADRO TO DAKAWA

Such were the conditions of imprisonment in which the mutineers were held without trial for almost five years, with the sole purpose of breaking their commitment to the democratization of the organization they loved. Occasional visits by the leadership of the ANC only served further to frustrate the rebel inmates, to drive them to admit their guilt and to reduce them to tools manipulated by enemy provocateurs. But, if anything, the conditions in Quadro confirmed the justness of their cause and strengthened their commitment to cleanse the ANC of such filth.

The conference on which the detained mutineers had banked their hopes materialized at Kabwe on 16 June 1985, but to their disappointment it never carried out the expected reforms. The delegation from Angola, the main centre of internal strife, was predominantly composed of selected favourites of the ANC military leadership, who drowned the few who were sent with them as a compromise to give the conference a semblance of representativeness and democracy. The presidential report of O.R. Tambo never even touched on the events that had rocked the ANC and led to so much bloodshed, and which had forced the convening of the conference. When the issues behind the mutiny were put on the table by some of the cadres from Angola, the matter was hushed up by Tambo under the pretext that it could divide the ANC. Mr Nelson Mandela had sent a statement to the conference appealing for unity and rallying support for the leadership of Tambo, and it was tactically read at the opening of the conference. It was a further weight against the rebels. Unity, as always, was pushed forward at the expense of a fair and democratic solution of the problems that had beset the ANC. The culprits were saved and further strengthened their positions within the ANC. It was a miscarriage of justice.

Members of the National Executive Committee were to be elected from a list of candidates drafted by Tambo. At the end of the conference we were confronted by our jailers in Quadro and some members of the leadership boasting about unity in the ANC. Our demands for free and fair elections and for an inquiry into the activities and crimes committed by the security apparatus were ridiculed, and they bragged about how isolated the rebels had found themselves in the conference. Pro, one of the camp commanders of Quadro, commented to the mutineers in the cells: 'The people in Lusaka did not even want us to send your lieutenants to the conference, but we insisted here in Angola that they should go, and they experienced bitter isolation when they wanted to raise the disruptive issues of *Mkatashingo*.' Andrew Masondo was the only one who was sacrificed on the NEC, and that was simply because he was so discredited in Angola that he could not be saved. But the masterminds remained intact.

On 16 November 1988, exactly four years and nine months after the beginning of their imprisonment, the mutineers were summoned to the biggest cell in Quadro. There were about 25 of them in all, and they were required to sign documents committing them to keep the crimes of Quadro a secret. A security officer signed the same documents, as a witness. After an emotional and angry address by Griffiths Seboni threatening to shoot anyone who repeated anything concerning such problems within the ANC, the rebels were transported to Luanda and kept secretly in a storeroom to avoid contact with MK cadres. [By this time the international negotiations concerning the removal of Cuban troops from Angola were well under way. The removal of the prisoners from Quadro preceded the departure of the bulk of ANC personnel from Angola — *Eds.*] After two weeks they were secretly taken to the airport and flown to Lusaka, where they were kept in the airport until late at night. The following morning they were transported in an ANC bus to the border between Zambia and Tanzania where, without documents, they were crossed into Tanzania to an ANC development centre at Dakawa, near Morogoro. The whole journey took place under the escort of the security personnel and upon arrival in Dakawa they were interviewed by the security officers in one of their bases called the Ruth First Reception Centre. The main purpose of the interview was for the security officers in Tanzania to check on the mutineers' commitment to what had landed them in prison in 1984. To the disappointment of the security officers, the rebels still justified their cause. Again to the disappointment of the security officers, the welcome they received when they came into contact with the community was unbelievably warm and unique.

The political mood within the ANC in exile had remained shaky since the mutiny of 1984. The divisions between the security personnel and the general membership had continued to widen in spite of cosmetic changes of personnel in the apparatus. Piliso had been shifted from heading security to chief of the Development of Manpower Department (DMD), replaced by Sizakele Sigxashe, who had been part of the commission set up to probe into the details about the mutiny in 1984. Workshops had also been convened to look into the problems of the Security Department, with the aim of reorganizing it in order to change its monstrous face. But these were half-hearted efforts, and could not improve the situation because they evaded the sensitive issues and left out the views of those who had been victims. The old security personnel were, above all, left intact. There was also the pressing issue of the running battles against UNITA that had resumed in 1987, in which MK cadres were losing their lives in growing numbers. Armed struggle inside South Africa, one of the central issues in 1984, was caught up in a disturbing state of stagnation. The leadership of the ANC had become more and more discredited among the exiles, and it was hard to find anyone bold enough to defend it with confidence, as was the case earlier. Even within the security personnel you could detect a sense of shame and unease in some of its members. But it was still difficult for the membership to raise their heads, and the ANC security was in control of strategic positions in all structures.

As a result of this political atmosphere within the ANC, frustration and disillusion had set in at most of the ANC centres. Dakawa, where the ex-Quadro detainees were taken after their release in December 1988, was also trapped in political apathy, with political structures in disarray. The Zonal Political Committees (ZPCs), Zonal Youth Committees (ZYCs) Dakawa, Women's Committees, Regional Political Committees and all the other structures whose membership was elected were either functioning in semi-capacity or were completely dormant. Only the administrative bodies were in good shape, and this was mainly because their membership was appointed by the headquarters in Lusaka, and was composed of either security or some people loyal and attached to it. These are the structures that, contrary to the ANC policy of superiority of political leadership over administrative and military bodies, wielded great powers in running the establishments and which suffocated political bodies elected by the membership. This state of affairs reveals clearly that after more than 15 years without democracy and elected structures, the ANC was finding it difficult to readjust itself to the democratic procedures it was forced to recognize by the 1985 Kabwe Conference. The leadership found itself much more at home when dealing with administrators than with bodies that drew support from the grassroots. This strangled political structures, and drove many people away from political concern to frustration and indifference.

BETWEEN DEMOCRACY AND DICTATORSHIP

When the mutineers arrived in Dakawa, the political mood began to change as they managed to show the people, and those who had taken part alongside them in *Mkatashingo*, the need to participate and to demand to participate in all issues of the struggle. They themselves took part in all the labour processes of the Dakawa Development Project and showed a sense of keen interest in political matters. When the ANC secretary-general Alfred Nzo visited Dakawa shortly after their arrival, he commended their example and called on the community to emulate them. He also announced in the same meeting that the ex-detainees should be integrated into the community and were allowed to participate in all structures. This never excited the ex-detainees, who took it for granted that they were full members of the ANC whose rights were unquestionable, even taking account of the leadership's half-hearted and concealed admissions of past errors, and even if the leadership still did capitalize on the methods used by the mutineers.

With the decision to revive the political structures, a general youth meeting was convened on 18 March 1989 and in the elections a Zonal Youth Committee was elected into office, dominated by former detainees and other participants in the mutiny. Out of its nine members, five were ex-prisoners who had mutinied in 1984, including three members of the Committee of Ten. This initiated the revival of other structures such as the Cultural Committee and the Works Committee (a trade union-like body for labourers in the project) at whose head we had former mutineers. The ANC leadership was clearly eyeing this situation with a sense of discontent, but it was difficult for it to interfere directly with the democratic process under way, without provoking indignation from the community. To them this was a move that absolved the people they had tried to destroy and have ostracised.

The first political encounter between the Dakawa ZYC and ANC headquarters was at the Third Dakawa Seminar, held on 24–25 April 1989. The first and second seminars had been held in 1983 and 1985 respectively and had provided guidelines for the development of the Centre. The objectives of the Third Seminar were to review progress achieved, to establish an autonomous administration for the Centre, to consider new project proposals and to establish proper co-ordination between the Centre and regional and national structures. The Dakawa ZYC was not invited to be one of the participants. It challenged that decision, and was ultimately allowed to send one delegate, Sidwell Moroka, its chairperson, who was able to deliver its paper. This paper was prepared after taking stock of the views expressed by the youth meeting of

7 April. Among the participants at the Third Seminar were heads of departments from headquarters including Piliso and Thomas Nkobi, the national treasurer. The paper of the youth of Dakawa was criticized by the leadership. The main theme of the seminar was the need for the setting up of bodies of local self-administration, with the youth pressing for elective bodies and the other side, led by Piliso, dismissing the idea as unrealistic. After lengthy discussions with the chairman of the ZYC uncompromising on the issue, Piliso noted that the chairperson of the ZYC was 'stubbornly opposed to appointed personnel.' However, the result was that a recommendation in favour of the position of the ZYC was adopted.

After this seminar, the ANC leadership was to reconsider its attitude towards the former detainees. In June 1989, when the ANC youth section was to attend a World Youth Festival in Korea, a telex was sent to Tanzania from headquarters in Lusaka cancelling the names of four delegates democratically elected by the youth in Dakawa to represent the zone. The four names were all of former mutineers. When an explanation was sought, nobody in the HQ claimed responsibility, but it became clear from discussions between the Dakawa ZYC and Jackie Selebi, chairman of the National Youth Secretariat (NYS), that this had the hand of security. The Dakawa ZYC and other upper structures in Tanzania expressed their discontent with this practice that undermined democracy and infringed on the rights of the membership.

The Dakawa Youth Committee had by this time already established its *Youth Bulletin* and was also making its ideas clear in the paper of the whole community, called *Dakawa News and Views*. The local security department and its administrative tools became very uneasy about the articles that began to appear sparing nobody from criticism and with a clear stand for openness and democracy. On several occasions the ZYC found itself a target of attack as instigators, and its office-bearers were intimidated to the point where some of its full-time functionaries, such as Amos Maxongo, were forced to abandon their post. Following a paper prepared by the ZYC in September on 'housing problems in Dakawa,' the committee was called to account to the Zonal Political Committee and Administration meeting, and its members were threatened that they should either terminate their contributions in the local newspaper or change their language. The ZYC refused to back away from its position and called for freedom of expression.

This state of political wrangling and the rise in popularity of the Dakawa ZYC approached its climax in September 1989. At this time, the Regional Political Committee (RPC) — a supreme body responsible for political guidance and organization in different ANC regions — was elected into office in a meeting attended by delegates from all ANC centres in Tanzania. Sidwell Moroka was elected its chairperson and Mwezi Twala its organizing secretary. Both of them were former members of the Committee of Ten elected by the mutineers at Viana in 1984. The closing session, on 16 September, was filled with tension as some of the ANC leading personnel who attended, including Andrew Masondo, Graham Morodi and Willie Williams, and the members of the ANC security, showed clear expressions of disapproval of the results. Morodi, then ANC chief representative in Tanzania, forced himself to occupy the platform and made a comment insinuating that the results should be sent to the NEC for approval. On 18 September he sent a letter to the incoming chairman, Sidwell Moroka, suspending accession of the new Regional Political Committee into office with the excuse that he was still awaiting approval from Lusaka. On 5 October the body was dissolved by order of the chief representative, Morodi, who stated that the decision had the backing of the office of the secretary-general of the ANC, Nzo. The reasons advanced were that there had been violation of procedures in the meeting and that nominees had not been screened prior to the election: meaning that the ANC security has powers to determine who is eligible for election to the political structures of the ANC. It has a right to dissolve a democratically elected structure if it dislikes those elected by the ANC membership.

Later a body was appointed from ANC headquarters called the Interim RPC, to replace the democratically elected RPC and to fill the 'political vacuum'. The ZYC circulated a letter in which it disapproved of the imposition of 'dummy structures' and suppression of the democratically elected ones. It further raised the matter at the annual general meeting of the youth on 14 December. Rusty Bernstein, head of the ANC department of political education, and his staff, and the regional chairman of the youth, Gert Sibande (that is, Thami Mali, who was responsible for the 1985 stayaway that rocked Johannesburg), had been invited to attend, and were present. At the annual general meeting, the youth in Dakawa called for the refusal of the personnel appointed to this structure to participate in it. Members of the department of political education and the regional chairman of the youth, Sibande, also expressed their disapproval of this undemocratic action and promised to consider their positions in relation to it. This meeting, which Bernstein admitted had shown unheard of openness in the ANC, signalled the doom of the Interim RPC, which had until then failed to take office due to its unpopularity and the hesitation of the appointed personnel to play the shameful political role allotted to them. At this point the ANC leadership collected its strength and could not restrain itself any longer.

THE DESTRUCTION OF DEMOCRACY

Under instruction from the NEC, Chris Hani and Stanley Mabizela arrived in Tanzania from the HQ shortly thereafter and called for ANC community meetings in Mazimbu, and on 24 December 1989, in Dakawa. At these meetings, Stanley Mabizela announced the decision of the NEC concerning groups of people who had been imprisoned by the ANC. There were three categories that they mentioned:

1. A group of self-confessed enemy agents who had been imprisoned and released unconditionally. These had a right to take part and even occupy office in ANC structures;
2. A group of enemy agents who had been imprisoned and released conditionally. These had no right to take office in the structures of the movement; and
3. A group of 1984 mutineers who had been imprisoned by the ANC. These were also not allowed to take office in ANC structures.

And hence, he concluded, the NEC had decided to dissolve the RPC. He then instructed the communities to support and strengthen the Interim RPC.

This announcement was immediately challenged by the people in the meeting and the former mutineers themselves, with the following arguments: (i) That the National Executive of the ANC was acting autocratically, as it had no moral or political justification for taking a decision so important that it infringed on the right of the membership without even prior consultations with the general membership; (ii) That the very issue of the mutiny and the causes behind it had never been opened for discussion by the entire membership of the ANC, and that the mutineers themselves had been denied platforms on which to explain their actions, and that they had never been tried by any court or competent body in the movement; and (iii) That the very people who took the decision to dissolve the RPC were still continuing with tortures and murder of detainees and their political opponents.

The last point related to two young men who had escaped from the prison in SOMAFCO at Mazimbu, and who had reported themselves at the Morogoro Police Station. One of them was Dipulelo, who had headed the *Dakawa News and Views*, and who had been accused of subversion, and detained and tortured by a security department man called Doctor. They arrived at the Tanzanian police station in handcuffs and naked, the way they had been kept in prison at SOMAFCO [where the secondary school principal by this time was Masondo]. They had been detained in July 1989, and they related horrifying stories about the torture to which they had been subjected until they escaped in November.

At the meeting at Dakawa on 24 December, Chris Hani felt he could not tolerate the confrontation and howled from the rostrum at those who challenged the decision. 'The decision is unchallenged, it is an order from the NEC,' he shouted, beating the table with his fist. A commotion ensued as Hani's security tried to arrest those who talked, and a reinforcement of the armed Tanzanian Field Force was called to the hall by Samson Donga. The meeting ended in confusion and the whole community was astonished by the autocratic behaviour of that ANC leadership delegation. On 28 December a paper was circulated, officially banning nine members of different committees in Dakawa. This time again, those who sought the democratization of the ANC were arrogantly silenced by a decree from the strong opponents of apartheid undemocracy. What an irony!

RESIGNATION FROM THE ANC

Widespread discontent filled the air in Dakawa, and it spread to nearby Mazimbu, as the leadership reversed the process of political and cultural renewal that had marked the period in which the ex-mutineers had been free to develop their ideas among the ANC membership. This process of renewal was suppressed, not because there was anything wrong with it but because it threatened the ANC leaders with democracy, which they were not prepared to tolerate. Some members of the department of political education, such as Mpho Mmutle and Doctor Nxumalo, were summoned by the security department and questioned about their association with ex-mutineers, and instructed never again to visit Dakawa. A sense that anything might happen at any time set in, as the community awaited the reprisals that might follow. The whole of the ANC in Tanzania was filled with tension. From sources close to the security department, word came to the ex-mutineers about meetings held to decide on action to be taken against those who embarrassed the ANC leader and the man who wanted to take Mandela's mantle, Chris Hani.

It was at this time, on 31 December 1989, that the ex-mutineers considered the issue of resigning from the ANC. The reasons are glaring to any realistic-minded person. There was a need to pre-empt the actions of the security department, which would have definitely followed. There was a need also to look for better avenues for continuing the struggle against apartheid, given that the ANC had banned the ex-mutineers from freedom of political expression. And there was also a need to relate this state of affairs to the leadership of the

ANC inside South Africa, to the leadership of the Mass Democratic Movement (MDM) and to all the people of South Africa.

We appeal to the people of South Africa and the members of the ANC to support our call for an independent commission to investigate these atrocities.

AN OPEN LETTER TO NELSON MANDELA FROM EX-ANC DETAINEES

YMCA Shauri Moyo
P.O.Box 17073
Nairobi.

14.04.90

Dear Cde Mandela
Revolutionary Greetings!

The news through the press about our horrific experiences at the hands of the ANC security organs must have left you in a state of bewilderment. Fully aware of that, we realise the need to write you this letter giving an account of our vicissitudes in combating the enemies of democracy within the ANC and putting across also our incessant efforts to have these problems resolved democratically with the full participation of the entire membership. By this we hope to dispel any misunderstandings regarding our decision to expose this disgraceful and shameful page in the history of our organisation, which we hold at high esteem, even at this hour.

First, it is a fact, indisputable indeed, that the 1984 mutiny was a spontaneous reaction of the overwhelming majority of the cadres of MK to crimes and misdeeds, incompatible with the noble and humane ideals of our political objectives, carried out by certain elements in the leadership of the ANC. These included, among other things, acts of torture and murder through beatings, committed by the ANC Security personnel under the leadership of Mzwandile Piliso; brutal suppression of democracy denying the membership of the ANC any opportunity, for a period exceeding thirteen years, to decide through democratic elections who should lead them; and misleading our people's army by locking it into diversional battles from which our struggle did not benefit, thereby weakening and destroying its fighting capacity.

Second, it remains our firm belief that, had the ANC leadership acted honestly at the very early stages of mutiny, and most of all, had President Tambo responded responsibly to our appeal for his immediate and direct intervention, many lives could have been saved. Regrettably, in a manner identical to our political enemy, the South African regime, the ANC leadership fished out the 'ringleaders' and their most plainspoken opponents and unleashed virulent brutalities against them.

Third, having gone through close to five years without trial in the most notorious prison within the ANC, and having endured the humiliating, dehumanising and hazardous conditions in which some of us perished, we remained committed to the ANC. This was in recognition of the justness of our cause, in honour of men like you and the multitudes in our beleaguered homeland who languished in racist dungeons and got murdered in this noble cause, and lest we forget our comrades whose lives were cut short by those who deceptively made noise and declarations about democracy on behalf of our people.

Fourth, embarrassed at the way the ANC community in Dakawa absolved us by electing us into the political structures in the Tanzanian ANC region, Chris Hani and Stanley Mabizela, acting on behalf of the National Executive Committee, then muzzled us by banning us from participating freely in ANC political life and dissolving democratically elected structures. Our efforts to challenge such an undemocratic action and to explain the causes of the 1984 mutiny for which we were being unjustifiably treated were answered by shouts from Hani himself, taking us down [from] the platform and even calling for armed Tanzanian Task Force Unit to surround the hall.

It's the realization of the last-named factor that sealed and shattered our long-standing commitments and hopes to reform the ANC from within, and we resigned in December last year. But let it be stressed still, that even at that time, we still limited our activities to consulting the internal leadership of our movement to avoiding embarrassing the organisation we so dearly loved. We contacted through letters and attempted to send our document (captured at the Dar es Salaam Airport by ANC and Tanzanian security) to such stalwarts of our anti-apartheid struggle as Frank Chikane, General Secretary of SACC, leadership from prison, and Archbishop Desmond Tutu.

Knowing you as a personality who distinguished himself by unflinchingly fighting and standing for human rights and ideals of highest democracy, we receive with bitterness your praises showered at these corrupt and atrocious elements, whilst a shroud of secrecy wraps around the noblest sons and daughters of South Africa who perished in pursuit of the same ideals as yours[,] at the hands of these fake custodians of our people's political aspirations. It is this that pricks our conscience to remove this shroud. Nothing can be more treacherous than to allow such crimes to go unchallenged and unknown. Nothing can be more hypocritical when some of us even at this hour are languishing in those concentration camps. Even much more disturbing is that these enemies of democracy are to be part of that noble delegation of the ANC to negotiate the centuries-long denied democratic freedoms of our people. What a mockery! What a scorn to our people's sacrifices for freedom! We back your tireless efforts and of all those peace-loving South Africans who see the need for a peaceful settlement of our problems, but we also believe that our people's yearnings for justice can only be competently secured by a morally clean leadership.

We know how difficult it is to accept these bitter but objective truths, and how mammoth the task is of taking appropriate actions against these individuals. But we know also how [undermined?] they are even within the ANC membership, and we are certain also that, if only they could talk, much more horrific stories will come out of those who tasted the bitterness of the ANC Security's treatment. Hence, our sincere call to you and the fighting masses in South Africa and within the ANC to back our demand for a commission to inquire into these atrocities. This, *contrary to short-sighted ideas*, will not weaken the ANC, but will demonstrate to our people and the world the ANC's uncompromising commitment to justice and democracy. No better guarantee can be made to our people that when our organisation ascends to power, their rights and freedoms will thrive in competent and responsible hands.

Amandla! NGAWETHU!!
POWER TO THE PEOPLE!!
Yours in the Struggle,
Ex-ANC detainees
(Copy from fax-message)

Authors' note, August 2009: The TRC Final Report concludes about the men executed at Pango camp in May 1984: 'Seven people were executed following an investigation and subsequent tribunal. They were Mr Edward Malope (MK Joseph Masimini), Mr Zwelethemba Magwa (MK Jongile Mzwandile), Mr Masibulele Tonisi (MK Hobo Walter), Mr Mandla Reuben Jele (MK Stopper Nyembezi), Mr Cekiso Hoyi (MK Ronald Msomi), Mr Irvin Ondala (MK Wandile Mashaqane), Mr Mlamli Namba (MK James Nkabi (Mkhambi)).' [Volume Two, Chapter 4, paragraph 156. Slightly adapted]

3 *A Death in South Africa**

THE PRINCIPLE OF MONARCHY

The Mandela myth was mainly the creation of the South African Communist Party. As the most important organizer of ANC politics within the country and internationally for thirty years, especially through the media, the SACP in the late 1950s and early 1960s set about the creation of a very specific cult of personality.

The 'M Plan' of 1953, in which 'M' stood for Mandela, did more to surround the leader's name with a mystique than reorganize the ANC on a cell-system, as it was supposed to do. Ten years later, after the arrest of members of the High Command of Umkhonto weSizwe at Liliesleaf Farm in Rivonia, the emphasis was not principally on a collective call: 'Free the Rivonia nine.' The fate of an entire generation of political victims was absorbed into the fate of a single individual: 'Free Mandela.' Such personification of thousands of individual acts of imprisonment by the state might have been good media politics, but it was the negation of democratic accountability. It represented the introduction of the monarchical principle as a staple into modern South African political life. More urgently, it was a trivializing of politics which took the issue away from matters of substance and concentrated attention on the persona of one man.

It is now clear that Mandela's last three years in prison were a secret cloister of discussions, cultivated by the state, in which the Olympian remoteness of the regime was imparted to the politics of its leading opponent. In essence the fate of the whole society devolved in isolation upon the judgement of one man, whom prison appeared not so much to exclude from the people as it served to exclude the people from the secret deliberations between this one man and the state. This was a spectacle, in which a single individual cast a shadow on a vast audience through his non-presence.

---

*First published in *Searchlight South Africa* Vol 2, No. 6 (January 1991), pp. 11–24 as 'A Death in South Africa: The Killing of Sipho Phungulwa'.

And thus we come to Caesar's wife. As the decades of Mandela's imprisonment went by, the mystique of royalty, the principle of divine right, passed by law of succession to his wife, who became the representative of the idea of the sacral on the earth of township politics. In so far as Mandela in prison was mystically always present through his absence, Mrs Mandela as consort played a very material Empress Theodora, or perhaps Lady Macbeth. The more the myth grew through Mandela's unworldly situation in prison — alive, yet dead to human contact, the unseen mover in the power play of southern African politics — the more an extraordinary status attached to his wife.

During the 1960s and especially in the 1970s, Winnie Mandela won widespread respect for her resistance to the government. She defied loss of husband, banning, banishment, prison and unremitting police harassment, emerging from the 1976 student revolt as an important political leader. She was an emblem of defiance. The fact that her political philosophy was shaped by a crude nationalism opened her to the abuses of the 1980s: a matter greatly facilitated by her unique status as oracle to the unseen leader on Robben Island. In conditions of unremitting social tension, culminating in near-insurrection in the period of the 1984–86 township revolt, these circumstances produced their own deadly result.

This would have been venal enough if her courtiers had principally been adults. It was in the nature of South Africa in the mid-1980s, however, that her retinue was composed largely of children. Old Socrates drank hemlock, by order of an Athenian court, on a charge of corruption of youth, but Mrs Mandela's corruption of youth proceeded under the title *Mama weSizwe*: 'mother of the nation'.

A principal automotive arm of the 1984–86 township revolt was the schools boycott, interlinked with other campaigns such as the rent boycott. The effect of the schools campaign was ultimately catastrophic; but this movement of the youth (the 'young lions') also put an immense head of pressure under the regime. Their organizing role in rents boycotts and in getting urban councils disbanded cannot be ignored. When unemployment stood at 40 per cent and over, and underemployment was very high; when 800,000 or more were employed in petty hawking; and when the youth themselves faced the prospect of miserable paid jobs or no jobs at all, the school was no magnet of attraction at the best of times. The schools boycott led to illiteracy, the bleakness of prospects made literacy irrelevant.

The schools boycott was associated with the slogan (endorsed in practice by the ANC) 'Liberation before education', also phrased as: 'Revolution today, education tomorrow.' Across the country, tens of thousands of children decamped permanently on the streets, a huge, amorphous army, a children's crusade, brought into existence by this mass of declassed youth merging with the very large stratum of the unemployed and the criminal *bohème* of the townships.

Educated by the streets, since they were amenable to no force of adults in the society, these children became the masters of their parents and the vehicle by which the ANC leaders acquired their ticket to the talks at Groote Schuur. Adults not in South Africa need only imagine the effect of permanent, unbroken school holidays in their own homes, and on their own streets, spiced with the sadism of South African social conditions. This was the milieu in which teenage armies, teenage generals, teenage courts and teenage executioners gave lessons in patriotism to the workers.

AN AUTOCRACY OF THE YOUNG

An inversion in culture was the dye in which all subsequent South African political life was stamped. Having fought the battle for the trade unions over the preceding decade, the workers worked while the children militarized themselves. In this way the township won political hegemony over the factory, the workless over the worker, the child over the adult. The revolt of the young — uninfluenced by any mediating influence of the trade unions — found its expression partly in the 'necklace' killings by means of a burning tyre soaked in petrol. Small left-wing groups critical of the new reasoning were ordered to shut up, or else. Critical individuals were silenced or driven out. It was in this environment of menace that a founder member of MK said during the period of the township revolt: 'I know where the government stands, I know where Inkatha [the political arm of the KwaZulu Bantustan] stands, but I don't know where the "comrades" stand. If the ANC radio from abroad ordered them to kill me, they would do it.' (personal communication, 1986)

Leadership by children of the streets was fatal to any bond (in Russian terms, *smychka*) between town and country. The phenomenon of a counter-revolt by migrant workers, in their tribally segregated barracks, in opposition to the revolt of the township youth had already appeared in 1976, both on the Rand among Zulu workers at the Mzimhlophe hostel in Soweto and among Bhaca workers in the hostels at Nyanga East near Cape Town. In each case, resentment by migrant workers at taunts and harassment by the politicized youth of the cities gave rise to pogroms against township residents, with the active connivance of the police. In the following fourteen years, the ANC learnt no lessons from this incubatory period of rural/urban slaughter, which reached its full horror in the PWV (Pretoria-Witwatersrand-Vereeniging) region in August and September 1990, and afterwards.

A further consequence of this paedontocracy, or government by the young, was the milieu out of which arose the Mandela United Football Team — a euphemism of the same order as the term Civil Co-operation Bureau for the secret assassination department run by the South African Defence Force . Mrs Mandela, who advocated liberating the country 'with our necklaces and our boxes of matches' during the 1984–86 township revolt, reigned as queen of the ghetto over this gang of youngsters, whom she housed and who functioned as an instrument of political control over the townships. This group, since linked to sixteen murders, was founded at the end of 1986.

THE EMPRESS OF THE DAMNED

It would take a novelist or dramatist of great power to illuminate the motives of this woman, enduring loss of husband, banning, exile and imprisonment, transformed into a scourge of mothers through her teenage wolf-pack. How far was the brutalized behaviour of the 'football' club simply an expression of the generalized brutality of South African conditions, brought about by its predatory social production relations? At what point did international adulation of Mrs Mandela feed the mania? Or the attentions of South African white bourgeois society, which introduced her to its salons as the townships burnt? Or the courts, which for several years declined to prosecute, despite agreement between prosecution and defence on evidence relating to Mrs Mandela in a case in 1988 resulting in imposition of the death penalty? Or the South African press, which never reported this and other matters? (This legal record, unreported in South Africa, was made public by John Carlin in an article, 'Terrorized by "Winnie's boys"', in the *Independent* (London), 21 September 1990.)

'Winnie's boys' were generally just that — boys. But boys transformed into killers. The rise of political violence as a means of political control in the townships, associated most blatantly with the Mandela team, became institutionalized at the same time as torture, imprisonment and murder of internal critics within the ANC had become routine practice abroad. The nature of the ANC security department in its exile camps — before, during and after the township revolt — was described in *Searchlight South Africa* No. 5. Serious historical research is needed before an accurate picture emerges of the nature and orientation of political violence in the townships in the 1984–86 period and afterwards. It is likely, however, that the methodology of Mrs Mandela's boy scouts in dealing with critics was reinforced by knowledge of how the ANC security department conducted itself abroad. According to court records agreed by prosecution and defence, Oupa Seheri, a trained ANC guerrilla, carried out a double murder in Soweto while staying in Mrs Mandela's house, where he also kept the murder weapon. Two other trained ANC guerrillas — Peter and Tsepo — were later killed in a shoot-out with the police in the home of Jerry Richardson, the 'manager' of Mrs Mandela's 'team,' who was sentenced to death for the murder of 14-year-old Stompie Moeketsi Seipei.

Seipei was himself typical of this army of youth. Having played his part in the township wars, he was murdered on or around 3 January 1989. Mrs Mandela's household — 'packed with youths… part barracks, part boarding school, part prison', in Carlin's description — was the arena in which an ad hoc disciplinary committee tried cases and ordered punishments, administered then and there by physical violence in the yard. After having been abducted from a white priest's house and brought to Mrs Mandela's house for 'trial' and a beating, Seipei was taken away by Richardson and disposed of. The image of this child, coupled forever with that of the 'mother of the nation', will remain a vignette of the period in which the ANC re-won political hegemony in the townships. And inextricably associated with these, a third image: of a young girl engulfed in flames before the television cameras, a victim of 'our necklaces and our boxes of matches'.

What repelled the residents of Soweto was a methodology of coercion, in essence no different from that which produced the 1984 mutiny in the ANC abroad. Within South Africa it was only less organized, given that the ANC lacked parastatal powers. A 'crisis committee' was set up by ANC loyalists in Soweto in July 1988 to watch over Mrs Mandela, according to Carlin: it was helpless against the 'football team,' and failed to save lives. The turning point came with Seipei's murder, which caught the attention of the media. Shortly afterwards, in a remarkable press conference on 16 February 1989, the acting general secretary of the United Democratic Front, Murphy Morobe, read a prepared statement on behalf of the Mass Democratic Movement (MDM). Speaking on behalf of the then most important network of ANC supporters in the country, Morobe said:

> We have now reached the state where we have no option but to speak publicly on what is a very sensitive and painful matter. In recent years, Mrs Mandela's actions have increasingly led her into conflict with various sections of the oppressed people, and with the Mass Democratic Movement as a whole. The recent conflict in the community has centred largely around the conduct of her

so-called football club, which has been widely condemned by the community. In particular, we are outraged by the reign of terror that the team has been associated with. (quoted by Carlin)

Since then, both before and after the release of her husband, the ANC made strenuous efforts to rehabilitate Mrs Mandela as the consort of the probable future president of South Africa. She was seen sweeping the streets of Alexandra township together with residents in a photo-opportunity prepared by the former Alexandra Action Committee, under the guidance of its most prominent activist, the trade union leader Moses Mayekiso (now a member of the central committee of the SACP). This process of political sanitizing was not confined to South Africa. In a press conference in London on 4 June, during one of her husband's international tours, not a single question was put to her by the world's press as she sat beside him, concerning the affair of Seipei and the football club. The mythology of political sanctity was international.

The ANC must have imagined that reality was what it willed it to be. It appointed Mrs Mandela as its 'head of social welfare' on 21 August this year-despite everything. To residents of Soweto that decision must have appeared equivalent to appointing a child molester to head an orphanage, and it produced an angry protest demonstration outside ANC offices in central Johannesburg by black social workers. That ANC leaders such as the secretary-general Alfred Nzo should have even considered attempting to 'rehabilitate' Mrs Mandela in this way, after the statement by the MDM, is an indication of the autocratic matrix in their thinking. It is an index also of a tension between the bureaucratic centralism of the ANC in exile and local organizations created spontaneously within South Africa before and during the 1984–6 period: a tension continuously present since the return of the ANC leaders, and one tending towards the negation of local democracy.

RETURN OF THE EXILES

It is not hard at this point to understand the political environment in which eight former members of the ANC in exile — six of them victims of the repressions abroad — returned to South Africa from Tanzania in April this year, as reported in *Searchlight South Africa* No. 5. Their return was mentioned in the article 'Inside Quadro,' which introduced 'A Miscarriage of Democracy: The ANC Security Department in the 1984 Mutiny in Umkhonto weSizwe', written by five participants in the mutiny, then (and at the time of writing this report, still) refugees in Nairobi.[1] The authors of the article — Bandile Ketelo, Amos Maxongo, Tshona, Ronnie Masango and Luvo Mbengo — first came public with an account of their experiences in a long interview published in a British newspaper, the *Sunday Correspondent*, on 8 April, while the other group of eight were being held in prison in Malawi after having fled Tanzania in an effort to reach South Africa.

Since May, when material for issue No. 5 was got ready for the printer, the ANC security apparatus in exile has moved in some strength back to South Africa, merging with the youth milieu from which the Mandela 'football club' was drawn. In part this took place illegally, through the ANC's underground channels, but it also took place through a special amnesty agreed between the government and the ANC within the negotiating process. One of the first to return legally — preparing the way for senior commanders of MK such as Joe Modise (commander) and Chris Hani (chief of staff) — was the ANC's head of intelligence, Jacob Zuma. These were the conditions in which Sipho Phungulwa, one of the group of eight who returned to South Africa in April, was murdered in a daylight public assassination in Umtata, the main town of the Transkei, early in June.

Phungulwa was one of the closest colleagues of the authors of the article on the 1984 mutiny. After active involvement in the 1976–77 youth uprisings in the Port Elizabeth area, he left South Africa to join MK with his close friend Amos Maxongo, one of the authors of the article. Under the 'travelling name' Oscar Sizwe, he was one of the first group of MK cadres posted to Lesotho to help establish and organize ANC underground structures in the Transkei and Border areas. This was appropriate since he knew the region, and his first language was Xhosa. At that time he was 'working very closely to Chris Hani and acting as his bodyguard' (letter from Ketelo, 17 July 1990).

Hani is reported to be a member of the Politburo of the SACP (*Front File*, October 1990). He appeared on the platform at the public launch of the SACP in Soweto on 29 July, speaking only in Xhosa. Ex-detainees regard him as a Xhosa chauvinist, a current vigorously resisted by the mutineers both before and after the mutiny. When Phungulwa was murdered, Hani had already returned to South Africa under amnesty and had begun to set up a base operation for MK in the Transkei 'homeland', working under very favourable conditions provided by the military regime of Major-General Bantu Holomisa, the first of the Bantustan leaders to adapt to the new dispensation. Even when the South African government withdrew Hani's amnesty in July and arrested leading MK figures following capture of large quantities of arms and computerized instructions relating to the so-called Vula military operation, Hani continued to enjoy protection in the Transkei. The indemnity was later restored by the government.

In exile, following his mission in Lesotho, Phungulwa had 'gone through the trying times in the struggle to democratize the ANC' (Ketelo). He took part in the 1984 mutiny in Angola, was next-door neighbour to Ketelo in the isolation section of the State Security Prison in Luanda after the crushing of the mutiny in Viana camp and then shared a cell with him in the ANC detention camp, Quatro (officially, 'Camp 32'). He remained in Quatro until the former mutineers were released in December 1988.

After they were transferred by the ANC to Dakawa camp in Tanzania in January 1989 and permitted to take part in normal exile activities, Phungulwa was the main person responsible for organizing sports and culture among the exiles, whom the ANC prisoners on their arrival found very dispirited and apathetic. Towards the end of last year he was elected Sports and Cultural Co-ordinator for all the exiles in Tanzania, 'known practically by every ANC member in the region'. In general, it was only the former mutineers, with their attachment to democratic principles and their pronounced notions of political commitment, who could breathe life into the moribund structures in the camps. It was not long before these pariahs, who were not permitted to mention the mutiny or the repressions they and their colleagues had suffered, became an alternative pole of leadership to the security-dominated ANC bureaucracy in Dakawa.

On 16 September 1989, one of the seminal events in the life of the ANC abroad took place. In an astonishing rebuff to the ANC leadership, two former mutineers were elected to the leading positions on the most representative body of all the exiles in Tanzania, the Regional Political Committee, at an annual general meeting attended by several top-ranking ANC leaders, including one — Andrew Masondo — regarded by the mutineers as among the ANC leaders most responsible for the reign of terror in the camps.

The two ex-prisoners from Quatro chosen to represent thousands of exiles in Tanzania were Omry Makgoale (the MK district commander in Luanda before the mutiny, elected chairperson of the RPC under his 'travelling name' of Sidwell Moroka, also known as Mhlongo) and Mwezi Twala (elected organizing secretary, under the travelling name Khotso Morena). Both had been members of the Committee of Ten, elected in Viana camp on the outskirts of Luanda to represent the demands of the armed personnel of Umkhonto to the ANC leadership in the middle period of the mutiny in 1984. Makgoale had been present in Quatro prison when the leading figure in the mutiny, Ephraim Nkondo (known to the mutineers by his travelling name, Zaba Maledza), was dragged through the prison with a rope around his neck, shortly before his death.[2]

By voting Makgoale and Twala to leading positions on the RPC, the ANC exiles in Tanzania effectively endorsed the standpoint of the mutineers of 1984 against the ANC National Executive Committee and the MK High Command, which had violently repressed their demand for a democratic conference. Twala was one of the group of eight who later escaped from Tanzania with Sipho Phungulwa in January this year, and was the main spokesperson when they gave a press conference in Johannesburg on 16 May after being released by the police.

Within days of the election, the ANC leadership set out to negate its embarrassing result, culminating in an administrative *ukase* of the NEC in October dissolving the RPC and attempting to replace it with an appointed Interim RPC which the ex-detainees correctly described as a dummy body. This was an event of the greatest importance for the future of democratic conditions in South Africa, since this dissolution of an elected body was the work of a small number of individuals who within six months were engaged in negotiating with the South African regime for a new form of government in the country. The question of the detainees proved to be a nerve signal indicating the future political complexion of South Africa itself.

THE STRUGGLE FOR DEMOCRACY

Phungulwa fought alongside his prison comrades from Quatro to reverse this system of administrative decree. At the annual general meeting of the Zonal Youth Committee (ZYC) in Dakawa on 14 December — in the presence of the SACP leader Rusty Bernstein, of the Regional Department of Political Education — he argued that ANC officials should not dictate 'who should be elected'. He opposed the idea that individuals elected to the RPC should agree to participate in an appointed 'dummy structure'. A person who was elected by the people, he stated, 'should serve the interests of the electorate not certain individuals. As the ANC has taught us, we should elect people of our choice'. (Minutes, signed by the ZYC administrative secretary, Neville Gaba, 28 December 1989)

At this meeting, one of the most important in the fight of the ex-mutineers against bureaucratic despotism, Bernstein pointed out that he was 'happy to see the spirit of democracy. In his opinion the meeting was conducted in the spirit of *perestroika* and *glasnost*, a spirit that requires truth about things'. (Minutes) It is not known how Bernstein reconciled these oily words, sanctioned from Moscow, with the silencing of the leading activists in the democracy movement in the ANC shortly afterwards, or with the manner in which they were driven into flight from the ANC and its host state, Tanzania, or with Phungulwa's murder.

A motion calling on an elected office-bearer of the dissolved RPC 'not to participate in the dummy interim structure' was passed by the ZYC, after contributions from Makgoale, Twala and Phungulwa setting out the history of the struggle for democracy within the ANC. By continuing the fight for electoral accountability through the ZYC, the former prisoners made it plain that they had not given up the principles of the mutiny, but that these now had a wider audience than ever. It was a forthright challenge which the ANC leaders were not slow to respond to. Within a fortnight, ANC headquarters in Lusaka sent two NEC members, first to the camp at Mazimbu and then to Dakawa on 24 December, in order formally to exclude the mutineers from office in any of the ANC structures, as reported in *Searchlight South Africa*, No. 5. The two delegates from the NEC were Chris Hani, who had played a major part in the suppression of the mutiny, and Stanley Mabizela, whose colleague from Fort Hare University College in the early 1960s, Sizakele Sigxashe, had concluded the mutiny with public executions.

On 28 December, following 'the decision of the NEC,' the ANC coordinator at Dakawa, Sidwell Khoza, insisted by letter that Phungulwa be removed from his position as cultural coordinator, along with eight others holding elected office in various local structures, including Ketelo, Maxongo, Makgoale and Twala. 'A sense that anything might happen at any time set in, as the community awaited the reprisals that might follow', the Nairobi refugees wrote in their history of the mutiny (pp. 8–45 in this book). 'There was a need to pre-empt the actions of the security department, which would have definitely followed.' Three days after being removed from office on Khoza's instruction, Phungulwa and the ex-detainees (but not Makgoale and some others) resigned from the ANC in order to remove themselves from its jurisdiction, and thus hopefully avoid arrest and possibly death.

At first they tried to place themselves under the jurisdiction of the UN High Commissioner for Refugees in Dar es Salaam, the Tanzanian capital. They received no assistance, a thread that runs throughout the history of the UNHCR in the face of appeals for help from the victims of the nationalist movements in South Africa and Namibia. Instead, they were arrested by the Tanzanian government and held in detention during the visit by Walter Sisulu.[3] The conviction that they could get no protection either from the UNHCR or from the Tanzanian regime, which they viewed as in league with the ANC apparatus, convinced the ex-mutineers that their only safety lay in flight.

Bandile Ketelo and Tshona succeeded in reaching Nairobi on 22 January, after having been deported three times back to Tanzania in handcuffs by the Kenyan immigration police, and 'threatened with death if we came back to

Kenya' (letter from Ketelo, Nairobi, 14 June 1990). Others arrived in two groupings in March, including Amos Maxongo and his companion Selinah Mlangeni, and their small baby. All suffered extreme hardship, including arrest, before being provided accommodation by the All-African Council of Churches at the YMCA in Nairobi.

The other group of eight, including Phungulwa and Twala, attempted to make their way from Tanzania back to South Africa via Malawi, on the principle that 'better a South African jail than the ANC "security"' (*Searchlight South Africa*, No. 5, see p 2 in this book). Arrested and imprisoned under very grim conditions in Malawi, they were interrogated there by South African security police, returned to South Africa by air by the government, detained by the police for three weeks in Kimberley and then released in Johannesburg on 15 May. The following day they presented the story of the mutiny and the repressions within the ANC at a press conference in Johannesburg organised for them by a Reverend Malambo, a figure with a political history allegedly associated with the South African government. While an ANC supporter accused them of being 'askaris' (former ANC members 'turned' by the police into secret assassins for the state) and to the disbelief of anti-apartheid journalists, they gave a detailed account of the mutiny and repressions within the ANC, confirming the information provided by the Nairobi group to the British press in April and the article appearing in *Searchlight South Africa* in July. Phungulwa at this time had only three weeks to live.

Friends of *Searchlight South Africa* were present at this press conference and had discussions with some of the ex-detainees afterwards. A fairly detailed report of the occasion, and of their allegations, appeared the following day in the Paris journal, *Liberation* (17 May). The group stated that they intended to form an association of 'parents of those who died or were detained in exile'. They had a duty to look after the interests of those they had left behind. It was necessary to obtain explanations from the ANC and to organize their comrades' return.

SHROUDING A MURDER WITH SLANDER

Days before Phungulwa's murder, the ANC's chief of intelligence, Jacob Zuma, took issue with the ex-detainees, claiming that a statement at their press conference that the ANC was holding more than 500 dissidents was false and that the correct figure was just over a hundred. He publicly smeared all the ANC prisoners, including the group of Twala and Phungulwa, with responsibility for 'participating in assassinations and spying'. The method of the Moscow

Trials was deliberately invoked against the ex-mutineers, in order to discredit their fight for democracy. 'There were people with instructions to sow discord within our forces and our membership, to raise complaints about petty things and to aid a situation of uncertainty, even with specific instructions to organize mutiny', he told *New Nation*, a pro-ANC weekly funded by the Catholic Church (25 May, reported in *ANC Newsbriefing*, week ending 3 June).

As stated in an open letter delivered to Nelson Mandela on his visit to London in July, these remarks by the ANC's chief of intelligence were 'a lie and an incitement to murder' (open letter to Nelson Mandela from Solidarity with ex-SWAPO detainees, London, 3 July 1990). A close colleague of the leading stalinist Harry Gwala during his imprisonment on Robben Island, Zuma is responsible for very important positions within the NEC in the negotiating process: he is a member, for instance, of the ANC working group responsible for determining political offences in association with the South African government, deciding on release of political prisoners and immunity for exiles (*South*, 10 May, reported in *ANC Newsbriefing*, week ending 20 May), and is on the ANC committee responsible for investigating the carnage in Natal (NEC statement, 25 July). One need only grasp the primacy over the ANC bureaucracy in exile of its security apparatus — staffed mainly with members of the SACP and trained by the KGB — to gauge the weight of Zuma as chief of security, and the implication of his slander on the former mutineers. For many in South Africa, the label 'enemy agent' has been a death sentence.

Not long afterwards, Twala was told that he had 'forfeited his right to live in the townships' because of his comments at the press conference, following a 'comrades meeting' in Evaton, where his family lives. His young accusers said later: 'We ordered the family he was visiting to kick him out immediately'. (*Weekly Mail*, 8–14 June) In fleeing Tanzania for South Africa, the group had failed to reckon with the township vigilantes, whose activities received heightened expression in Mrs Mandela's football club and correspond nicely to the political theory of Mr Zuma. The phrase 'forfeited the right to live' rings ominously: it appears to have been a commonplace of township jurisprudence.

Zuma's statement could only mean that the ex-detainees were being set up for murder, either at the hands of township thugs or by ANC security personnel returned from abroad. Either way there would be no problem. The ANC/SACP was in the process of transferring security personnel from Mazimbu in Tanzania to South Africa, one of whom (travelling name Lawrence) was shot dead and others arrested by the police. In general, Umkhonto seems to have used its security personnel on numerous clandestine missions within South Africa, partly at least because of their greater loyalty to the SACP.

Phungulwa was killed in the territory he had previously helped to organise for military operations by MK. He had gone to the Transkei with Nicholas Dyasophu, a colleague from the mutiny and one of the group who had returned with him via Malawi, in order to explain to ANC members about the situation of the ex-mutineers. An appointment was made to speak to the chief representative in the ANC office in Umtata. A report from South Africa explains what followed:

> On the day of the appointment, when the comrades arrived in the office they were told that the man they were supposed to meet was not present and therefore they were asked to wait a bit.
>
> When the comrades realized it was getting late they began to leave, but officials insisted that they should wait until six o'clock as there was going to be a meeting and the man they were looking for would surely attend. But as the comrades could not wait any longer they left.
>
> Outside the office there was a car with two occupants who sternly looked at them. On their way to the location they saw the same car following their taxi. At the point of their destination, the car overtook and blocked the taxi and that was where Sipho Phungulwa was shot. Dyasophu managed to flee and tell the story.

The use of the car and the weapon (a Scorpion machine pistol) recalls evidence agreed between prosecution and defence concerning the same means used in a double murder in Soweto in 1987, involving Oupa Seheri — a trained ANC guerrilla, infiltrated back into South Africa from abroad — operating from Mrs Mandela's house. Further, on leaving the ANC offices in Umtata shortly before he was shot, Phungulwa had recognized one of the two men in the car as a former ANC guerrilla whom he had himself trained in a military camp run by MK in Angola. This information became available when Dyasophu was able to alert his comrades to what had happened.

AN EXPENDABLE LIFE

After the murder, some of the ex-detainees living in Soweto appeared on South African television and explained their case. As chief of staff of MK, Hani, who was in South Africa at the time of the murder setting up his own base of operations in the Transkei, was interviewed on the same programme and obscured the issue in the same manner as Zuma by presenting the ex-detainees as killers acting on behalf of the South African state. Without exception, former mutineers whether inside or outside South Africa considered Hani to have been ultimately responsible for Phungulwa's murder. They consider that

Phungulwa — with his detailed knowledge of MK operations in the Transkei and his past role as Hani's bodyguard — was killed because he knew too much and because he had infringed on territory where Hani was setting up his own local military fiefdom, separate from the Johannesburg base of Joe Modise, the Umkhonto commander.

A month later, Nelson Mandela was confronted with information about Phungulwa's murder and the demand for an investigation by the ANC in an open letter from a small group set up in London, Solidarity with ex-SWAPO Detainees (SWESD). When the same issues were raised before journalists from all over the world at a press conference in central London on 4 July, during his world tour, Mandela 'brushed aside' the question in a 'steely' manner, according to a front-page report in the British press the following day. His comment was cynical: 'I have never known a dead man to be able to identify the person who killed him'. (*Guardian*, London 5 July) A letter delivered personally to Archbishop Desmond Tutu on 21 June in Oxford, where Tutu was receiving an honorary degree, asking him to support an inquiry into Phungulwa's murder, likewise failed to get a reply.

During the same period, ANC security in the camps in Tanzania told exiles that the ex-mutineers who had returned to South Africa or were living as refugees in Nairobi were 'true enemy agents who came to cause confusion amongst our ranks'. The language is very similar to that employed by Zuma, as ANC security chief, shortly before Phungulwa was shot. Security officials (nicknamed 'Selous Scouts,' after a notorious detachment in Ian Smith's forces in the last years of white rule in former Rhodesia) also stated that Phungulwa had been killed 'because he went to attack ANC offices in the Cape' (private communication in possession of the author). This transparent falsehood was an implied admission that he had in fact been killed by the ANC.

Despite having been presented by ex-detainees with a document setting out the history of suppression of the struggle for democracy in the ANC during his visit to Tanzania in January, Walter Sisulu at the most senior level of the ANC's old guard from Robben Island — second only to Mandela — also publicly repudiated the ex-detainees in much the same way as Zuma and the security apparatus in Tanzania. There is a systematic refusal, or inability, on the part of the ANC to confront its own history, which is somewhat akin to the ambiguity of Mandela in confronting the history of his wife. Instead, the big lie serves as a means to repress further, and even — as in the murder of Phungulwa — to prepare and justify assassinations. A leading MK commander, Tokyo Sexwale, who spent 18 years on Robben Island, effectively conceded that ANC members had been involved in Phungulwa's murder when he met the Nairobi group on 31 August in Nairobi to urge them to rejoin the ANC: he stressed, however, that this had not been on instructions from the leadership (letter from Bandile Ketelo, 11 September).

Shortly after Phungulwa's murder, following a similar approach by Sexwale and the ANC national organizer and former MK leader from the 1960s, Wilton Mkwayi, the six surviving members of the group which had returned via Malawi — not including Dyasophu — were reported to have agreed to rejoin the ANC (*New Nation*, 29 June). When the Nairobi group were asked to rejoin the ANC by Sexwale, they refused. In the event of any meeting with the ANC leadership, they wanted to be independent. That is how the matter rests before the ex-detainees, among an estimated 40,000 exiles, return.

A PREMATURE TRUTH

Zuma and Hani are men with whom capital can deal. None better than such as they to police the embers of revolt! As men of the political generation of the 1960s, they could not forgive the mutineers for holding up to them the principles of the youth of 1976 — above all, its inability to compromise on democracy. For the earlier generation of the time of Zuma and Hani, stalinism was a magnetic pole of attraction: not so for the youth of 1976, who imbibed some of the spirit of the changed world politics of 1968. This clash of political generations, as much as anything, explains the opposing places in the conflict between the 'mother of the nation' and the children of 1976.

The return of Sipho Phungulwa, after thirteen years' exile, was the return of one of the children of that period — one of the most thoughtful and dedicated of its children. In the meantime, the hope and promise of that time had given birth to strange fruit, both in South Africa and abroad. A study of the period from 1976 to 1990 would indicate that it produced initially the most democratic process of self-organization in the country's history, the formation of the black trade unions. It was a period as full of promise as in any country's history. The contribution of the ANC to this process was minimal. The formation of the unions into a force within the society was achieved, if anything, despite obstruction by the ANC and the SACP in exile (see 'Two Lines within the Trade Unions,' *Searchlight South Africa* No. 3). The independence of the unions presented itself initially as a major obstacle to ANC political hegemony, a barrier to be knocked down before the country could be made safe for the present negotiations.

The means by which this was achieved required that the principles of the generation of 1976 be barbarized — in other words, that their revolutionary sting be drawn. The suppression of the generation of 1976 by the ANC security department in exile in the mid-1980s, alongside the rise of political hoodlumism as a way of death within the country, marked a political reaction against the most radical tendencies within the society: a campaign of repression which, in the manner of the 20th century, branded its victims as the counter-revolution. It is Zuma and Hani, not the ex-detainees, who shake the hand of the South African state, dripping in blood.

South Africa, too, has its revolution betrayed, and the mutineers of 1984 are witness to it. Thus the response: Off with their heads! Wipe out the infamy! from the ANC security apparatus. Alongside the myth of Mandela and the sinister figure of his wife, one must place also the corpse of Sipho Phungulwa. He had been back in South Africa for less than two months, half of that time as a prisoner of the state, the other half as a marked man by the ANC. The great majority in South Africa will shortly discover how little they are to gain from the current changes. Precisely because of that, the mutineers endure the fate of those who tell a premature truth. It may be asked why attention should be focused on this one death, when the period since the unbanning of the ANC has produced so rich a harvest. It is because this murder, like none other so far, reflects back on the principal mythology of the transition period: the myth of the ANC, reaching its most celestial heights as the Mandela myth.

Author's Postscript, 2009: The Amnesty Committee of the Truth and Reconciliation Committee granted amnesty on 13 August 1998 to 'three members of the African National Congress's military wing, Umkhonto weSizwe (MK)' for the murder of Sipho Phungulwa (whom it described as a 'defector', a loaded term with pejorative implications) and the attempted murder of Nicholas Luthando Dyasophu. (Application AC/98/0034).

The Amnesty Committee states that Ian Ndibulele Ndzamela, Pumlani Kubukeli and Mfanelo Dan Matshaya 'were part of a group of four MK members who decided to kill Sipho Phungulwa and Luthando Dyasophu, former exiles who defected and became "askaris"'. This description by the Committee of Phungulwa and Dyasophu as 'askaris', i.e. operatives of the apartheid state, was a calumny. The TRC defamed the victims in order to exonerate their murderers, despite having had access to my article in *Searchlight South Africa* No. 6 (January 1991), published seven years previously, and to other sources of reliable information.

The statement continues: 'The Amnesty Committee said in its decision that upon their return to South Africa, the two defectors [that prejudicial term again] held a press conference, slating the ANC [also a prejudicial description].

The applicants decided to kill them, warned the local ANC leadership in Umtata about their deployment in the area and put them under surveillance'. [The term 'deployment' is also prejudicial, suggesting that Phungulwa and Dyasophu were acting under military orders physically to attack members of the ANC in the Umtata area.]

In awarding amnesty, the Committee — under the chairmanship of Judge Ronnie Pillay — concluded that Phungulwa's murder and the attempted murder of Dyasophu were offences 'committed for political reasons in the interest of an anti-apartheid stance.'

So that's alright then. Founded on a calumny, the two-faced apologetics of the TRC in this judgment suggested serious problems for the future of the judicial process in South Africa.

The statement makes clear, however, that the murder of Phungulwa, the former bodyguard of Chris Hani, was an official act sanctioned by the ANC in the Transkei at a time when Hani was in the region as the most senior officer commanding. It confirms the character of the mutiny in the ANC in 1984, in which Phungulwa and Dyasophu were participants, as a moral act directed against an often murderous autocracy.

NOTES

1. As explained in the article in *Searchlight South Africa* No. 5, the ANC's prisoners in Angola renamed the detention Camp 32 after a hated prison in South Africa, the Johannesburg Fort, known colloquially as 'Number Four.' This then became transformed into the Portuguese for the word four, 'Quatro' — which we spelt incorrectly as 'Quadro.' There were other errors in the article, in which real names were occasionally confused with the pseudonyms (or 'travelling names') that ANC exiles received when they left South Africa. ANC combatants whose real names were confused with their travelling names include Mwezi Twala, Vusi Shange and Bandile Ketelo.
2. Ephraim Nkondo was the younger brother of Curtis Nkondo, the former president of the Azanian People's Organisation (AZAPO) and current president of the national teachers' organization, NEUSA. He was known to the mutineers by his travelling name, Zaba Maledza, the name in which he appears in *Searchlight South Africa* No. 5. In 1976 he had been a student at the University of the North at Turfloop, active in the black consciousness students' organization, SASO. A published report on the mutiny, the pamphlet *Fighting the Crazy War*, by an anonymous participant, is dedicated to Nkondo under the hope that in a democratic South Africa 'the ghost of Zaba Maledza and others will be laid to rest'.
3. A picture of the grim conditions in the prison system of Tanzania is provided in the autobiography of the former leader of SWAPO, Andreas Shipanga, held without trial in Tanzania from 1976 to 1978. Shipanga was falsely charged by SWAPO with having spied for the South African government. His account of his years in prison in Tanzania appears in *In Search of Freedom: The Andreas Shipanga Story, as Told to Sue Armstrong*, 1989, Ashanti, Gibraltar.

4 *The ANC Prison Camps: An Audit of Three Years**

To the memory of

EPHRAIM NKONDO and MLAMLI NAMBA

VINDICATION OF SEARCHLIGHT SOUTH AFRICA

Searchlight South Africa has been vindicated by three recent reports and one major press investigation into the system of prison camps run by the African National Congress in exile.

Still more, the participants in the mutiny in the ANC army Umkhonto we-Sizwe (MK) in Angola in 1984 have been vindicated. There is clear recognition in all three reports that a major motive for the mutiny was the demand for democracy in an army tyrannised by the ANC Security Department. Not a shred of credibility remains for the slur that the mutiny was 'instigated by enemy agents'.

At the same time, there has been no investigation worth the name into abuses in the camps run by the South West Africa People's Organisation of Namibia (SWAPO) in southern Angola, or in camps run by the Pan Africanist Congress (PAC) in Tanzania and elsewhere.

The three reports into abuses in the ANC appeared between October 1992 and January 1993. The most reliable and significant of these reports, by Amnesty International (2 December 1992), drew more than half its material from information previously published in *Searchlight South Africa* in issues 5 to 9. This information was subsequently confirmed by Amnesty, conducting its own independent investigation through a full-time professional researcher, Richard Carver, with whom *SSA* was frequently in touch.[1]

The ANC was compelled at the highest level to acknowledge its imprisonment, torture and execution of members in exile as a means of suppressing

*First published in *Searchlight South Africa* Vol. 3, No. 2 (April 1993), pp. 8–30 as 'The ANC Prison Camps: An Audit of Three Years, 1990–1993'.

critical opinion. It was compelled also to acknowledge the role of *Searchlight South Africa* in exposing these abuses. The *Weekly Mail*, the leading liberal newspaper in South Africa, also acknowledged reliance on material published in *SSA* more than two years previously, as a source for its own exposure of torture and executions by the ANC.

After long delay, the work of this journal has become front-page reading in South Africa. It has entered the archives and everyday political knowledge and debate.

The reality of the ANC's system of prison camps and the nature of its Security Department, iMbokodo ('the boulder that crushes'), has been established without question. The ANC is no longer portrayed almost universally by the left and the liberals as a saintly Robin Hood riding to the rescue of humanity on a dashing (Hollywood) charger. Where previously there was silence, or uncritical celebration of the perpetrators of abuses, there now is routine reference in the South African and international press to the issue of 'the camps'. It is a truth that can no longer be suppressed.[2]

This work was carried out in conditions of extreme difficulty. The Amnesty report was the culmination of two and a half years of exhausting campaigning, in all but total isolation, mainly by two people. Amnesty had to be threatened with exposure before it undertook to carry out this investigation. Even then there was no certainty that its inquiry — which was taken out of the hands of its South Africa desk — would result in publication.

Whole-hearted, generous and unstinting collaboration was provided to this magazine by a single British colleague, the former Westminster borough councillor, Bill McElroy — an outstanding human being worth an army in any campaign. Southern Africa owes this remarkable man a debt of gratitude. He is known and loved by many former ANC and SWAPO detainees.

THE STATE OF THE LEFT

The campaign provided a painful lesson in the lack of concern for human rights among socialists and liberals, when relating to nationalist and stalinist politics in southern Africa. Only one left-wing socialist group in Britain, the Workers Revolutionary Party (WRP), and its affiliated organisations internationally, actively and continuously drew attention to suppression of political dissent by murder, torture and imprisonment by the ANC and by SWAPO (now the party of government), during the decades of exile.

The other trotskyist groups in Britain, the United States, South Africa and elsewhere nearly all maintained a stony silence. So did the British Labour and Liberal parties, which were informed at the highest level of what had happened in the camps. This was done by Bill McElroy and myself, as co-editor of *Searchlight South Africa*, working together in the umbrella organisation Justice for Southern Africa. The few individuals who read our journal and expressed support for our stand were exceptions to the rule. We welcomed them, but they were as isolated in this matter as was *SSA*.

These groupings and individuals either justified the methods of stalinist dictatorship when practised by the ANC and SWAPO, or turned a blind eye. This failure of moral judgement, in countries where press freedom and freedom of association are well established, made the work of exposing abuses extraordinarily difficult. Greater humanity was shown on this issue in Britain by Baroness Chalker at the Foreign Office. It is sad, but true. The extraordinarily comprehensive resistance to the fairly straightforward moral issues posed in this campaign, especially in Britain, indicates a substantial problem in modern society at the level of thought, of philosophy, of intellectual culture and ideology. Hopefully, this can be explored in a future issue.

In one instance, the biggest left-socialist group in Britain, the Socialist Workers Party (SWP), knowingly preserved silence over the assassination in South Africa in June 1990 of Sipho Phungulwa, a former ANC detainee, even though a leading member of the SWP had met Phungulwa in Johannesburg only three weeks previously. This member of the SWP passed information to *Searchlight South Africa*, published in issue number 6 (January 1991), which the SWP excluded from its own press.

At a meeting in the London School of Economics in February 1992, at a discussion on South Africa convened jointly by *SSA*, the Revolutionary Communist Party (RCP) and the journal *Critique*, a leading officer of the RCP, suggested from the platform that I 'deserved a bullet' after I had spoken to the meeting about the ANC prison camps. Two-thirds of the audience, members and supporters of the RCP, cheered vociferously.

Another trotskyist group, based in the US, in its weekly newspaper described the editors of *Searchlight South Africa* as 'New World Order socialists' serving the interests of the Bush administration, because of our criticism of the prison camps and the criminality of Mrs Winnie Mandela.

It was much the same within South Africa. When Baruch Hirson, co-editor of *SSA*, raised the issue of the ANC security department and its prison camps in his opening address to the Conference on Marxism in South Africa at the University of the Western Cape in September 1991, the audience froze. No-one referred to the issue in general discussion. Other attempts to open the discussion at the University of the Witwatersrand never happened: there was apparently no time in the busy academic year for a talk on the subject.

Frozen out in silence or vilified by the left, *Searchlight South Africa* was simultaneously subject to arbitrary seizures by security officials in South Africa, having been banned for commercial distribution in its first three issues. We have no idea how many copies were confiscated or destroyed.

Individual copies nevertheless percolated through to university libraries in South Africa and to individuals in the townships and suburbs. In particular, the article on the 1984 mutiny in the ANC by Bandile Ketelo and four other former ANC guerrillas in *SSA* No. 5 was widely circulated within the country by *Samizdat*, mainly through extensive photocopying.[3] Each copy of this issue entering the country was read by many readers, passing from hand to hand. The article was later published as a pamphlet by Justice for Southern Africa under the title *Mutiny in the ANC, 1984*. This pamphlet was produced jointly with the WRP in Britain, which sold it through its bookshop in south London.

To many hundreds of people in South Africa, *Searchlight South Africa* provided the first authoritative account of the mutiny and the fate of its victims. In several instances, *SSA* and Justice for Southern Africa, working together, provided families with their first glimmer of hope for the fate of relatives whom they had last seen, as youngsters, fourteen or more years previously. In several instances, we provided friends and relatives with the first reliable account of a death.

LIFE IN ARREARS

In the years immediately before and after the return of the exiles, this was the only South African journal that gave impartial airing to the truth that everybody in the camps knew by word of mouth, or as the brand of servitude on their own backs. Despite a few (very few) inaccuracies, inevitable in the conditions under which the journal is produced, our reporting was and remains trusted by the exiles.

Several prisoners of the ANC in Central and East Africa were released as a result of the efforts of *SSA* and Justice for Southern Africa. Slightly safer conditions of life were secured for former detainees within African states, and more especially in South Africa itself. Our achievements, however, only throw into relief immense continuing unmet needs.

Two former ANC detainees with whom we were directly or indirectly in touch were murdered almost immediately on their return 'home.' These were Sipho Phungulwa (shot dead in Umtata in the Transkei in June 1990, 'allegedly by named ANC officials', as Amnesty states, p 17) and Bongani Ntshangase, 'shot dead by unidentified assailants', as Amnesty records, at Msinga in Natal on 21 May 1992. More details can be found about the lives and deaths of these two men in *Searchlight South Africa* Nos 5, 6, 8 and 9, and in the Amnesty report. The bulk of the former victims of the ANC security department who have returned to South Africa live miserable lives. Some in disappointment and desperation have turned to alcohol.

It has been a chilling experience. We have struggled in isolation to try to save the lives of brave and democratic people in South Africa, for whom existence, as one said recently, in desperation, is merely 'living in arrears'. In this we have received no help of any substance from the left, or from liberals, or from academics, in Britain, South Africa or internationally — rather, obstruction.

It is an issue that involves a mark of shame on nearly all the socialists and liberals who uncritically championed the ANC and failed to take the measure of their own convictions. To this general truth an exception must be made in the case of those individuals who, against the current in South Africa, together with the courageous publisher of this magazine in South Africa, Kevin French, gave their support to our protests against the crimes committed by the ANC and by SWAPO.

Former detainees now fear that a future ANC/National Party coalition government, bringing together these two dominant undemocratic political traditions, will be the most authoritarian in the country's history. They stand in a very dangerous exposed position as this new fusion government comes into being. Its first task must be to damp down expectations among millions of blacks for an improvement in their immediate conditions of life. Under these circumstances, the former detainees' critical understanding of the real nature of the ANC and its corruption in exile may well prove intolerable.

Their experience of the ANC was and is a learning resource concerning South Africa's future. By shutting their eyes to this, future oppositional individuals and groups — socialists, liberals, trade unionists, convinced Christians, civic-minded individuals and more independent-minded nationalists — deprive themselves of an opportunity for arming themselves morally and intellectually in advance.

In exile, the former detainees fought the battle for democracy under the most difficult and dangerous conditions. They are precious educators of the society about the need for defence of its civil rights, since they opposed both the racist, capitalist abuses of the National Party and the stalinist abuses of the ANC (directed in large part by its guiding brain, the South African Communist Party). As such, they cannot be trusted by either of the future main parties of government.

The problem is: who wants these democratic nuisances? They know too much. That is why they are dangerous for the powers that be, as members of the generation that went from the school students' revolt of 1976 to the ANC mutiny of 1984, and which humorously named the ANC's worst prison after the Fort prison in Johannesburg. ('Number Four' in Sowetan argot, translated into Portuguese, became 'Quatro' in Angola.)

Despite the work of *Searchlight South Africa*, and despite the three recent reports on ANC abuses, former detainees remain severely in danger because of the world's indifference. Vindication by three reports has not brought former detainees, or this journal, any relief. Nor has it yet brought any new courageous support in the form of fresh contributors, distributors or even subscribers. Yet *SSA* continues to be the sole disinterested centre for liberal and socialist international support for the former ANC and SWAPO detainees, despite our own pitiful human and material resources. This journal has on principle refused to attempt to 'use' the detainees for any ideological, political or organisational end.

Our dilemma will appear more clearly after a closer examination of the three reports, and the public naming of individual ANC torturers and murderers by the *Weekly Mail* in its issue of 21 October 1992.

CONFLICT WITHIN THE NEC

The first report to appear was at once conclusive and yet very far from conclusive. In this report the ANC had no alternative except to condemn itself out of its own mouth. In September 1991, Nelson Mandela as president of the ANC responded to extensive pressure from returned exiles, from leading members who had not been in exile and — no doubt — from certain foreign governments, by naming a three-person commission of inquiry into abuses within the ANC in exile. This was in effect an inquiry by the ANC into itself. It was reported in a footnote in *Searchlight South Africa* No. 8, January 1992, in which I stated: 'Political observers and victims of the ANC security apparatus alike expect nothing to come of it'. (p 24)

What could not be known at the time was that the decision to establish the commission of inquiry and, then later on, the further decision to publish its report, was the result of an intensive struggle within the National Executive Committee of the ANC.

A very sharp conflict took place between NEC members who had run Umkhonto weSizwe and the security department in exile — who desperately tried to prevent any inquiry (and, later, still more, publication of its findings) — and other NEC members who wanted the truth to be known. These were mainly more civic-minded ANC activists who had led the campaign of the United Democratic Front within the country during the 1980s. Exile leaders who adamantly opposed an inquiry were Chris Hani (general secretary of the South African Communist Party, former deputy commander of Umkhonto and the person most responsible for suppression of the mutiny in Umkhonto), Joe Nhlanhla (head of the ANC's Department of Intelligence and Security from 1987, and thus head of security while Quatro prison was in operation) and Jacob Zuma (a leading member of the SACP in exile, and head of counter-intelligence in Umkhonto from 1987). The ANC president, Nelson Mandela, gave his support to those in favour of holding the inquiry and, later, of publishing its report; and this grouping prevailed.

Taking place behind closed doors, this struggle was of immense importance for the future of democracy and civic conditions generally in the whole of southern Africa. At stake were two different styles of leadership within the ANC, the one — of the 'external' leaders — deriving from three decades of closed, autarchic, command society in the camps with its model derived from the Soviet KGB and the East German Stasi; the other, of the 'internal' leaders, from the more open and pluralistic culture developed in the trade unions and civic associations within the country during the 1970s and 1980s.

A major concern of the 'internal' leaders was that in a future electoral campaign, under a new constitution, the state security forces would use secret information to discredit the ANC because of past human rights abuses by 'external' leaders in the camps. There was no way 'internal' leaders could know the background of their exile colleagues, in advance of the selection of candidates, without an inquiry by the ANC itself. That decided the matter.

The commission appointed by Mandela was headed by a respected South African barrister, Advocate Thembile Louis Skweyiya, SC. Its official title was The Commission of Enquiry into Complaints by Former African National Congress Prisoners and Detainees, and was known as the 'Skweyiya Commission'.

Its report, conveyed to Mandela in August 1992, noted extensive concern that the commission would carry out a 'tame' investigation. This was principally because in this inquiry the ANC was investigating itself. In addition, Skweyiya is a member of the ANC, and his brother, Zola Skweyiya, is a high-ranking member of the ANC's legal department, As Officer of Justice in the ANC in exile, Zola Skweyiya had been frustrated in his brief to investigate the prison camps. However well intentioned personally, he had been totally ineffective because the camps remained closed to him. A second member, Ms Brigitte

Mabandla, like Advocate Skweyiya, is a member of the ANC and a member of its Constitutional Committee. The third initial member, Mr Charles Nupen, resigned and was replaced during 1991 by Advocate Gilbert Marcus.

The Commission had no powers to subpoena witnesses, or to compel them to answer questions. It was dependent on the willingness of witnesses to come forward, which — given South African conditions — proved in the Commission's words its 'greatest shortcoming'. Its hearings were not in public.

Mr Marcus, gave proof of personal impartiality in a discussion in Johannesburg in October 1991 with the researcher appointed by Amnesty International, who attended some of the sessions of the Commission. The Commission's independence was however gravely threatened by the fact that its secretariat was initially in the hands of a young lawyer, Mr Dali Mpofu, later revealed in the press to be the lover of Mrs Winnie Mandela, then head of the ANC's Department of Social Welfare and a voracious threat to the former detainees.

As the scandal concerning Mrs Mandela's personal life rose to the boil, Mr Mpofu left the commission. With him, however, also disappeared its secretariat, seriously compromising its work. The ANC had undertaken that it would appoint an 'independent lawyer to conduct investigations, interview witnesses, visit detention camps and lead the evidence before the commission and to do all things reasonably incidental to the foregoing'. Advocate Elna Revelas of the Johannesburg Bar, who was not a member of the ANC, was appointed to this investigatory post. A relatively extensive investigation then followed — given the crucial limitation that this was an internal inquiry by a commission appointed by a political party to look into its own abuses.

The reluctance of witnesses to come forward was not, in fact, the Commission's greatest weakness. Its central flaw lay in its terms of reference. These had been set in a letter by Nelson Mandela to each of the three commissioners, referring them in effect to complaints only by living prisoners about their own previous conditions of detention. By definition this excluded what needed investigation at least as much: the murder and disappearances of others. An absurd and arbitrary division was thus created for the Commission from the beginning. Its report was by its very nature partial, flawed and massively inadequate. In the eyes of the commissioners, their brief from the ANC placed the central event in the three decades of the exile — the mutiny in the ANC in Angola by 90 per cent of its trained troops — out of purview. It was as if Hamlet's investigation into the troubles in his family were constrained to omit his father's murder.

The consequences of this flawed brief were very serious. Of the three reports, that of the Skweyiya Commission received by far the greatest attention in the South African press. ANC leaders such as Hani were not only exonerated without proper inquiry but were able to hold up the report afterwards as providing them with a clean bill of health. In this sense, it served the classic function of an official fudge.

AN ABUSE OF POWER

Nevertheless, the Commission concluded that within the ANC in exile for the greater part of the 1980s, 'there existed a situation of extraordinary abuse of power and lack of accountability'. It confessed to 'staggering' brutality by the ANC security department. (pp. 65, 39) The silence of the left and the vilification of this journal are striking in the light of this admission. Nelson Mandela accepted the Commissions's conclusions — reluctantly, and without grace — at a press conference on 19 October 1992. He stated that the ANC leadership acknowledged 'ultimate responsibility for not adequately monitoring and, therefore, eradicating such abuses'. (*Guardian Weekly*, SA, 23 October 1992) This was an evasion. As will be seen, there is evidence that the top leadership in exile, up to the level of Oliver Tambo as president, condoned and participated in the practice of abuses. A clear function of the Skweyiya report was to deflect that impression.

The Commission's treatment of written evidence was dilatory. As one of the editors of *SSA*, I posted the history of the mutiny in Umkhonto published in *SSA* No. 5 to Messrs Mashile Ntlhoro, Attorneys, the Johannesburg firm representing the Skweyiya Commission, on 19 May 1992. This was despite reservations that the full truth could not be revealed in an internal ANC inquiry. Having worked for an independent international commission of inquiry since early 1990, I felt it necessary to make it as difficult as possible for an internal inquiry to suppress information. I therefore tried to place this document on record before the Commission, and in correspondence urged former ANC detainees to place as much testimony as possible before it as well. I later received a registered letter from Mr Brian Mashile of Mashile Ntlhoro, thanking me for providing the Commission with 'valuable information'. The letter added: 'We will be corresponding with you in due course and shall keep you posted of developments.' (Letter, 3 June 1992). No such communication followed.

In the event, the Skweyiya report made no reference to the article on the mutiny in *SSA* No. 5. This was a significant and unjudicial lapse. The article in *SSA* remains the single most important first-hand published account of repressions within the ANC and of the mutiny, which took shape mainly in response to these repressions.

The authors of the article had addressed a letter to Mr Mandela, then in London, on 14 April 1990. This letter was later reprinted in *SSA* No. 5, where it was available to the Commission. In this letter, Ketelo and his colleagues called on Mandela to support their demand for a commission to inquire into 'atrocities' in the ANC camps. (p 68) It was their own first-hand revelations of tortures and killings, published in the British press the previous week, that impelled Mandela to make his first public repudiation of torture by the ANC, at Jan Smuts airport on 14 April 1990.

For the Commission, or its attorneys, to neglect this article — written by the individuals who first drew Mandela's attention to the need for an inquiry — was beneath the level of judicial practice. Because of this lapse alone the investigation was neither 'full' nor 'thorough,' as Mandela had requested.

The report states that it was 'not within the scope of this Commission to deal with the causes of the mutiny'. (p 55) In so far as repressions and maltreatment were a very major cause of the mutiny, the limitation is absurd. The report adds however that there were

> a number of published accounts on the mutiny including a chapter in the recently published book by Stephen Ellis and Tsepo Sechaba entitled *Comrades Against Apartheid*. The authors record that included in the demands of the mutineers was the suspension of the ANC security apparatus and an investigation of Quatro. (pp. 55–56)

This chapter in the book by Ellis and Sechaba (reviewed in *SSA* No. 9) was heavily based on the article by Ketelo and his colleagues. In this way, despite the neglect of the 'valuable information' placed before the Commission by this journal, the work of *Searchlight South Africa* could not be avoided.[4]

In the event only 17 detainees gave evidence to the Commission. One was Pallo Jordan, a leading figure in the ANC's negotiating team, who was held in isolation for six weeks by the ANC security department in Zambia in 1983. According to the report, he was arrested following criticism of the security department for conducting itself 'like a repressive police force'. (p 66)

The Commission was 'eventually' also furnished with a copy of the report of the so-called Stuart Commission into the 1984 mutiny in Angola. The Skweyiya Commission noted that the contents of this previous internal ANC inquiry had 'never been made public and, it seems, not formally tabled before the ANC National Executive Committee'. (p 56) This bears out the account published in *SSA* No. 6 of the sinister and farcical nature of the 1985 ANC national conference at Kabwe in Zambia in 1985 which, as stated in *SSA*, neglected to table the Stuart Commission report.[5]

The Skweyiya Commission in fact vindicates the motives of the mutineers, and exculpates them from the charge of having been 'enemy agents'. Ellis and Sechaba, it notes, state in their book that it was widely known that the Stuart Commission 'attributed blame for the mutiny on the excesses of the security department, poor political education, poor recreational facilities and quality of food and the yearning to go home and fight'. The Skweyiya Commission then places its own stamp of verification on these remarks. 'These are indeed the findings of the Stuart Commission', it states. (p 56)

The Skweyiya Commission did not publish the report of the Stuart Commission, though it recommended publication. (So far, this appears not to have been done.) Revelations quoted from the Stuart report make it plain that ANC leaders imprisoned, tortured and executed the mutineers in full knowledge that they were innocent of the smear of being South African government agents. The Skweyiya report states that the Stuart Commission had 'clearly identified' the malaise of brutality in the ANC. (p 65) It quotes the Stuart report as having stated that force had become 'the rule rather than the exception' and that coercion was 'indiscriminately used not only as a punishment but even when carrying out interviews and debriefings'. (ibid)

The then ANC president, Oliver Tambo, certainly knew this when he inspected the inmates at Quatro in 1987, as reported in *SSA* No. 5 and confirmed by the Skweyiya Commission. (p 36) Yet neither he nor any other leader relieved the prisoners of their misery, knowing well they were innocent of the charge of being 'enemy agents'. In his report as former president in exile to the ANC national conference in Durban in July 1991, Tambo repeated against the mutineers the brutal and now discredited assertion: 'Enemy Agents!' (*Sunday Star*, Johannesburg, 21 July 1991) It was then, as it had been in exile, an incitement to murder and brutality.

THE SKWEYIYA COMMISSION'S CONCLUSIONS

Contrary to Tambo, the report concludes:

(i) Those witnesses who were detained without trial should have the allegations against them unequivocally and unconditionally withdrawn… These witnesses deserve, in our view, a clear and unequivocal apology for the wrongs that they have suffered.

(ii) All witnesses who suffered maltreatment while being detained in ANC camps should receive monetary compensation for their ordeal.

(iii) Some of the witnesses who appeared before us were, in our view, in need of medical and psychological assistance. Such should be offered and provided by the ANC.

(iv) Some of the witnesses expressed the desire to continue their education which had been interrupted by long periods of detention. We recommend that the ANC provide assistance in this regard.

(v) Detainees who lost property should be compensated for such loss.

(vi) It is apparent to the Commission that many people suffered in the ANC camps... We suggest, therefore, that consideration be given to the creation of an independent structure which is perceived to be impartial and which is capable of documenting cases of abuse and giving effect to the type of recommendations made in this report...

(vii) We are aware that allegations have been made concerning the disappearance and murder of prisoners... (The) allegations are of the most serious nature and demand investigation. We therefore suggest that the impartial and independent structure referred to in paragraph (vi) above, or some other appropriate body be charged with the responsibility of investigating all allegations of disappearance and murder.

(viii) We strongly recommend that urgent and immediate attention be given to identifying and dealing with those responsible for the maltreatment of detainees... It is clear that several persons against whom serious allegations of brutality have been levelled are currently employed by the ANC in the security department. A list of such persons will be supplied to the President of the ANC. It would be wrong in our view to limit the responsibility to such persons. There are clearly persons in the senior ranks of the security department who were responsible for the situation in the Camps and who should not escape the net of accountability. We consider this recommendation to be of the greatest importance, particularly in the light of the role that the ANC is likely to play in a future Government. No person who is guilty of committing atrocities should ever again be allowed to assume a position of power. Unless the ANC is prepared to take decisive action, the risk of repetition will forever be present. The best formula for prevention is to ensure that the perpetrators of brutality are brought to account and are seen to be brought to account.

(ix) [The Commission here recommends that secret ANC internal reports into the death of Thami Zulu in Zambia in 1989, and of the Stuart commission into the 1984 mutiny in MK, be made public].[6]

(x) [The Commission finally recommends that in keeping with its terms of reference, its report be released to the public 'as soon as possible'. In the event this was to take two months, while ANC leaders debated how to handle these damning conclusions.] (pp. 68–74)

The principal blame for the conduct of the ANC security department was placed by the Commission on a single individual, Mzwai Piliso, head of the ANC's Department of Intelligence and Security until 1987. Piliso admitted personal participation in tortures. His task, in his own words, was to extract information 'at any cost'. The report states that Piliso was 'relieved of his duties' in 1987, and that the views and attitude of his successor at the head of a provisional directorate of security, Joe Nhlanhla, 'contrasted sharply' with those of Piliso. No evidence is provided for this assertion.

Sizakele Sigxashe, head of the military tribunal which ordered public execution of mutineers at Pango camp in 1984, is cited as a member of the 'new department' which, according to the report, was 'charged with remedying the past'. (p 63) There is no reference in the report to Sigxashe's prominent role in ordering executions, which is clearly stated in the article by Ketelo and his colleagues. [*SSA* No. 5, p 28 in this book] Nor therefore is there any explanation how a person responsible for ordering executions could be 'charged with remedying the past'. At this point the Skweyiya Commission report becomes a whitewash. The failure of the Commission to place on record the 'valuable information' provided by *SSA* No. 5 reveals itself here as prejudicial.

THE CURIOUS HISTORY OF CHRIS HANI

In the same way, the Commission was able to exonerate Chris Hani, the then Umkhonto commissar. Hani was permitted to express his 'feelings of revulsion' at oppressive practices in the ANC without becoming subject to normal cross-examination. (p 60) This is particularly important because of Hani's current status as general secretary of the SACP and his former position as Umkhonto chief of staff, with a major following among its commanders. There are several explicit references to oppressive conduct by Hani in Ketelo's article. These too were ignored by the Commission, which reported that Hani

> told us of his increasing concern for what he described as '**the horrors of Quatro**' [in bold type in the report] and how he and others had insisted on the adoption of the Code of Conduct of 1985. [This Code was a dead letter — PT] He described some of the members of the security department as '**really vicious**', a description which was amply borne out by the evidence. He felt that the ANC as an organization built upon respect for human rights had an obligation to acknowledge and redress the wrongs of the past and to prevent them from happening in the future. (pp. 60–61)

The article by Ketelo and his colleagues includes the following references to Hani.

1. In the second stage of the mutiny, during the democratic and peaceful drawing up of grievances at Viana camp outside Luanda in February 1984, Hani 'with an AK submachine gun, made his appearance on the side of the loyalists chasing and firing at those who wanted to join the mutineers' (p 44)

2. Standing beside two members of the Liberation Committee of the Organisation for African Unity, Hani made a speech to the troops at Viana in which he denounced the mutiny and its demands as 'an adventure instigated by disgruntled elements'. (p 47)

3. Hani and the Umkhonto commander Joe Modise 'accompanied a group of security personnel to round up those who had escaped arrest at Viana. When a captured mutineer tried to explode a grenade in the military vehicle in which Hani and Modise were escorting their prisoner, 'Hani issued instructions to the security personnel to shoot [the prisoner] on the spot, but Modise intervened saying 'he [the prisoner] must go and suffer first'. (p 48) The prisoner, Muyisile Maseko (real name Xolile Siphunzi), was last known by the authors of the article to have been left in Luanda State Prison when the mutineers were released in December 1988.

4. Mwezi Twala (travelling name Khotso Morena), a member of the Committee of Ten which was elected to lead the mutiny, was 'shot from behind in the presence of Joe Modise and Chris Hani during their round-up of other mutineers'. (p 50) Twala survived.

5. Following the decision by the military tribunal headed by Sigxashe to execute seven of the mutineers at Pango camp in the third and final stage of the mutiny, Hani 'endorsed their execution' which he appears to have witnessed himself. (p 53) Another member of the tribunal was Morris Seabelo, 'a former commander and commissar at Quatro and at that time chief of security in the whole of the Angola region of MK'. (p 52) Seabelo (real name Lulamile Dantile) has been described by participants in the mutiny as Hani's 'closest lieutenant'. Prisoners at Quatro were told by guards that Hani was in fact a member of the tribunal himself, and that he was present at the executions. (personal communication) Similar allegations were made to the Douglas Commission, discussed below. Hani denies this. *SSA* has not been able independently either to verify or

disprove these allegations. They are matters that the Commission did not investigate.

6. Finally, together with Stanley Mabizela, a fellow member of the ANC National Executive Committee (NEC), Hani personally suppressed all elected structures at Dakawa camp in Tanzania in late December 1989, in order to depose former mutineers who had been freely elected by ANC exiles. These included the chairman and organising secretary of the elected committee representing all the exiles in Tanzania.

AN ADMISSION

Hani and other top ANC leaders were spared by the Skweyiya Commission's terms of reference and by its decision to place responsibility for investigating details of torture, murders and disappearances, and for naming names, on yet another commission.

Prior to the Skweyiya report, the most serious investigation into abuses in the camps published in South Africa was an article by Hein Marais in the journal *Work in Progress*, in its issue of June 1992. Marais gives an impartial assessment both of the book by Ellis and Sechaba and of the article in *Searchlight South Africa* No. 5, which he acknowledges by name at several points. An editorial explains the editors' decision to 'look closely at the dark chapter, both in the interests of the ANC itself, and in the interests of democracy in the long-term'. It urges ANC leaders to 'come clean', arguing that the organisation could not afford to have its image tarnished at election time by the National Party, which would exploit every weakness. Appearing in the closing months of the secret sessions of the Skweyiya Commission, this issue of *WIP* bears the marks of a strenuous efforts by 'internal' leaders of the ANC and the SACP to force the Commission to publish. Marais nevertheless does address the central moral issues.

Next to a photograph of Hani, the journal cover ran the headline: 'ANC Camps: Hani opens up'. There is very little opening up by Hani. Forgetting his own role in damning the first ANC detainees to return to South Africa as 'enemy agents' (on South African television, in mid-1990), Hani presents himself as the person most responsible for ending executions in 1984, which he says he had always opposed. He declares that while certain ANC members should not be part of a new security force in South Africa, and that a parliamentary committee should oversee the security apparatus, abuses in the ANC had happened only 'to a very small extent'. The more the evidence is studied, the more it appears that Hani has adapted himself chameleon-like to every terrain.

Within days of its publication of the Skweyiya report, the *Weekly Mail* summed up its inadequacy in a major front-page article. It headed its exposure: 'The names the ANC tried to hide'. (21 October 1992) The article by Ketelo and others in *SSA*, the major suppressed document of the Commission, formed a principal basis to the *WM*'s investigation. In the preceding week, a journalist on its staff phoned Ketelo in Britain to question him in detail about the article. He was intensively questioned about his relation to *Searchlight South Africa*. (It must be stated emphatically that Ketelo has no relation to *Searchlight South Africa* beyond having been the principal author of the article in issue No. 5.)

An interview with Ketelo then appeared as part of the three-page investigation by the *WM*. About half the names and details of torturers cited by the *WM* confirmed information published over two years earlier in *SSA* and posted to the paper at the time. It was not until after the ANC published the Skweyiya report that the *Weekly Mail* moved to publish its own investigation, confirming and supplementing Ketelo's article in detail. Even then, despite citing Ketelo, it carried no reference to *Searchlight South Africa*. There was nothing in the *WM* referring readers to Ketelo's article, despite its central place in the literature on ANC abuses. In its own fashion, and for its own reasons, the *WM* thus continued the strange relegation of this journal to the land of the living dead.

In almost comical fashion, the *WM* was then forced to acknowledge the existence of this journal the following week. This was at the instance of the ANC itself. As the *WM* reported, its revelations 'sparked outrage' from the ANC. For the first time, the ANC now publicly acknowledged the work of *Searchlight South Africa* in exposing its abuses. Its spokesperson, Carl Niehaus, stated:

> The names, some of which are completely unknown to us, are clearly drawn from a magazine article published in *Searchlight South Africa* Vol. 2 No. 1, 1990, and is [sic] therefore available for all people to read. We find it regrettable that a newspaper such as *The Weekly Mail* with its own outstanding record of exposing abuse and corruption should not have seen fit to pay attention to accuracy and detail. Among other things it states that Maurice Seabelo died mysteriously in Lesotho. Now again the *WM* lifts this terminology from the magazine article, whereas even a superficial investigation or an inquiry to the ANC would have revealed what is a matter of public record. Maurice Seabelo was among those killed in SADF raids on Maseru in December 1985. (*WM*, 30 October 1992)

Seabelo was the first commander at Quatro, which was known formally both as 'Camp 32' and after his death as the 'Morris Seabelo Rehabilitation Centre'.

Substantial detail is provided in *SSA* No. 5 about Seabelo, who at the time of the mutiny was chief of security of the whole of the Angola region of Umkhonto. As Hani's closest lieutenant, Seabelo sat on the tribunal which ordered death by firing squad for the seven mutineers at Pango. He later boasted to prisoners in Quatro that he had personally taken part in the executions, blasting his victims with an RPG anti-tank bazooka rocket. Survivors were compelled to witness the mutilation of their comrades. (personal communication)

Without citing its source, the *WM* article of 23 October had repeated a phrase by Ketelo and his co-authors in *SSA* No. 5, concerning Seabelo's death. They had stated that in late 1985 Seabelo had 'mysteriously lost his life in an underground ANC residence in Lesotho, where none of those he was with, including Nomkhosi Mini, were spared to relate the story'. (p 54) Ketelo did not state that this mass killing took place in an SADF raid, but it could easily be inferred. It was indicative of the ANC that it chose to make an issue over such a phrase.

In reply, the *WM* stated that as well as drawing on *SSA* its report had been based 'on a variety of sources, and no names were included unless they were corroborated by more than one source'. It argued cogently that where people in authority had knowledge of torture being carried out by individuals directly under their command, this amounted to complicity. It asked:

> If the minister of law and order, the commissioner of police or a senior officer under his command, knew that certain detainees were being tortured in security police detention and chose not to intervene, do we not accuse them of the same crime?

A TYPE OF AMBIGUITY

The *WM* suggests a much broader scope for inquiry concerning Hani's activities than provided by the Skweyiya Commission. Hani's role, it stated, was 'ambiguous.' It notes that

> according to several affidavits and accounts by former detainees he endorsed the decision by the Military Tribunal for the execution of seven of the rebels (which he denies) and was present at the subsequent execution of four others. They also say that he was present when Mwezi Twala was shot in the back in Angola in 1984.
>
> Former ANC detainees also say that at times he suppressed their right to speak and hold office (after their release) and did not keep the promises he had previously made to them. They say he also did little to help them while they were in detention in Quatro.

Investigation of the role of ANC leaders in executions appears to be part of the remit of a new commission named by the ANC a month after publication of the Skweyiya report. It includes Mr Sam Motsuenyane (an elderly South African businessman), Mr David Zamchiya (a former Zimbabwean government official) and Ms Margaret Burnham of the United States. (*Weekly Mail*, 27 November 1992)

SSA has no additional information about the working of this new commission. It suffers the same defect as the Skweyiya Commission: whatever the merits of its members, it represents an organisation investigating its own malpractice. The evasiveness of the Skweyiya Commission in relation to Hani does not inspire confidence in the will or ability of the new commission to name names comprehensively, to specify crimes committed and to recommend firm measures for exclusion of the perpetrators from office.

As the *WM* pointed out, several high-ranking torturers and killers continue to work in the ANC security department operating out of party headquarters in Shell House, Johannesburg. These include Nelson Mandela's personal bodyguard, M.B. Mavuso (Umkhonto travelling name 'Jomo'), a former guard at Quatro who is 'widely alleged to have been directly involved in torture'. (ibid)

Another torturer currently working in ANC headquarters, travelling name Sizwe Mkhonto — a former student at the Moscow Party Institution, trained in intelligence in East Germany and the USSR — was camp commander at Quatro for several years, starting while still in his teens. This brutalised youth called the principal leader of the mutiny, Ephraim Nkondo, from his cell in Quatro on Saturday 26 May 1984. This was shortly after the crushing of the mutiny in Pango camp. Nkondo was seen the same day being pulled through the camp with a rope around his neck. (personal communication) The next day he was found dead in his cell, with a rope around his neck. Without strict accounting for the torture and murder of individuals such as Nkondo, the ANC continues to carry the mark of Cain. It remains to be seen whether the new commission headed by Mr Motsuenyane — a director of ICI (South Africa), president of the Boy Scouts in South Africa and founder and chairman of the National African Chamber of Commerce (NAFCOC) — can honestly confront this past.

As its title indicates, the report by Amnesty International, the second to appear, is far more adequate to the subject. Entitled: 'South Africa: Torture, ill-treatment and executions in African National Congress camps', this was the most balanced of the three reports. It notes that officials of politically impartial human rights bodies in South Africa had informed Amnesty that they would have been 'willing to establish a genuinely independent commission of inquiry had they been approached by the ANC'. (p 21) The ANC did not approach them.

Amnesty is very forthright that the ANC's torturers and killers should never be

> allowed to hold positions of authority within the organization or under any future South African administration. In particular, they should never be in a position where they have responsibility for law enforcement or custody of prisoners. (p 26)

Such a cleansing of the stables has yet to begin.

Amnesty is lucid in pointing out weaknesses in the terms of reference and operation of the Skweyiya Commission, particularly its failure to 'analyse the chains of command within the security department and MK, and between these bodies and the ANC leadership, in order to establish political responsibility for what went on in the camps'. (p 23) This is the most sensitive issue for the leaders in exile, and therefore least accessible to an internal closed inquiry.

The Amnesty report indicates that the ANC's system of providing nearly all its black members in exile with travelling names, or *noms de guerre*, continues to screen the identities of both victims and their persecutors. This is shown by the continued effective anonymity of torturers such as Sizwe Mkhonto and of the seven men executed at Pango. (They are not anonymous of course to South African state security officials, or to iMbokodo, only to the general public.)

The names of the seven people executed at Pango are taken by Amnesty from Ketelo's article. But these are travelling names, fictions, and therefore serve to obscure the fate of these people to their relatives.[7] The best known of these men, referred to in *Searchlight South Africa* and in the Amnesty report by the travelling name James Nkabinde, was Mlamli Namba. (personal communication) Along with several other members of iMbokodo, Namba resigned from the security department in 1980 in protest at its authoritarian behaviour and because of corruption at ANC headquarters in Lusaka. As stated in Ketelo's history of the mutiny, he had been a personal bodyguard to Tambo in Lusaka. Namba's fate is therefore a personal reproach against Tambo.

THE RESPONSIBILITY OF OLIVER TAMBO

The third of the three reports summarises the results of an inquiry by a Durban advocate, Robert Douglas SC, commissioned by an explicitly pro-capitalist organisation based in Washington DC, the International Freedom Foundation (IFF).[8] Its most important section consists of extracts from about 60 sworn depositions made in the second half of 1992, mostly from survivors of the camps. These depositions need to be carefully checked and assessed in their original form, since witnesses were not cross-examined and their statements may well contain some individual errors as well as unfounded assertions. In time, however, and in the course of thorough historical research, they will provide a major source of information for a fuller historical picture of the ANC in exile. Outside the archives of state security and the ANC itself, they represent the biggest body of first-hand statements yet collected about the life of the ANC in exile. Judging from extracts from witnesses whose experiences were previously recorded in this journal, the material presented as evidence by Douglas does appear to reflect the actual statements of survivors of the camps and generally does not appear to have been falsified. Survivors of the mutiny and victims of the security department think highly of the evidence, though not necessarily of Douglas' method of drawing conclusions. (personal communication)

The report is particularly damaging to the reputation of Tambo. Witness 25 (they are not named) is described as having joined the ANC inside South Africa in 1978, eventually becoming a senior member of the intelligence wing after leaving the country. He states:

> I am fully familiar with the command structure of both the security and intelligence wings in the ANC during those years. At the head of both was Oliver Tambo, the President of the ANC. The security wing was commanded by Mzwai Piliso [condemned by the Skweyiya Commission for his forthright advocacy of torture] and the intelligence wing by Sezekele Sigxashe [head of the tribunal that ordered the execution of the mutineers at Pango]. (p 45)

A former medical officer in the camps, interviewed by Douglas, is also cited as saying that after the influx in 1976, 'President Tambo appointed him to a senior position in the security department to assist with the screening of new recruits'. This witness is then quoted as saying that:

> The security system was directly under the President. We reported to the President directly and his secretary Duma Nokwe was the one we first reported to. (pp. 58–59)

Tambo has a powerful case to answer. As president he was no remote, purely formal figure in the ANC — that is, principally a figurehead or symbol, like a modern constitutional monarch. He was more in the manner of the president of the United States, head of the executive: and in this case, at the time of the mutiny, an unaccountable and largely unelected executive, unrestrained by checks and balances. As ANC president he was commander in chief of MK and one of the three senior office-holders in the ANC. (The other two were Alfred Nzo, secretary-general after Nokwe, and Tom Nkobi, as treasurer). Directly under his authority came three sub-departments: (1) army; (2) security and intelligence; (3) information and publicity. As president, he thus had more information than anyone else in the whole organisation.

Tambo presided over a crucial session of the High Command of MK, meeting in Luanda, either in the last week of January or early February 1984. This meeting took place immediately after the first stage of the mutiny at Kangandala on the eastern front in Malanje province — when troops refused to go into action against the Angolan rebel movement UNITA — and immediately before the second stage of mutiny at Viana camp on the outskirts of Luanda in February, when a Committee of Ten was elected and demands were drawn up.

Present at this session of the High Command besides Tambo were Nzo; Nkobi; MK commander Joe Modise; MK chief of staff (and SACP general secretary) Joe Slovo; SACP leaders Reg September, Mac Maharaj and Cassius Make (real name Job Tlhabane, assassinated by apartheid state agents in Swaziland in 1987); Timothy Mokoena, MK chief of personnel; Ntate Mashego (real name Graham Morodi), regional commander; and a number of ranking military and security officers, including Peter Seeiso. (Hani was not present.) The meeting discussed the grievances already being expressed by the troops, Tambo taking a leading part.

The top political leaders of the ANC, the SACP, and the top military leaders of MK, most notably Tambo and Slovo, were therefore well apprised of the discontent among the overwhelming majority of the ANC's trained troops. They knew the feeling of the troops, then gathering in Viana, before the outbreak of full-scale mutiny, and took no adequate measures to meet their demands. As Ketelo and his colleagues recorded, these were:

1. An immediate suspension of the Security Department and establishment of a commission to investigate its all-round activities. Included here are also the investigation of one of the most feared secret camps of the ANC, Quatro.

2. A review of the cadre policy of the ANC to establish the missing links that were a cause for a stagnation that had caught up with our drive to expand the armed struggle. [This was in essence a demand to be withdrawn from the civil war in Angola, and to be sent to fight in South Africa against the forces of the state — PT.]

3. To convene a fully representative democratic conference to review the development of the struggle, draw new strategies and have elections for a new NEC. (*SSA* No. 5, p 45)

It is most probable that the High Command, acting as a body, and headed by Tambo, directed the suppression of the purely peaceful gathering of the mutineers at Viana, where these demands were formulated in a series of open, public mass meetings. The ANC suppressed this phase of the mutiny principally by summoning the Presidential Brigade of FAPLA, the army of the ruling MPLA party, to storm the camp. In all likelihood this followed a personal appeal by Tambo to the Angolan president. Close questioning of all those present at this meeting of the High Command, by commission of inquiry, meeting in open session, is needed to determine precise responsibility for the tortures, imprisonment and deaths that followed.

THE EXECUTIONS AT PANGO

In his report, Advocate Douglas suggests further dimensions of responsibility on the part of the ANC leadership. He quotes a very important passage from the interview with Hani in *Work in Progress* (June 1992) concerning suppression of the mutiny in its third and final stage, at Pango camp in May 1984. Hani states:

> The loyalists (if I may use that term) overran the camps. Lives were lost on both sides. Very sad, because these were all members of the ANC, fellow South Africans. And that was the end of my role. I was never a member of the tribunal which tried them. A tribunal was set up by the ANC to try them, and some of them were sentenced to death. And executed — it was a big number, about eighteen or nineteen, I can't remember. I rushed back to Lusaka and said to the leadership: Stop the executions. (pp. 54–55)

This is the first high-level acknowledgement that the number of people executed at Pango was much higher than indicated in the article by Ketelo and his colleagues. Their account was clearly restrained.

Secondly, Hani makes plain in this statement that authority for stopping the executions lay with the top political leadership of the ANC at the organisation's headquarters in Lusaka. This suggests primarily Oliver Tambo himself. Hani's statement is the most important public comment on the mutiny so far by any leading figure in the ANC in exile. It is puzzling, however, because as Army Commissar of MK and as the sole member of the NEC in the region, Hani was himself already the senior leader of the ANC at Pango. It was left to a relatively far less influential figure in the NEC, Mrs Gertrude Shope, to relieve the suffering of the prisoners, as reported by Ketelo and his colleagues in *SSA* No. 5. (p 29 in this book) As Douglas observes, Hani's statement raises more questions than it answers. Nothing except questioning, in open commission, of all relevant ANC officials can satisfy the need for justice in this matter. No ANC leader of the exile can be trusted with authority until full knowledge of this individual's conduct is made available to the public.

The principal flaw in the Douglas Commission report relates to instances of over-straining of the published evidence, to support conclusions condemning leading figures in Umkhonto: principally Slovo and Ronnie Kasrils, both leaders of the SACP.[9] In the opinion of this writer, the existing evidence, including evidence accumulated by Douglas, provides very strong supposition that both men had extensive knowledge of the system of human rights abuses in the camps. But the evidence which is publicly available at present is not yet conclusive. It can not be concluded on the available evidence that they had direct, personal, first-hand responsibility.

Slovo is cited in one deposition as having visited Quatro at night. (p 43) Prisoners from the mutiny in Quatro were indeed told this at the time by guards. An Umkhonto soldier, Zondi, whose jaw had been broken at Pango, told fellow prisoners in Luanda State Security Prison that he had been sent to military hospital in Luanda on Slovo's orders, following a visit to Quatro. Zondi later suffered severely at Quatro, where guards repeatedly hit his still broken jaw, and where he developed epilepsy. (personal communication)

Kasrils is cited as being responsible for visiting a prison camp at Nampula in Mozambique in 1982 and for incarcerating fourteen Umkhonto soldiers in a basement at Quibaxe in northern Angola, following their refusal to obey orders in 1977. (pp. 7, 43, 60) The prison at Nampula was deep in the bush, surrounded by wild animals and in an area heavily affected by malaria. The majority of prisoners were MK veterans of the war in Zimbabwe, where they had fought in the military wing of the Zimbabwe African People's Union (ZAPU). When they refused to be transferred to fight in the civil war in Angola, demanding to be sent to fight in South Africa itself, they were confined to Nampula, where some went mad. Kasrils did not deny knowledge of this camp in a press conference in Johannesburg in January 1993. At this conference, he and two former participants in the 1977 'mutiny' at Quibaxe denied that the men imprisoned in the basement had been affected by noxious fumes. (*Weekly Mail*, 29 January 1993) Slovo and Kasrils bear responsibility as senior officers of Umkhonto. The precise limits and extent of their responsibility for abuses remain unclear.

Douglas unfortunately made no headway in tracking down the drugs Mafia within iMbokodo, a line of inquiry that may well hold the key to the murder of several ANC personnel in Zambia in 1989, including the high-ranking Umkhonto commander Thami Zulu who died under ANC guard in Lusaka in November 1989.[10] Until the criminal network within Umkhonto weSizwe, and especially in the security department, is uncovered, the precise extent of infiltration by South African Military Intelligence must remain unknown.

Whatever the flaws in the report, these are insignificant by comparison with the additional information it makes available to South Africans about the organisation which now prepares to govern them. The report is full of suggestive leads, which need to be followed up by careful, investigative, historical research. This cannot be done in detail here.

The editors of this journal were invited by letter to assist the investigation by Mr Douglas. We did not respond, as there was no way of knowing what kind of hidden agenda lay in his commission by the IFF. Paradoxically, the report by Douglas was the only one to quote directly from the article by Ketelo and others in *SSA*, and to cite this magazine by name as its source, There is a long, extended extract from this article in the report — a description of the mutiny, which Douglas describes as a 'vivid and detailed account.' (pp. 20–23) It is the longest quoted passage in the report.

Some former detainees whom we know of provided depositions to Douglas, others declined. There can be no imputation of 'selling out' against those who gave evidence to Douglas. They were completely within their rights. So too of course was Stephen Ellis, who gave the benefit of his knowledge to Mr Douglas in Leiden.

That said, it must be stated that it seems extremely likely that the IFF in South Africa stands close to Inkatha and Chief Mangosuthu Buthelezi, and therefore also to the wrecking strategy directed against the ANC and the SACP by South African Military Intelligence. This is no reflection on the standing of Mr Douglas as a barrister or on the quality of his evidence, but it does indicate the serious weakness of liberal and human rights organisations in South Africa, which all too frequently have compromised their principles through uncritical support for the ANC. There is urgent need for these individuals and organisations to reassess their mode of thinking and activity.

For many ANC detainees there is nowhere to turn for support, except to an organisation tainted by its relation to the far right. Criticism must be directed, not to these detainees (many of whom are in despair), but to people and organisations in South Africa and abroad who abandoned them. In the absence of liberals and socialists who are prepared to conduct these investigations, this is left to the IFF and individuals such as Advocate Douglas.

There is a major need for a campaign to compel the ANC to implement the recommendations of the Skweyiya Commission calling for disclosure of the names of the guilty and for real, practical monetary restitution to the detainees. The majority of the former detainees are in desperate poverty. It is a South African and international disgrace, a pall on the conscience of anyone concerned with civil rights in the region. Likewise, this journal supports the demand of former detainees (and of Advocate Douglas) for the commission headed by Mr Justice Richard Goldstone — investigating murders and abuses by the security forces of the state — to extend its inquiries to human rights abuses by the ANC and SACP in exile.

The matter becomes all the more urgent, since a merger between the old South African state security forces and members of the ANC security department is on the order of the day. Nhlanhla, the head of the ANC's Department of Intelligence and Security — and one of the leading opponents of the Skweyiya inquiry — is reported to be in line 'for a top job' in the new combined force. (*Weekly Mail*, 29 January 1993)

MALADMINISTRATION OF JUSTICE

Like Amnesty, this journal deplores the government's Further Indemnity Act, which was passed shortly after publication of the ANC commission's report. The effect of this act is to provide state protection for its own torturers and murderers and those of the ANC alike. We endorse the call of the Douglas Commission for those responsible for human rights abuses in the ANC camps to be prosecuted — but as part of comprehensive prosecution of the infinitely greater number of murderers and torturers paid by the South African state. There can be no justice in South Africa without this. Yet it is all but impossible that it will happen.

The former detainees have real cause to fear for their future. This can be seen in the Transkei. As the Amnesty report reveals, two and a half years after the political assassination of the former detainee Sipho Phungulwa in the Transkei, nobody has yet been brought to trial. This is despite the presence of witnesses and ballistic evidence, and the fact that two men were belatedly arrested, charged and released on bail.

Amnesty cites a report in the South African newspaper *City Press* in late 1992 to the effect that the office of the Transkei Commissioner of Police had circulated a directive signed by the deputy chief of the Criminal Investigation Department, ordering police not to arrest ANC members on criminal charges without first consulting an Umkhonto liaison officer. (p 18) The Transkei police have denied the report. It seems all too likely to be true. To former detainees from the camps, it is a foretaste of South Africa to come. There is urgent need for connections to be made between former detainees in South Africa and Namibia, and human rights organisations in South Africa and the world. Without full and public justice for the victims of the prison camps run by the ANC and SWAPO, there is no future for civil rights in the region. Future abuses cannot be combated by people who endorse (or are silent about) past abuses. An issue of this kind can not be buried in a shallow grave.

NOTES

1. Report of the Commission of Enquiry into Complaints by Former African National Congress Prisoners and Detainees, Johannesburg, August 1992. Amnesty International, South Africa: Torture, ill-treatment and executions in African National Congress camps, London, December 1992 (Al Index: AFR 53/272). The Report of the Douglas Commission, Durban, January 1993.
2. The *Guardian* in Britain carried a sharp rebuke on its letter page on 19 February 1993 from Mr Bill McElroy, of Justice for Southern Africa. He pointed to factual errors and bias in a eulogistic article by Victoria Brittain on Chris Hani, the SACP general secretary, concerning his role in the mutiny in Umkhonto in Angola in 1984.
3. Ketelo, Bandile, et al (1990), 'A Miscarriage of Democracy: The ANC Security Department in the 1984 Mutiny in Umkhonto weSizwe', *Searchlight South Africa* No. 5 (July 1990).
4. Ellis, Stephen, and Sechaba, Tsepo (1992), *Comrades Against Apartheid: The ANC and the South African Communist Party in Exile*, James Currey and Indiana University Press.

   Ellis and Sechaba note that their account of the mutiny 'relies heavily' on the article in *SSA* No. 5 by Ketelo et al. (p 128, n 3) The reviews of this book were interesting. The ANC newspaper, *New Nation*, funded by the Catholic Church, waited until immediately after publication of the Skweyiya report before printing a very favourable review which took note of the 'stalinist socialism' of the SACP and commended the book's 'wealth of new information and insights.' (30 October 1992) By contrast, the review by Garth Strachan — formerly close to the ANC security department — in the SACP journal *African Communist* (second quarter, 1992) — is concerned mainly to question the motives of the authors, and avoids the central issue of suppression of democratic discussion by the security department through a bland reference to 'mistakes.' Strachan's review makes no reference at all to the mutiny.
5. Mkatashingo (letter to the editors), 'The ANC Conference: From Kabwe to Johannesburg', *Searchlight South Africa* No. 6 (January 1991).
6. For the mysterious death of Thami Zulu (real name Muzi Ngwenya), poisoned with a chemical Diazonin [should read 'Diazinon' — PT, 2009] used by South African Military Intelligence while under ANC guard in Zambia in November 1989, see Paul Trewhela, 'A Can of Worms in Lusaka: The Imprisonment of Hubert Sipho Mbeje,' *Searchlight South Africa* No. 9 (August 1992). A definite criminal network existed within the ANC in Angola, Zambia and the frontline states. (See note 10.)
7. The following appear to be the real names of some of the people executed at Pango: Mlamli Namba, Vusumzi Maxwell Tonisi, Loyiso Victor August, Lucky Samuel Twala, King George Matshika. These names are derived from named photographs of Umkhonto members published in an 8-page Fact Sheet titled 'ANC Hell Camps', abstracted from the *Aida Parker Newsletter* No 141, Johannesburg. Names and photographs are almost certainly from the files of South African Military Intelligence.
8. The Johannesburg newspaper *City Press* has stated that the IFF is headed by US Congressman Jesse Helms, whom it describes as 'a renowned ANC-basher and supporter of Renamo

in Mozambique, UNITA in Angola and other rightwing causes elsewhere in Africa and Latin America.' (18 October 1992)

9. Kasrils is described in the Douglas report as deputy commissar of Umkhonto in Angola, head of Umkhonto special operations and head of its military intelligence (1983–88). He played a prominent part in events leading to the massacre by Ciskei troops at Bisho in September 1992. (See Paul Trewhela, 'A Massacre of Innocence', *Searchlight South Africa* No. 10 (April 1993), pp. 39–50.)
10. Earl, a senior figure in iMbokodo in Angola and Tanzania, fled to Kenya in 1990 with his wife after they rejected efforts by a leading figure in iMbokodo to recruit them into an operation involving smuggling of drugs into South Africa. The United Nations High Commissioner for Refugees moved them to the United States. (personal communication) Earl was based at this time in Zambia, where a series of mysterious deaths took place around the same time, in some cases involving security personnel. One of those murdered was Jackie Mabusa, a member of the security directorate and nephew of the iMbokodo security chief, Joe Nhlanhla. Mabusa was poisoned in Lusaka in 1989 while attempting to investigate corruption in the National Executive Committee. (See note 6) A major scandal involving the top ANC leadership in Lusaka has still to break (see pp. 115–126 of this book).

*

Author's note, August 2009: This essay was published in *Searchlight South Africa* No. 10 in April 1993, before publication of the report of the Motsuenyane Commission, which had been appointed by the ANC to investigate human rights abuses within its ranks. The report of the Motsuenyane Commission was later issued by the ANC in August 1993, subsequent to the report of the Skweyiya Commission (which had been appointed for the same purpose), which appeared in August 1992, and prior to the convening of the Truth and Reconciliation Commission by the first post-apartheid government under President Nelson Mandela.

The open letter to Nelson Mandela by five former members of Umkhonto weSizwe, written on 14 April 1990 and delivered to him at his hotel in London very shortly afterwards (p 43 in this book), was one of the first published calls for a commission of inquiry into abuses which the authors and others had suffered.

One of the five authors, Amos Maxongo, was probably the first victim of Quatro prison camp to talk about these experiences with Mandela, and to call on him in person to convene a commission of inquiry. Then staying in London with Bill McElroy, Maxongo stood up and confronted Mandela with 'ANC atrocities against their own fighters' at a public meeting in Commonwealth House in London, in 1991, resulting in 'consternation among the platform party' which included Thabo Mbeki, Pallo Jordan (subsequently Arts and Culture Minister) and Mendi Msimang, then ANC chief representative in

London, and husband of the subsequent disgraced Health Minister, Dr Manto Tshabalala-Msimang. (See interview with Maxongo in Bob Myers, 'Challenging Mandela', in Bob Myers [ed], *Revolutionary Times, Revolutionary Lives: Personal Accounts of the Liberation Struggles*, Index Books, London, 1997. p 103). Mandela then asked Maxongo to speak to him in private.

Trenchant criticism of the failures of the TRC appears in R.W. Johnson, *South Africa's Brave New World: The Beloved Country since the End of Apartheid* (Allen Lane, London, 2009); Terry Bell, with Dumisa Buhle Ntsebeza, *Unfinished Business: South Africa, Apartheid and Truth* (RedWorks, Observatory, South Africa, 2001); and Anthea Jeffery, *The Truth about the Truth Commission* (South African Institute of Race Relations, Johannesburg, 1999).

Baruch Hirson, Bill McElroy and I were amazed that as much historical reality did in fact get revealed in the Skweyiya and Motsuenyane Commissions, and in the TRC, as proved to be the case. The report of the Stuart Commission (1984) into the mutiny in Umkhonto weSizwe in Angola in 1984 and the report of the ANC commission of inquiry into the death of Thami Zulu (1990) were made public along with the report of the Motsuenyane Commission, in August 1993.

In his study, *A Country Unmasked: Inside South Africa's Truth and Reconciliation Commission* (OUP, 2000), Alex Boraine revealed the sharpness of the struggle that took place within the National Executive Committee of the ANC, at each stage in the development of the TRC, up to and beyond publication of its final report. His first-hand study of the turbulent history of the TRC confirmed the account in the essay, above — written in 1993, several years before the convening of the TRC — of the intense struggles within the NEC, over whether or not any of its abuses in exile should be disclosed.

5 *The Dilemma of Albie Sachs**

A DEATH IN EXILE

Three months before the unbanning of the ANC and the release of Nelson Mandela, a senior commander of Umkhonto weSizwe died in exile at the headquarters base of the ANC in Lusaka, Zambia. He died of the effects of TB, AIDS and very possibly poison. He died suddenly, five days after having been released from detention by the ANC security department, and was under close ANC guard when he collapsed.

Soon afterwards a top-level commission of inquiry of four commissioners — all leading ANC members — was set up by the National Working Committee of the National Executive Committee (NEC), following a great deal of hostile speculation in the ANC about the circumstances and cause of the man's death. The commissioners did not begin their investigation until three months later. This was at the beginning of February 1990 — the same time as the legalisation of the ANC (on 2 February) and the release of Nelson Mandela. The four commissioners signed their report on 16 March 1990, Presumably it was presented to the NEC immediately afterwards.[1]

Through a combination of circumstances, this report from the exile makes possible a more searching inquiry into the credibility of the ANC in its constitutional negotiations. It permits a close evaluation of the gap between words and deeds. Though withheld from the public until August 1993, when it was released with the report of the Motsuenyane Commission into executions and torture in the ANC in exile, this report was effectively a document of the legal ANC. The ANC was by this time a party to the negotiating process. The report could only have been written with the changed circumstances of the ANC strongly in mind.

Among the four commissioners were two senior political and legal advisers to the ANC in its constitutional discussions. Of these, one was among the best-

*First published as 'The Dilemma of Albie Sachs: ANC constitutionalism and the death of Thami Zulu' in *Searchlight South Africa* No. 11 (October 1993), pp. 34–52.

known international personalities representing the ANC in the decades of the exile: Albie Sachs, former Professor of Law at Eduardo Mondlane University in Mozambique, Director of the South African Constitution Studies Centre at the Institute for Commonwealth Studies, London, a member of the ANC Constitutional Committee and author of a number of books. We have here an insight into ANC military and security operations during the exile, produced in the spirit of its open, public constitutional proposals.

The tension between these opposite dimensions provides a means of testing the ability of the ANC to confront its past, and of deciphering the phraseology of its constitutional proposals. The reader is engaged not so much in uncovering a history, as deconstructing current discourse. An inquiry into the ANC's past, the report is still more an index to its semantic integrity at present, and its means of operating in the future. It permits a critical judgement on the texts, spoken and unspoken, of ANC negotiators in their conclaves at the head of state, as well as on its security practices in exile.

The dead man was Muziwakhe Ngwenya, who grew up in Soweto and was then in his mid-thirties. He is better known by his pseudonym or exile 'travelling name' of Thami Zulu, or TZ. Throughout the report he is referred to as TZ. I will refer to him as Zulu, or Thami Zulu. The commission's report will be referred to either as the Thami Zulu report or as the Sachs report, since Sachs chaired the inquiry.[2] Like certain other essential details, Zulu's date of birth and age at death are not recorded in the report. Nor are the precise date and and time of his death, a bizarre omission from an inquiry of this kind. Eighteen months after presentation of the commission report, an article in the Johannesburg *Weekly Mail* by Phillip van Niekerk gave his year of birth as 1954. An article on the same day in the London *Guardian* by its South African correspondent, David Beresford — clearly coordinated with the article in the *Weekly Mail*, and carrying similar but not identical material — gave his date of death as 16 November 1989.[3] No ordinary police inquiry would have omitted such details.

The death of Zulu resulted in so much dissatisfaction within the ANC that it could not be hushed up. This was a major, but not the sole, reason for the relatively extensive inquiry by the ANC that followed. The report leads into the labyrinthine world of secret military operations, counter-operations and counter-counter operations in the contest between the ANC and the South African state during the 1980s, a world familiar — in another continent — from the fiction of John le Carré.

Zulu came from 'a well-educated and relatively comfortable home in Soweto'. (p 8) His mother, Mrs Emily Ngwenya, was a primary school head teacher.

(*Sunday Times*, London, 4 March 1990) His father was also a head teacher. They were sufficiently well-off to send him for most of his secondary-level education to Waterford, a fee-paying boarding school in Swaziland modelled on the English public school system. He thus escaped the worst effects of Bantu Education in South Africa. In the words of the report, his life experience as a youth was 'different from that of most of the persons' in Umkhonto. His immediate family are members of the developing black middle class in South Africa, which has most to benefit from the current political changes. Following his death in Lusaka, these were not people to be kept quiet with sinister allegations or threats, or who had only limited access to the means of public discussion.

Zulu was a person of stature in the exile. A witness to the inquiry stated that Zulu was 'always used to being in command and never to being commanded'. He gave himself 'the airs of a Napoleon'. After abandoning his studies at the University of Botswana to join Umkhonto in 1975, he was appointed leader of a batch of young exiles who left Swaziland for Tanzania for military training. Two years later he led the 'first group of the Soweto generation to receive military training abroad [in East Germany]. Further training followed in the Soviet Union. He then became chief of staff at Nova Katenga military training camp in Angola, where he was distinguished by his brutality, coldness and cruelty towards the troops. (personal communication) Torture of Umkhonto soldiers in Camalundi camp in Malanje province and the death under torture of Oupa Moloi, head of the political department, took place in 1981 under his authority as camp commander. Zulu brazenly threatened others in the camp with the same treatment.[4] This was followed by his appointment to the post of Regional Commander, covering the whole of Angola, the only country where the ANC was then engaged in any substantial combat. As such, he held senior responsibility for the deployment of ANC troops in the civil war alongside government MPLA forces against the rebel army of UNITA, with its infrastructure provided by South Africa.

Zulu was finally appointed commander of what was known as the 'Natal Machinery'. This was a grouping, based in Swaziland, responsible for what the report describes as the secret 'irrigation' of armed combatants into Natal and their military activity inside that area. (p 7) He was a crucial frontline commander responsible for conducting guerrilla and sabotage operations within South Africa. After his death, Joe Modise and Chris Hani (commander and chief of staff of Umkhonto) wrote a tribute which stated: 'Under your command, Durban earned the title of the most bombed city in South Africa… You performed your task with distinction and remarkable courage'. Saluting this 'giant and gallant fighter,' they recalled his 'efficiency and competence'.[5]

FEAR AND LOATHING IN LUSAKA

Zulu held this post from 1983 until 1988, when he and virtually the whole of the Natal Machinery were withdrawn to Lusaka for investigation by the security department, following severe losses to the South African state. Shortly before his arrest, nine ANC guerrillas under his command, including three women, were murdered in cold blood, at point-blank range, by a South African hit squad in two separate ambushes as they crossed from Swaziland into South Africa. One of Zulu's deputy commanders — known as Comrade Cyril, or Fear (real name Ralph Mgcina) — had been detained earlier by the ANC security department in Lusaka and interrogated. A summary of a confession by Mgcina, allegedly made at the end of May 1988, a month before the slaughter on the Swaziland border and Zulu's subsequent arrest, is attached to the Sachs report.

According to this document, Mgcina stated that he had worked for the South African Special Branch since 1973, had joined Umkhonto and been deployed as a 'leading cadre in one of our military machineries' in Swaziland. From this position, he had set up the assassination by a South African hit squad of Zulu's predecessor as commander, Zwelakhe Nyanda [brother of the present Minister of Communications in the Zuma government, retired General Siphiwe Nyanda, first Chief of Staff of the SANDF] in 1983. The summary by ANC security of his alleged confession, dated 3 August 1988, states that the strategic goal of SA intelligence was to allow infiltrated structures in Swaziland to grow

> and then cut them down, but leave an embryo for the ANC to build on and within that embryo leave its own forces so that the new structure is also controlled. This would go on indefinitely.

Mgcina subsequently died mysteriously in the custody of his ANC captors. Beresford states he had 'refused to sign a confession that he was a South African agent'. His wife, 'Jessica', was also detained and questioned. The Sachs report states that during the investigation in Lusaka, 'two leading members of the Machinery admitted to having worked with the enemy'. The question was whether Zulu was a 'third person' also working for South African security. (p 8)

In their account of the ANC in exile, Ellis and Sechaba state that Zulu was a member of the South African Communist Party (SACP), and was present at the extended meeting of the central committee in East Berlin in 1979 which elected Moses Mabhida to the post of general secretary.[6] He came close to joining the Umkhonto High Command, with 'strong backing' from Chris Hani, then

Umkhonto commissar. (p 170) At the ANC consultative conference at Kabwe in Zambia in 1985 — its first for 16 years — he chaired 'some crucial sessions' of the Internal Reconstruction Committee. Zulu was clearly an important figure in the ANC, destined for high office, until his recall to Zambia. He was then held prisoner in Lusaka by the ANC security department for 17 months, from June 1988 until his release on 11 November 1989. Curiously, the Sachs Commission, which had access to his interrogators, state he was in detention for 14, not 17, months.

The commissioners are listed in the report as follows:

Z.N. JOBODWANA. Convener and presently member of the Dept of Legal and Constitutional Affairs; formerly an attorney in South Africa.

ISAAC MAKOPO. First Chief Representative of the ANC to Botswana, 1978–83; formerly chairperson to the Regional Political Committee, Lusaka; presently Head of the National Logistics Committee in the Teasury Department of the ANC.

TIM MASEKO. Worked as a Research Chemist in Swaziland; formerly principal and Chief Administrator of Solomon Mahlangu Freedom College, Morogoro, Tanzania.

ALBIE SACHS. Formerly an advocate and Law Professor in South Africa; currently Director of the South African Constitution Studies Centre at the Institute of Commonwealth Studies in London.

The commission has special interest because of the legal background of Jobodwana and Sachs. In addition to them, the ANC in its negotiating strategy now has the benefit of a whole corps of constitutionalists. These include Kader Asmal, professor of Human Rights Law at the University of the Western Cape, and like Sachs a stalwart of the exile. Asmal spent most of the period of exile as a lecturer in law and as a senior administrator at Trinity College Dublin, and was a central figure in the Anti-Apartheid Movement in Ireland. Among his recent publications is an article entitled 'Democracy and Human Rights: Developing a South African Human Rights Culture', to which is appended the first draft of the ANC's Bill of Rights of November 1990.[7] At a conference on Ethnicity, Identity and Nationalism in South Africa held at Rhodes University, Grahamstown, in April this year, Asmal presented a paper on the current constitutional negotiations, reprinted in a long extract in the *Southern African Review of Books*.[8] The stress on human rights in the ANC constitutional proposals is obviously very important. The manner in which the ANC has actually approached the matter of human rights, in practice as well as theory, may be seen from the case of Thami Zulu.

HUMAN RIGHTS, FOR SOME

The ANC produced its Constitutional Guidelines in 1988 while numerous members remained imprisoned, without trial, in its prisons and detention camps in several African countries. Its Bill of Rights of November 1990 was drafted and published while a smaller but still substantial number — including some later described as 'genuine comrades' by Nelson Mandela — remained prisoners in an ANC prison at Mbarara in southern Uganda, prior to their release in August 1991.

In his paper at Grahamstown, Asmal quoted the declaration by the ANC that its Bill of Rights would guarantee a society upholding

> fundamental rights and freedoms for all on an equal basis, where our people live in an open and tolerant society, where the organs of government are representative, competent and fair in their functioning, and where opportunities are progressively and rapidly expanded to ensure that all may live under conditions of dignity and equality.

What is at issue is his comment, reprinted in the SARB, that there are 'no hidden agendas' in such claims. This is the importance of the position of Albie Sachs in the Thami Zulu Commission. From comparison with his published writings, a major part of the report, if not all, appears to have been written by Sachs. He currently holds senior political office in the ANC, after election to the NEC at the ANC's national conference in Durban in July 1991.

On 9 May 1990, days after returning from exile after leaving the country 24 years previously, and after a near-fatal attempt on his life by South African Military Intelligence in 1988, Sachs admitted to a mass meeting of students at the University of Cape Town that the ANC was still holding prisoners. He said he had been moved to tears by a recent visit to a detention camp, and admitted that the ANC had 'mistreated' prisoners in the past.

> If people come back and say they have been mistreated by the ANC, it is not necessarily lies. But if people come back and say that is the ANC [policy], that is lies. (*Times*, London, 11 May 1990)

The previous month, five former ANC guerrillas (Bandile Ketelo and his colleagues) told the world press about torture, murder and imprisonment for dissent in its prison camps in exile. A week later Nelson Mandela conceded that torture had indeed taken place in exile (but erroneously claimed that those responsible had immediately been punished). From the Thami Zulu report, it now becomes possible to evaluate the relation of Sachs, as a leading constitutionalist in the ANC, to the issue of its human rights abuses.

Several months after his return from exile and his speech at UCT, Sachs published a book in Cape Town entitled *Protecting Human Rights in a New South Africa*. The preface is dated 'London and Cape Town, August 1990' (i.e. four months after the revelations by the former ANC detainees, and three months after Sachs' speech at UCT).[9] It contains not a word about the ANC's prison camps or its human rights abuses. Nor is there any reference to this in Sachs' autobiographical account, *The Soft Vengeance of a Freedom Fighter*, published in Britain, also in 1990.[10]

The book on human rights presents important, though unofficial, guidelines on ANC perspectives for human rights in South Africa. It appears to be an expanded version of an address presented earlier by Sachs at the London School of Economics, at an occasion named in honour of the British stalinist lawyer, the late D. N. Pritt.

During the heyday of the ANC prison camps, from 1978 to 1988, a chasm opened up between the declared aims and beliefs of the ANC and its actual practices, a history of semantic distortion bearing on the crisis of violence within South Africa over the past few years. Put simply, the ANC's manner of dealing with internal dissent during the exile does not breed confidence among its political rivals and opponents — among blacks as well as whites when they look to their future.

The story of a single individual makes the point. In their history of repressions within the ANC published in *Searchlight South Africa* No. 5 (July 1990), Ketelo and his colleagues recalled the experiences of three ANC colleagues whom they describe as the 'very first occupants of Quatro prison'.[11] The 'travelling names' of these three exiled members of Umkhonto weSizwe were given as Ernest Khumalo, Solly Ngungunyana and Drake. After increasing dissatisfaction among troops in Fazenda training camp in Angola in 1978, these three are said to have left the camp in 1979 to go to the capital, Luanda, to demand their resignation from the ANC. In Luanda they were beaten in the street by ANC and Angolan security officers, bundled into a truck and taken straight to Quatro.

According to Ketelo, Ngungunyana was released after two years, Khumalo in 1984 while the fate of Drake was described as still unknown. These men endured the worst period in Quatro. Khumalo had the appalling experience of being released from the prison in 1983, only to be re-arrested and returned to Quatro the same day. He served about five years. There was no trial, no charge, and no means by which the prisoners could defend themselves. They were subject to constant brutality. The sharpest edge to this history of arbitrary practice, however, is this: 'Ernest Khumalo' was the exile pseudonym of a half-brother of the king of the Zulus, King Goodwill Zwelithini, the titular head of the KwaZulu Bantustan and Patron-in-Chief of the Zulu nationalist party, Inkatha. Khumalo's real name is Immanuel Zulu. He completed a course of study in Liverpool in Britain over a year ago and has resisted efforts by his close relative, Chief Mangosuthu Buthelezi, the head of Inkatha, to return to South Africa to deploy his experience in exile to discredit the ANC.[12] (personal communication)

PERCEPTIONS IN KWAZULU

Through the unbridled arrogance of its security department, the ANC sent a message to Inkatha leaders over ten years ago in this single episode that may well have helped inflame near-civil war within the country, at the cost of thousands of deaths. The KwaZulu Bantustan, like all such regions within South Africa's borders, was and is a one-party state run under a blatant ideology of ethnic chauvinism, with shameless patronage to the advantage of the ruling political elite. Nothing could have been better calculated to breed distrust among Buthelezi and Zwelithini in the constitutional character of the ANC than its treatment of their relative, Immanuel Zulu. For these men, the liberal phrases of the ANC as pronounced by Asmal, Sachs and others ring hollow. The horrors of the past six years involving countless murders by members and supporters of Inkatha may well have happened anyway. There are deep social and political causes. But no amount of killings by both sides in the conflict should be permitted to obscure the crucial point. If this was how the ANC treated their relative, a loyal member of the ANC who rejected the Bantustan philosophy, what hope could there be for KwaZulu leaders in a centralised state ruled by the ANC?

Their response was to develop and trust in their own armed might, rather than the possibility of an effective civil polity in which the ANC would form the majority party. In the light of ingrained suspicion of ANC motives deriving from its treatment of its own members in exile, the adequacy of its attempt to address the death of Thami Zulu (Muziwakhe Ngwenya) has more than an emblematic significance.

Sachs, who was among the best-known ANC legal figures during the exile, is unusual for the manner in which he has attempted to relate to the issue of 'the camps'. It is unlikely that any of the ANC constitutionalists know more than he does about the operations of the security department. To some extent, Sachs was the liberal and juridical 'conscience' of the ANC in exile. The manner in which he used his knowledge is therefore a crucial measure of the organisation as a whole.

The Sachs report quotes an ANC doctor in exile, Dr Pren Naicker, 'the main person in charge' of Thami Zulu's medical needs while in ANC custody from the time he manifested symptoms of ill-health until his death. According to Naicker, conditions for ANC detainees in Zambia were in a 'truly parlous state' before the appointment of the new head of ANC security, Joe Nhlanhla, in 1987. No details are given. Conditions, 'poor as they were, had improved immeasurably' compared with the previous period (under Mzwandile Piliso). Some months earlier Naicker had had to raise with Nhlanhla the 'appearance of bruises on the arms and wrists of certain of the detainees'. (pp. 12, 15) That is all that appears in the 22-page report referring to actual instances of human rights abuses in ANC custody — a matter now richly documented in the report of the ANC commission headed by Advocate Thembile Louis Skweyiya SC (August 1992), the report by Amnesty International (December 1992), the report of Advocate Robert Douglas SC (January 1993), the article by Ketelo and his colleagues (July 1990) and the report of the second ANC commission of inquiry into its human rights abuses, headed by Mr Sam Motsuenyane, which reported in August.

[*Author's note,* 2009: Dr Pren Naicker, who trained in medicine in Moscow, is the son of the late SACP and ANC leader, M.P. Naicker, a major political mentor of President Jacob Zuma when he was a young man in Durban. On return from exile, Dr Naicker became Brigadier-General Pren Naicker, head of the Military Health Service of the South African National Defence Force.]

The Sachs Commission presents a convincing account that Zulu was not tortured during his detention. But the context in which it investigated the possibility of torture was deficient. As a former advocate in the South African Supreme Court, it should have been obvious to Sachs and his fellow commissioners that the question of whether or not Zulu had been tortured could not adequately be investigated unless they were able to establish whether or not torture had previously been widely practised in the ANC.[13]

This they did not do. Instead of carefully establishing a general context, against which the specific experience of Zulu might be more precisely located, the commissioners filled pages of the report with abstract principles. These are worth quoting, because of the problematic relation of words to deeds in the ANC.

Section 3 of the Thami Zulu report quotes from the ANC Code of Conduct, with a summary and commentary by the commissioners. There is no indication here that 'mistreatment' — Sachs' phrase at UCT — was in fact widely practised by the security department, as this journal has recorded.[14] The character and limits of 'intensive' interrogation are also not defined, either in passages quoted from the Code of Conduct or elsewhere in the Sachs report.

THE SACHS COMMISSION AND THE KABWE CONFERENCE

The report goes on to state that the Code of Conduct was adopted at the Kabwe conference in 1985, 'precisely to deal with the question of human rights within the organisation'. It states:

> The delegates at the Conference firmly rejected any notion that any means whatsoever, however cruel, could be used in defending the physical integrity of the organisation, or that members surrendered their basic human rights once they joined the ANC. Similarly, delegate after delegate stressed that the viciousness of apartheid in no way justified viciousness on our part. (p 4)

The problem of ANC constitutionalism is wrapped up, a riddle inside an enigma, in this passage. Whatever was said at the Kabwe conference — and it is the responsibility of the ANC to produce full and complete minutes — this event marked the lowest point in the history of its deliberative proceedings. This magazine has published an account of the packing of the Kabwe conference by the security department, the suppression of meaningful debate and the silencing of critical opinion that took place there.[15] By the time it was convened in June 1985, those ANC members who had most insistently called for a conference over the previous five years had been silenced by the firing squad or were subject to constant brutality in prison. They remained prisoners at Quatro for a further three years after it concluded.

The conference was the direct result of the ANC mutiny the previous year, which demanded an end to human rights abuses in the organisation. In all probability drawn up with major assistance from Sachs himself, the Code of Conduct was mainly a fig-leaf covering a brutal practice of suppression of dissent. The report of the Stuart Commission into the causes and nature of the mutiny was not tabled at Kabwe. Up to the time of writing, it has still not been made public. The Skweyiya Commission found that it had apparently *not even been placed before the* nec by August 1992, when it reported its own findings.[16] This was 18 months after the unbanning of the ANC, and a full year after the national consultative conference in Durban in July 1991.[17] Vital knowledge about the history of the ANC remained restricted knowledge, excluded from elected members of its highest constitutional body. The presentation of the Kabwe conference as a forum for defending human rights by the Sachs Commission is not credible.

A PERSONAL STATEMENT

Sachs is a humane man, who genuinely desires an impartial and non-vengeful system of justice. That is why he wishes for 'soft' vengeance for the bomb that maimed him. In his account of the bombing and its aftermath, he describes his feelings after hearing that Mozambican and ANC security had arrested a man who had allegedly confessed to planting the bomb in his car. The man was described as a black Angolan working for South African Special Forces (a sub-department of Military Intelligence). In a radio interview, Sachs said that his most fervent wish was that the alleged assassin should be

> tried by due process of law in the ordinary civil courts, and if the evidence was not strong enough for a conviction, he be acquitted. The risk of an acquittal was fundamental, since the creation of a strong system of justice in Mozambique, one in which the people had confidence, which operated according to internationally accepted principles, would validate all our years of effort...

This was an honourable standpoint, offering guidance for the future of judicial conditions in southern Africa, all the more stirring because in rejecting the norm of an eye for an eye ('hard' vengeance), Sachs as political exile, as jurist and as victim was making a statement of his deepest convictions. Due process, he said, would be a 'personal triumph over the bomber, the ultimate in my soft, sweet vengeance'.

The problem lies in Sachs' blurred perception of what he calls 'our values'. It would be mean-spirited, insulting and wrong to doubt his sincerity over the need for due process for the man believed to have maimed him. There is no doubting also his desire to eliminate torture, imprisonment without trial and executions by his colleagues in the security department and the military. He genuinely feels anguish at the malpractices of his own side, 'all our years of effort', to which he gave half a lifetime in exile, and an arm and an eye. But the constraints upon him — political constraints, both external and personal — are too heavy, and they wear away judicial principle.

This appears in the Sachs report when it refers to the creation of the post of Officer of Justice under Section B of the ANC Code of Conduct, acting under overall supervision of the NEC and in collaboration with the President's Office.[18] The function of Officer of Justice was to:

(A) maintain the principles of legality within the organisation;

(B) supervise investigations when they reach the stage that charges are being contemplated against members; ...

(I) ensure that no person in the custody of or under investigation of officers of the organisation is treated in a cruel, inhuman or degrading way;

(J) make regular inspections of the way persons deprived of their liberty are treated, with a view to ensuring that the purposes of re-education rather than vengeance are fulfilled; . . .

(K) see to it that no undue delay takes place between completion of investigations and the date of trial; . . .

(M) take all steps to minimise the period of waiting. . . (p 5)

Excerpts from the Code of Conduct were published last year by the Skweyiya Commission in its report, including several of the clauses set out here. (pp. 16–24) A matter nowhere taken up in the Sachs report, or referred to anywhere in Sachs' books, but published in the Skweyiya report, is the clause in the Code of Conduct dealing with 'exceptionally serious cases'. This states that 'where no other penalty would be appropriate, maximum punishment may be imposed'. The Skweyiya Commission concludes: 'By maximum punishment, is envisaged the sentence of death'. (p 18)

This crucial passage is omitted in the Sachs report, despite its relevance. It is the legal formulation of the death penalty by the ANC: no small matter for a country regarded as the hanging capital of the world, where violent death is everyday. The Sachs report quotes instead a passage from the Code of Conduct stipulating that the 'rights and privileges' of prisoners should be based on the 'humanist traditions of the ANC'. (p 5) Once again liberal legal phraseology obscures a thorny truth. The Code of Conduct and creation of the post of Officer of Justice were clearly the result of strenuous efforts by individuals such as Sachs. There is no cause to doubt their sincerity in wishing to establish legality in the ANC, so as to rein in the abuses that had provoked the mutiny, with its further cycle of executions, torture and large-scale imprisonment of loyal members. In its lengthy citation of legal norms, however, the Sachs report conceals the fact that the post of Officer of Justice was an almost total dead letter. Two years after the Sachs report, the Officer of Justice, Zola Skweyiya, told the inquiry chaired by his brother Thembile Skweyiya that his efforts to visit Angola in 1986 and 1987 had been 'blocked at every turn' by the then head of the security department, Piliso, and that he himself had been in danger of being arrested. He had been allowed to visit Angola late in 1988, but was denied access to Quatro. Efforts to visit Uganda were also blocked. (pp. 63–64) Severe abuses continued unchecked, well on into 1991.

From the Sachs report it is clear that Zola Skweyiya did not at any stage visit the detention centres where Thami Zulu was held. The commission is critical that the Code had 'not been fully implemented'. It was most unsatisfactory, the report goes on, that no clear time-limit had been placed on detention without trial. (p 6) The period over which Zulu was held as a suspect was far too long. It finds no evidence to suggest that Zulu had otherwise been improperly treated, and no information has emerged to suggest otherwise. The investigation had been carried out in a 'serious and professional manner'. (p 19) The commissioners conclude that there was sufficient evidence to justify Zulu's detention; that there was no proof that he had in fact been a state agent; but that he had been guilty of 'gross negligence' and possibly also personal misbehaviour. (p 18) I am not aware of any cause to doubt these conclusions. The commission appears to have operated on these matters in a judicial fashion.

THE FINAL DAYS

Zulu had entered detention, in the words of the report, as a 'large, well-built slightly overweight person, and come out gaunt, frail and almost unrecognisable'. (p 10) On his release on 11 November, he was taken to stay at the house of a friend, Dr Ralph Mgijima. He told Mgijima that his condition had deteriorated drastically while he was in an isolation cell, lying all day on a mattress on the floor. In previous years Zulu had suffered from TB. Having developed diarrhoea, mouth sores (thrush) and a spiking fever towards the end of his time in detention, he was taken in the charge of Dr Naicker to University Training Hospital (UTH) in Lusaka for X-rays on 1 November. Nothing was detected on the X-rays, but a blood test taken at the same time showed he was HIV positive. The Presidential Committee (Tambo's office) then ordered his release. Mgijima considered Zulu's condition on arrival at his house to be shocking but not suggestive of imminent death. The following day Mgijima fell seriously ill and had to be taken to hospital for an emergency operation.

Zulu died of heart and lung failure four days later on 16 November, while Mgijima was still in hospital. The histopathological analysis after his death showed advanced TB in various organs, including the sac around the heart. Medical opinion in Lusaka, London (where specimens of blood and stomach contents were taken for analysis) and South Africa enabled the commission to decide that he was a victim of AIDS which had destroyed the immune system, permitting rapid advance of TB.

The problem for the commissioners was that samples of Zulu's blood and stomach contents sent for analysis at UTH in Lusaka showed traces of diazinon, an organic phosphorus pesticide, in both specimens.[19] The blood also contained 84 milligrams percent alcohol, the equivalent of about three pints of beer. A forensic scientist in London who was given the same specimens for analysis three months later said that diazinon has a strong and unpleasant taste. It does not dissolve in water or tea, but is soluble in alcohol. 'Three pints of beer taken within a twenty-four hour period and each containing a teaspoonful of diazinon could have been fatal'. (p 13) Diazinon is not however accumulated in the body; it is excreted out. 'Thus if it had been given to TZ it would necessarily have been given within a day or at most two days prior to his death'. The commissioners state that while they cannot express any certainty as to whether Zulu had been poisoned, they felt 'the likelihood is that he indeed was'. (p 14)

At this point the investigation breaks down. There could not be a greater contrast between the scrupulous manner in which medical forensic detail has been accumulated and assessed, and the absence of forensic investigation subsequent to these findings. If diazinon could only have been administered to Zulu within one or at most two days before his death, then the identity of his murderers had to be established through a careful trawl of all people who had access to him over that time, and who might have provided him with poisoned beer. There is no indication in the report that any such inquiry was made. No information is provided about who visited Mgijima's house during that time. The investigation disappears into a hole. The commissioners state: 'If TZ was poisoned, then we cannot see that anyone other than South African security could have been responsible'. (p 14) The obvious point is avoided: if poison was administered to Zulu in three bottles of beer, those who supplied it were almost certainly members of the ANC, and perhaps very senior members.

This point is simply not canvassed. There is no attempt to compile a list of people who had seen Zulu in the two days before his death. The commission further suppressed information which appeared later in the South African and British press. The identity of one individual who did see Zulu during those two days is known. It is Chris Hani, then Umkhonto chief of staff.

After his return to South Africa, Hani seems to have given details of his own account of the lead-up to Zulu's death to Van Niekerk of the *Weekly Mail* and (in the same briefing) to Beresford of the *Guardian*. This appears to have been the immediate stimulus for their coordinated stories in Britain and South Africa on 6 September 1991. Following Hani's murder in April 1993, there is an onus on Van Niekerk and Beresford to make plain exactly what their relation to Hani was in compiling their accounts.

The countdown to Zulu's death appears to be as follows:

Saturday 11 November:

Zulu released from detention and brought, very ill, by the security department to Mgijima's house.

Sunday 12 November:

Mgijima taken ill and rushed to hospital for emergency operation.

Monday 13 November:

Mgijima phones Hani from hospital and tells him to check up on Zulu. Hani and Modise, the two senior commanders in Umkhonto, go to the house, find the gate locked and 'vault over a high fence to get to TZ', whom they find in a very sick state. 'After that two MK men were sent to look after him'. (Van Niekerk) These were men loyal to Hani. (personal communication) They are so far unidentified, and there is no way of knowing whether or not they were interviewed by the Sachs Commission. This is obviously crucial for any serious inquiry into possible murder by poisoning. Failure to establish the precise role of these two men vitiates any judicial inquiry.

Tuesday 14 November:

Hani returns to the house and finds Zulu still in a bad state. Zulu does not want medical help but 'appeared to be worried that the Security Department is going to "finish me off" if he got into their hands'. (Beresford) This is clearly Hani's own account, and points a finger directly at the security department, then headed by Joe Nhlanhla (director), Jacob Zuma (head of counter-intelligence) and Sizakele Sigxashe. (Skweyiya report, p 63, and Beresford) Both Van Niekerk's and Beresford's accounts suggest Hani pointing an accusatory finger at Zuma, now assistant general-secretary of the ANC and one of the five-man team originally charged with conducting negotiations with the government.

Wednesday 15 November:

Hani calls in a doctor to attend to Zulu in the night 'and left two MK members to keep watch at his bedside'. (Beresford) Zulu suffers attacks of vomiting and diarrhoea.

Thursday 16 November:

Zulu starts gasping and is rushed to UTH, where he dies.

The Sachs Commission refers to 'lack of cooperation between Military HQ [i.e., Modise, Hani] and security [i.e., Nhlanhla, Zuma, Sigxashe]' on the issue of Zulu's detention and death. (p 19) This is a bland understatement. Beresford writes that under the ANC's command structure, the security department was responsible for detentions, was completely separate from the military command and had overriding investigatory powers.

> Thami's detention, which came as a shock to the military, was without the sanction of either Modise or Hani. The two commanders made furious demands inside the ANC National Executive to know the basis of Thami's detention and to have access to him. Both were refused.

Beresford writes that unless Zulu committed suicide, 'the finger of suspicion points to those in attendance on him in the final hours of his life ... which includes members of Umkhonto weSizwe itself'. He speaks of 'bitter, if unspoken antagonism' on the part of the military towards the security department. If South African intelligence had infiltrated an agent into the upper echelons of the ANC who was responsible for Zulu's murder, 'the potential for manipulation is obvious'.

Van Niekerk quotes an unnamed commander (probably Hani):

> TZ's detention was not discussed with us... Our response was one of bitterness and led to a straining of relations between the army and security. Security was very powerful — it had the powers of life and death. The death of TZ is an indictment of the methods we used against suspects, ignoring his track record and the views of those who worked with him closely.

The central issue for this article, however, is not the matter of determining the exact details in the last years and days of Thami Zulu, or even inadequacies in the investigation by the Sachs Commission. Many of these difficulties are probably irreducible, given the nature of a secret war.

What is at issue is Sachs' publication of a major book on perspectives for human rights in South Africa that makes no reference to human rights abuses in the ANC in exile — problems which he was very aware of at the time, at first hand. Even if he wished to explain the context in which these abuses took place in terms of his own understanding of the issue, this is not a matter that is irrelevant to the subject of his book. It is its most difficult and complex dimension. For a legal figure of his stature not to have mentioned the matter is to mislead his readers. He creates further difficulties for the already dreadfully burdened issue of human rights in South Africa. Kader Asmal's ringing declaration about 'no hidden agendas' is untrustworthy, and this book shows it. Sachs' sophistication, his legal training (both academic and practical), his fluent writing style and his familiarity with the legal system, the universities and the media in major western countries, together with his appealing personality, serve to mask the most sensitive problems for human rights investigation in South Africa, rather than clarify them.[20] The distinction between Sachs' role in protecting human rights inside the ANC and in concealing its abuses is difficult to make. His work is part of the problem, not its solution.

THE PURSUIT OF JUSTICE

There is no need to give extensive extracts from Sachs' book, *Protecting Human Rights in a New South Africa*. A great deal of it is sound and needs no further comment. Other parts give proposals for adaptation of the ANC programme to the hard realities of South Africa's capitalist structure. These are not matters that I am concerned with here. What is at issue is a rosy liberal prose that obscures what it should illuminate. A few references will be sufficient.

Sachs claims, for instance, that the

> frequent and massive human rights violations in our country, together with a vigorous movement of contestation and considerable international attention, have produced on our part [i.e. the ANC] unusual sensitivity to and a passionate interest in the safeguarding of human rights. (p 40)

Would it were true!

> For those of us who have suffered arbitrary detention, torture and solitary confinement . . . , the theme of human rights is central to our existence. The last thing any of us desires to see is a new form of arbitrary and dictatorial rule replacing the old. (ibid)

And yet. . . .

In a chapter on 'The future of South African law', he writes of the 'legal freedom fighters in our past' — Gandhi, Schreiner, Krause, Seme, Mathews, Fischer, Nokwe, Berrangé, Kahn, Muller, Mandela, Tambo, Slovo and Kies — people who saw their legal careers as being 'inextricably linked up with the pursuit of justice'. (p 98) No reference to the problematic relation of at least three of these to the ANC's system of prison camps in exile. No reference either to the fact that a number of these jurists for decades justified the tyranny of the Soviet Union, the model for Quatro and its clones. He writes of the qualities of professional legal integrity, including that of 'never consciously misleading the court'. (p 99) But to mislead a whole population. . . .

One could go on, but this is enough. If the ANC gets its way in its constitutional embrace with the National Party, or even part of its way, Sachs is likely to have an important place in the judicial system of the 'new' South Africa, perhaps even a place in the cabinet. In relating to Sachs, one is relating to the ANC at its most spell-binding. The matter of this article is the future of the legal system in South Africa, perhaps for decades to come.

Like those notables in the west who sang the praises of the Stalin Constitution of 1936, Sachs is victim of a romantic fallacy: of asserting a desired ideal, clothed here as a legal norm, as if it were a factual truth.[21]

His inspiring prose soars overhead and discredits the human rights objectives to which he earnestly and genuinely aspires. The ANC publicist is internally at war with the jurist, and the publicist frequently wins out. One sees the personal moral anguish of the activist reared in the old-style certainties of the SACP (he first visited the Soviet Union in 1954, the year after Stalin died), in conflict with the yearnings of a decent man. Thus the tears to which he gave acknowledgement at UCT. Between the 'comrade' and the activist for human rights, an internal conflict sparkles like static electricity.

Several things need obviously to be done. Sachs should write an honest, straightforward account of his own efforts (and those of others) within the ANC to secure better observation of human rights. As a member of the NEC, he should insist that the minutes of the Kabwe conference be published. As he writes in his book on human rights, 'it ill behooves us to set ourselves up as the new censors. . . .' (p 183) He should act on these words.

Finally, it is a scandal that the ANC should have refused to carry out the recommendations of the Motsuenyane Commission — above all, that torturers and killers should be removed from office in the ANC, and that compensation should be paid to victims — until such time as the National Party takes action against the state's own killers and torturers. The decision by the NEC to defer action on its own abuses until the convening of yet another commission, a so-called 'Commission of Truth', is an act of hypocrisy at the highest level of the ANC.[22] By this decision the ANC shakes hands with the NP in a pact of blood. As a member of the ANC, Sachs must take some responsibility for this deeply cynical measure.

The 'conscience of the ANC' is looking worn.

REFERENCES

1. 'Report of a Commission of Inquiry set up in November 1989 by the National Working Committee of the National Executive Committee of the African National Congress to Investigate the Circumstances leading to the Death of Mzwakhe Ngwenya (also known as Thami Zulu or TZ)', Lusaka, March 1990.
2. Reported by Phillip van Niekerk, 'Who killed Thami Zulu?', *Weekly Mail*, 6 September 1991. Van Niekerk refers to the commission's findings as the 'Sachs report'.
3. David Beresford, 'Poison in the ANC's ranks', *Guardian*, London, 6 September 1991. I take the spelling of Muziwakhe ('his house', or family, in Zulu) from the articles by Van Niekerk and Beresford, who had access to Ngwenya's parents. Both journalists are highly respected. Van Niekerk was visited in hospital by Nelson Mandela after being shot in the head by gangsters following the massacre at Boipatong.
4. Bandile Ketelo et al, 'A Miscarriage of Democracy, The ANC Security Department in the 1984 Mutiny in Umkhonto weSizwe', *Searchlight South Africa* No. 5 (July 1990), pp. 40–41.

5. Text and attribution from *Sunday Times, Weekly Mail and Guardian*.
6. Stephen Ellis and Tsepo Sechaba, *Comrades Against Apartheid: The ANC and the South African Communist Party In Exile*, James Currey/Indiana University Press, 1992.
7. Kader Asmal, 'Democracy and Human Rights: Developing a South African Human Rights Culture', *New England Law Review*, 27 (1992), pp. 287–304.
8. Kader Asmal, 'Making the Constitution', *Southern African Review of Books*, Vol 5 No 3, May/June 1993.
9. Albie Sachs, *Protecting Human Rights in a New South Africa*, Oxford University Press, Cape Town, 1990.
10. Albie Sachs, *The Soft Vengeance of a Freedom Fighter*, Grafton, London, 1990. This is a remarkable and moving book, one of the best of a large number of autobiographical accounts by leading individuals in the 'liberation struggle'. Its strength derives from Sachs' emotionally honest description of the experience of being very nearly murdered by a car bomb in Maputo in April 1988, placed by South African state agents, and of his efforts to recover personal and public poise after loss of an arm and the use of an eye. The danger of indulgent self-dramatization, common in a certain type of South African exile literature, is mainly set aside here by the nature of the subject, which is his own trauma. It marks a moment of transition from the tendentious public prose of previous writing by South African political figures, towards the truth of inner feelings, and a vivid acknowledgement of the sensuous pleasures of life.
11. Ketelo et al, op. cit., p 38.
12. Only one of the leaders of the mutiny in the ANC in Angola in 1984, Mwezi Twala, appears to have gone the distance of joining Inkatha. Twala has become an organiser for Inkatha in the Vaal region. Another detainee who has been amply described in the South African press as a real agent of South African security before he was arrested and tortured in exile by the ANC, Patrick Hlongwane, has delighted in making a nuisance of himself. Released from the ANC prison in Uganda in August 1991, Hlongwane formed a grouping on his return — almost certainly with state funds — called the Returned Exiles Committee (REC) which operated out of Inkatha premises north of Durban. At a recent meeting of the National Party Youth Congress, he embarrassed President F.W. de Klerk by claiming to be the NP information officer in Soweto. He claimed afterwards to be also a military member of the fascist Afrikaner Weerstandsbeweging (AWB). (*New Nation*, 16 July 1993). If a character like Hlongwane had not existed — half criminal, half clown — he would have had to be invented.
13. Sachs' book, *The Jail Diary of Albie Sachs* (1966, since reissued) was adapted for the stage by the British dramatist David Edgar. Edgar's dramatised version was performed by the Royal Shakespeare Company and appeared subsequently on television and radio in Britain.
14. See *Searchlight South Africa* numbers 5, 7, 8, 9. See also Amnesty International, South Africa. *Torture, Ill-treatment and Executions in African National Congress Camps*, London, December 1992 (AI Index AFR 53/27/92). The Skweyiya report (see note 16) noted 'gratuitous and random violence perpetrated on the detainees by camp guards' at the ANC prison in Uganda, well on into 1991. (p 47).
15. Mkatashingo, 'The ANC Conference: From Kabwe to Johannesburg', *Searchlight South Africa* No. 6 (January 1991), pp. 91–94.

16. Report of the Commission of Enquiry into Complaints by Former African National Congress Prisoners and Detainees (the 'Skweyiya report'), Johannesburg, Aug. 1992, p 56.
17. The date was mistakenly given as July 1992 in Paul Trewhela, 'The ANC Prison Camps. An Audit of Three Years, 1990–1993', *Searchlight South Africa* No. 10 (April 1993), p 17. In the same article the name 'David Moshoeu', MK regional commander in Angola at the time of the mutiny, should have read David Mashigo. His real name is Graham Morodi. The Stuart Report acknowledged that the mutiny was caused very largely by 'excesses of the security department'. (ibid, p 16) Thus its suppression.
18. As executive president, Tambo was responsible for the army, the security department and information and publicity. For a discussion of Tambo's responsibility, see Paul Trewhela, 'The ANC Prison Camps', op. cit., pp. 24–26 (pp. 81–84 in this book). Tambo was buried in South Africa in May this year in an atmosphere worthy of a Christian saint. Standing beside Nelson Mandela during the ceremony, in combat fatigues and giving the Umkhonto salute, were two of the leaders from the exile most heavily implicated in abuses: Joe Modise, commander, and Andrew Masondo, former national commissar and founder of one of the most brutal security organs, the People's Defence Organisation.

    The Skweyiya report quotes a statement made by Tambo on behalf of Umkhonto weSizwe at the headquarters of the International Commission of the Red Cross on 28 November 1980. Tambo solemnly undertook to respect the conventions and undertook in particular to apply the Geneva Convention on the treatment of prisoners of war, by which he meant 'regular armed forces of the South African regime captured by the cadres of Umkhonto weSizwe'. This excluded spies. The Skweyiya Commission found there had been 'shocking and persistent violation of the Code of Conduct by certain members of the security department of the ANC' (p 24), a violation also, by implication, of Tambo's undertaking in Geneva. Tambo made this undertaking during one of the most terrible periods of oppression of ANC members in Angola, when — among others — Immanuel Zulu was in Quatro. It was made for international political consumption, and perhaps in the hope of providing a modicum of safety for captured guerrillas in South Africa. But it had no relevance in the camps.
19. I mistakenly spelt this 'Diazonin' in my article in *SSA* No. 10 (p 30, n 6).
20. Having obtained his PhD at the University of Sussex after arriving in Britain, Sachs became senior lecturer in law at the University of Southampton. He received an honorary award of LLD from the university. Following his work as professor of law at Eduardo Mondlane University in Maputo, Mozambique (1977–83), he became director of research in the Mozambique Ministry of Justice. After the car bomb attempt on his life, he taught at Columbia University in New York as well as directing the South Africa Constitution Studies Centre at the Institute of Commonwealth Studies in the University of London. Since returning to South Africa, he has been attached to the University of the Western Cape and the University of Cape Town .
21. For a typology of the species, see David Caute, *The Fellow-Travellers*, Weidenfeld and Nicolson, 1973.
22. 'ANC torturers are granted a reprieve by Mandela', *Daily Telegraph*, 31 August 1993.

6 *Zulu Proves an Albatross around Zuma's neck**

There is very serious material in the public domain concerning Jacob Zuma — material that was published in the early '90s, before the Truth and Reconciliation Commission, which Zuma has not addressed in any way.

The principal focus remains the murder in Lusaka, Zambia, of Thami Zulu (real name, Muziwakhe Ngwenya, also known as 'TZ') a former commander of Umkhonto weSizwe, the military wing of the ANC and the South African Communist Party in November 1989.

I discussed the matter in an article in October 1993, in a banned exile journal, *Searchlight South Africa* No. 11, under the title 'The dilemma of Albie Sachs: ANC constitutionalism and the death of Thami Zulu'.

The subject was also dealt with this month by one of South Africa's most highly regarded journalists, Patrick Laurence, in an article in *The Star*, 'Jacob Zuma and the trail of blood' (March 3, 2009).

Zuma has not responded publicly to this material, which appeared in print in South Africa in the early '90s in different sources.

He similarly failed to respond to the pleas of Zulu's parents, Philemon and Emily Ngwenya, both school teachers from Soweto, for information about the death of their son. Their request was repeated publicly in their testimony to the TRC on July 26 1996.

In an article in the *Weekly Mail*, 'The question remains: who killed Thami Zulu?' (October 23, 1992), Paul Stober wrote: 'It is known that Zuma opposed Zulu's appointment as commander of Natal MK operations in 1983 because he favoured a Natal-born candidate for the position.

'Zulu was born and bred in Soweto. And by the time Zuma assumed the powerful position of head of ANC intelligence in the late 1980s, he was among those convinced that Zulu was a South African agent.'

Referring to the 'persistent allegation that (then) assistant ANC secretary-general Zuma was involved' in the detention of Zulu for 17 months by its

* First published in the Johannesburg *Sunday Times*, March 15 2009.

security department, iMbokodo (in which Zuma had been head of counter-intelligence), Stober reported that the ANC was treating the matter as 'particularly sensitive'.

Stober noted that an ANC-appointed commission of inquiry into Zulu's death, headed by Judge Albie Sachs, 'cleared him of being a state agent, and concluded that he died from unnatural causes. But it failed to answer the question: who killed Zulu?'

Stober wrote that there was a 'reluctance to come clean' about Zulu's death, which was being 'noted by ordinary ANC members who fear a cover-up'.

Forensic laboratory analysis, he wrote, had 'found traces of a deadly pesticide, diazinon' in Zulu's blood.

'The poison had to have been administered during the five days between Zulu's release from detention by iMbokodo and his death because it was a quick-acting drug.

'For whatever reason, Zulu was poisoned, it is assumed.'

Prior to Stober's article, the *Weekly Mail* and the *Guardian* (London) had already jointly reported on the likely involvement of the ANC in the murder of Zulu.

The article in the *Weekly Mail*, written by Phillip van Niekerk, is remarkable for its account of a very sharp, direct, personal criticism made by the late Chris Hani, the then chief of staff of MK, about the arrest, detention and death of Zulu.

Hani's comments on this matter can only be read as an implied criticism of Zuma, the ranking head of ANC security in matters such as the arrest of Zulu.

There has never been any suggestion of direct involvement in this matter of Joe Nhlanhla or Sizakele Sigxashe, the other two heads of the ANC's intelligence and security departments at the time, who had other responsibilities.

Hani's words sounded a warning about the abuse of power by iMbokodo, as led by Zuma.

Van Niekerk wrote: 'A suggestion has been made that there was rivalry between TZ and intelligence chief Zuma over control of Natal operations. The journal *Southscan* reported that Zulu 'won the post (as head of Natal command) in the teeth of opposition from Zuma, who favoured a Natal-born candidate'.

Van Niekerk added that Hani 'apparently raised the issue of TZ's detention at the level of the ANC's national executive committee'.

He went on to quote Hani from what appeared to have been the outcome of a personal interview.

Van Niekerk quoted Hani as saying: 'TZ's detention was not discussed with us. Our response was one of bitterness and led to a straining of relations between the army and security.

'Security was very powerful — it had the powers of life and death. The death of TZ is an indictment of the methods we used against suspects, ignoring his track record and the views of those who worked with him closely.'

Van Niekerk reported further that, at the time of his release, Zulu feared he was going to be murdered.

This is exactly what appears to have happened.

Zulu's friend, Ralph Mgijima (in whose house TZ was poisoned, while Mgijima himself was in hospital) told Van Niekerk: 'Thami did not want to go to a doctor because he said the intelligence guys were going to finish him off.'

Van Niekerk continued: 'Despite being one of the most senior commanders of Umkhonto weSizwe, Zulu was given a lonely burial in Swaziland.

'The ANC only paid for the body to be moved from the government hospital to a funeral parlour in Zambia. The family had to foot the bill to move the body to Swaziland, where he was buried with few ANC comrades in attendance.

'A statement by Hani was read at the funeral eulogising TZ, saying "we will never forget your theoretical and practical contribution to our armed struggle".'

The remarks by Hani, as quoted by Van Niekerk, are all the more remarkable since at the time Hani was general secretary of the SACP, chief of staff of MK and a member of the ANC's national executive committee.

The reporting by *Southscan*, Van Niekerk and Stober is in accord with feelings of concern about the TZ matter, as described by Tsepo Sechaba in the still unrivalled study by him and Professor Stephen Ellis in *Comrades against Apartheid: The South African Communist Party and the ANC in Exile* (James Currey, 1992).

Sechaba was the ANC *nom de guerre* of Oyama Mabandla, who was the primary source for this book and a former 'member of the ANC intelligence apparatus'. Mabandla's perceptions about the opposition within Umkhonto weSizwe to TZ, by implication referring to Zuma, can be taken as representing the understanding of the matter from inside iMbokodo.

Mabandla, who subsequently trained in law at Columbia University, is chairman of the Vodacom group in South Africa and was deputy chief executive of South African Airways until 2004.

Mabandla and Ellis wrote that, although Zulu was a 'senior commander of Umkhonto weSizwe and prominent in the party, there were those who disliked him'.

'The reasons for this dated back to his appointment to head the Natal underground machinery in 1983.'

They add that 'few in the ANC believe Zulu really was a spy, but blame his death on the excessive zeal of the ANC security apparatus.

'It shocked many that in 1989 the security department could act with such impunity to hound to death a very senior official without having to give any account of its actions.'

In the following years, Zuma made no accounting to the TRC about the detention and death of Zulu, despite references to him in the public domain which indicated his at least formal responsibility as head of ANC counter-intelligence.

No amnesty was sought or granted.

Discussing the role of the intelligence department within the politics of the ANC, Ellis provided a considered conclusion in his academic paper on iMbokodo.

He wrote: 'It was the specific contribution of the SACP during the years of its ascendancy… to introduce into the ANC… a direct input from the scientific Marxist-Leninist method.

'A stalinist notion of the correct political and ideological education of soldiers spread to other parts of the ANC, and tended to penalise critical thought even among non-soldiers. In the hands of political commissars and zealous young security officers, persons suspected of failing to conform to this line were equated with security suspects.

'In the ANC, particularly after 1969, this gave to the practices of the security organ a coherent ideological justification.'

The failure, or rather refusal, by Zuma, the ANC and the erstwhile leaders of the ANC, now leaders of the Congress of the People, to do a proper moral accounting for this crime, suggests there is a potential threat to civil liberties in the region should Zuma become president.

In the poem 'The Rime of the Ancient Mariner' by Samuel Taylor Coleridge, a sailor is doomed forever to carry the curse of having killed a great sea bird, the albatross, for no good reason.

The death of Zulu may prove to be the albatross around Zuma's neck.

7 *State Espionage and the ANC London Office**

ENEMY AGENTS

In *Searchlight South Africa* No. 10, published in April 1993, I discussed infiltration of the ANC in exile by South African Military Intelligence (MI) and noted that a 'major scandal involving the top ANC leadership... has still to break' (p 30, fn 10).

In May the ANC admitted that its chief representative in London in the 1980s had, before his death in April, confessed to being a spy for MI. On receiving the man's confession following his return to Odendaalsrus, South Africa, in 1991, the ANC had suppressed the information and allowed him to continue as chairman of the ANC's northern Free State region from 1991 to 1992. His constituency members had no knowledge of the affair, nor were they informed by the ANC after his death.

This real 'enemy agent' in the leadership of the ANC was known abroad under his exile pseudonym, Solly Smith. (In London he was 'Uncle Solly'.) His real name was Samuel Khanyile. Shortly after his death in Odendaalsrus in early April, a German magazine, *Top Secret*, published a facsimile from the Companies Registration Office in London indicating Smith's ten per cent stake in a South African state-funded media service in London, Newscope Limited, which published a now defunct magazine, *African Preview*. The company was run by a Ghanaian exile in London, Major Kojo Boakye-Djan. After his secret had thus posthumously been exposed, an ANC spokesman, Ronnie Mamoepa, stated that Smith had approached the ANC voluntarily after his return from exile and 'admitted he had been compromised and coerced into working for the regime' (*Sunday Times*, Johannesburg, 30 May).

At the same time, the South African press published information linking Smith's espionage operation on behalf of MI to a second leader of the ANC and the South African Communist Party, Dr Francis Meli, who died shortly after

---

*First published in *Searchlight South Africa* Vol. 3, No. 4 (June 1995), pp. 42–51. Slightly adapted and amplified, 2009.

his return from exile in a Johannesburg hotel room in October 1990. Born in East London in 1942, and a former student at Fort Hare University College in the early Sixties, he was in his late 40s at the time of his death. Meli, whose real name was Wellington Madolwana, wrote a once near-official history of the ANC[1] and was editor in London of *Sechaba*, the official exile journal of the ANC.

He was a member of the ANC's National Executive Committee and had been a member also of the SACP Central Committee, and possibly also its Politburo. As the first political commissar at Nova Katenga camp in Angola from the end of 1976, he held prime responsibility for ideological indoctrination of young recruits from the generation of the 1976 Soweto school students' revolt. He had earlier acquired his doctorate (in history) at the University of Leipzig in the German Democratic Republic, and was a classic product of the stalinist Party School system of political training. His exile pseudonym, Meli, was apparently derived from the initials of the Marx-Engels-Lenin-Institute.

In their account of the ANC and the SACP in exile, Steven Ellis and Tsepo Sechaba (real name, Oyama Mabandla) charitably describe Meli's history of the ANC as 'highly sanitised'.[2] It is indeed a shabby piece of non-research. They go on to state that Meli had written his thesis on the history of the Comintern and had 'impeccably orthodox Marxist credentials'. At the time of his appointment as commissar in Angola, where he was responsible for 'licking the new recruits into political shape',

> Meli was already regarded as an expert on the national question. In this, as in many other things, Meli was a fervent disciple of Stalin. The SACP has traditionally considered that if there was one sphere in which Joseph Stalin may be said to have had a correct approach in the Soviet Union, it was in successfully incorporating all the diverse nationalities of the USSR into a socialist state. (p 88)

No amount of evidence of the repressive nature of the Soviet state, its Great Russian chauvinism and the forced removal of whole peoples as a result of Stalin's politics of 'ethnic cleansing' could shake the faith of the SACP in the USSR as a model for South African conditions, or in Stalin as their philosophical guide. This stubborn faith remained impervious to the facts until the whole edifice came crashing down, revealing a snakepit of ethnic hatreds. As editor of *Sechaba* (one of the few journals available to ANC members in the camps) and as one of the SACP's leading 'theoreticians', writing under the names Phineas Malinga and Nyawuza, Meli was influential in elaborating ANC/SACP ideas on the 'national question' relating to South Africa.

He fed into the central area of ideological debate in the country.

Like Smith, Meli had a very serious alcohol problem. Ellis and Sechaba state that he was removed from the SACP central committee 'on account of his alcoholism' and was put under investigation by a party committee 'because of his lapses in preserving Party security'. At Engineering Camp at Nova Katenga (shared by Cubans and Angolans as well as the ANC), he was very sarcastic and rude to the recruits, who frequently dozed off in his lectures (personal communication). The boredom induced by his lectures was no disqualification to his eminence.

At party schools such as Meli attended in the Soviet bloc, among other subjects cadres were taught 'MCW' (Military and Combat Work). This concerned underground work and intelligence, and normally involved connections with the Stasi and the KGB. People attending these courses were closely monitored by the intelligence organs of the eastern bloc states, which kept files on them. Meli would have been held in high esteem by the East German authorities and was a big fish for the anglers of South African MI.

In May 1993, Major Boakye-Djan was revealed to be the crucial link also between Solly Smith and MI. He was placed under scrutiny by the ANC in 1988 following revelations in a London newspaper, the *Independent*, that he had received ANC documents from Meli.[3] In fresh revelations in *Top Secret*, both Smith and Meli were said to be involved in a disinformation campaign headed by Boakye-Djan and funded by MI.

IN THE LONDON CENTRE

Like most ANC chief representatives in important station posts during the exile, Smith belonged to the higher ranks of the ANC security department, iMbokodo ('the boulder that crushes'), now known as the Department of Intelligence and Security(DIS). London was the crucial coordinating centre for ANC activities internationally. As chief representative, Smith was like an ambassador of a Soviet bloc state. He was in charge of everything in the mission, including security. He was chief of iMbokodo in the London office, and coordinator of all ANC security in Britain.

All black ANC members (but apparently not white members) in Britain were required to surrender their passports to the chief representative's office in London, in other words to Smith. These passports were then kept locked up and their owners were deprived of their use until authorised by iMbokodo — that is, Smith — who had access to and control over the passport records of ANC members in Britain, whether they arrived to study or were passing through en route to conferences, All private mail arriving in Britain for ANC members and addressed to the ANC office was vetted by iMbokodo staff, and was available first of all to Smith.

At ANC headquarters in Lusaka in 1980, Smith had been a member of an iMbokodo directorate that discussed current dissension among young security personnel. Their dissatisfaction was directed at corruption among top officials, stagnation of the military struggle and repressive conduct by the security department.[4] Through Boakye-Djan in London, Smith was thus in a position to provide MI with copious ongoing information about the whole of the ANC in exile, including its central nervous system, iMbokodo. In the battle for security, the ANC was disastrously out-gunned. The 'turning' of a high-level political and security official like Smith made nonsense of the arrogance of iMbokodo, as self-asserted guardian of the struggle. ANC members in exile had cause to fear iMbokodo not only because of its brutality but for the scope it gave to penetration by the South African state. The nature of its control over ANC members made it doubly dangerous to them.

This was indeed what very many rank and file ANC members — especially in Umkhonto — did fear and suspect. The revelations about Smith and Meli bear out the charges and suspicions of ANC mutineers in Umkhonto in Angola in 1984 that the organisation had been infiltrated from the top by South African intelligence. The mutineers' first demand was for suspension of the suspect security department and for a comprehensive investigation into its activities.[5] These suspicions were forcefully articulated by a group of loyal and dedicated former members of the security department — also members of Oliver Tambo's personal bodyguard — who had resigned from iMbokodo at ANC headquarters in Lusaka in 1980 in protest both against its failure to protect the movement and at corruption among ANC leaders, including Tambo. After resigning their posts as security officials and resuming duties within the ranks of Umkhonto, some of these men continued to protest at the abuse of power by iMbokodo.

The fate of these former members of the security department — all from the generation of the 1976 Soweto school students' revolt — illuminates the real relations of power within the ANC in exile, its ideology and methods of rule, and its incapacity to listen to its most serious-minded younger members.

One, Mlamli Namba (MK name, James Nkabinde), was shot by firing squad on the orders of a tribunal staffed by members of iMbokodo after the third and final phase of the mutiny, at Pango camp, in May 1984. Head of the tribunal was Sizakele Sigxashe, who like Meli had studied at Fort Hare in the early 1960s. (Sigxashe received his doctorate in Moscow.)[6]

A second, Sidwell Moroka, or Mhlongo (real name, Omry Makgoale), was elected spokesperson by the June 16 detachment of Umkhonto and was delegated to call on the leadership to convene a conference of the whole organisation to discuss its problems, (No such conference was called until five years later, after the critics had been crushed and silenced). By 1984 Makgoale was MK district commander in the Angolan capital, Luanda. He was elected a member of the Committee of Ten that was chosen to lead the mutineers in Viana camp in February 1984, helped negotiate the surrender of the mutineers, was arrested, and spent nearly five years under continuous tortures in Quatro penal camp. On his release he was elected chairman of all ANC exiles in Tanzania in September 1989, before being forced out of office by Chris Hani and Stanley Mabizela, representing the National Executive Committee, based in Lusaka.

A third former member of Tambo's bodyguard, known as Earl (or McCann), fled to Kenya from Zambia with his wife in the early months of 1990, after being approached by senior members of iMbokodo to participate in a drug smuggling ring, He had been a camp commander in Angola, and had participated in arrests of his colleagues during the mutiny.

The warnings and insights of these former security officials were systematically ignored by the leadership of the ANC, in particular by Tambo, but above all by the security department. Instead, these young men were themselves hounded by iMbokodo as 'enemy agents'. It was the concerns of these men, and others, that Smith had rejected as a member of the iMbokodo directorate in Lusaka in 1980. Now he and Meli are found to have been deeply compromised.[7]

Smith's family has said he died of natural causes and that he had been very ill for some time. He had been admitted to hospital in Johannesburg and Bloemfontein several times in 1993. A Bloemfontein state pathologist, Dr Jan Olivier, found that his death was caused by cardio-respiratory failure. He said he had checked for traces of poison but had found nothing suspicious. A Bloemfontein doctor who treated Smith earlier in 1993 said he was not surprised to hear that he had died of heart failure. Smith, he said, had 'an enlarged heart, high blood-pressure, poor kidneys, degenerative arthritis, diabetes and Parkinson's disease' (*Sunday Times*, 30 May). His appalling state of health could only have been aggravated by his alcohol abuse.

Many ANC members, however, are suspicious. According to an ANC 'intelligence source', Smith had been warned by state intelligence agents not to reveal his past role on behalf of MI, and was in fear of his life. 'He had reached a point where he did not know whether they or his health were going to get him first', according to this ANC source (*Sunday Times*, Johannesburg). Smith had approached the ANC after important documents had been stolen from his home in June or July 1992. His son-in-law stated that Smith had been 'extremely worried' about the missing documents, because only he and ANC headquarters knew about them. The ANC appears to have left these documents in Smith's keeping even after he had told the organisation about his work for MI.

POISONS IN THE BLOODSTREAM

The unnamed source in ANC intelligence said it was '80 percent convinced' that Meli had been poisoned by a drink at the Carlton Hotel, even though he 'ostensibly died of heart failure' (*Sunday Times*). Major Boakye-Djan, the Ghanaian agent of MI, is believed by ANC members to have been with Meli in Johannesburg shortly before his death. Meli was seen in a drunken stupor with a suspicious friend in the Eastern Cape, by members of the ANC, according to *Top Secret*, and was to appear for questioning when he was found dead.

No conclusive evidence exists at present to show that either man died by poisoning. It is obvious, however, that both could have been susceptible to blackmail by MI in exile, because of their alcoholism. Anything could have been planted on these men, or extracted from them, in their habitually drunken state. They were wide open to exploitation by MI, and with them a huge swathe of the ANC membership.

This appears not to have been perceived as a critical problem by ANC security in exile, nor by the NEC and the SACP central committee. Neither man appears to have been able to get adequate counselling for his addiction problem, to their own cost, and that of their closest relatives, and also of the organisations in which they held senior rank, with access to top-grade confidential information involving life and death for many people (including, ultimately, perhaps also themselves). Meli was regularly 'dried out' in East Germany, but it is questionable whether this even began to help him in confronting his addiction problem. Addiction is notoriously intractable. It is doubtful whether much sensitivity or understanding was shown in the closed world of the ANC/SACP hierarchy. Chances for recovery would have been problematic, even had this been so.

The real question here, however, is political. Duma Nokwe was removed from his post as ANC secretary-general in 1969, following the Morogoro conference in Tanzania, because his alcoholism rendered him unsuitable for the post. (According to Ellis and Sechaba, Nokwe's alcoholism was 'eventually to kill him', p 60.) Smith and Meli retained senior posts, however, with access to confidential information.

The ANC has yet to make a full public account of the relations of Smith and Meli to Boakye-Djan, of the problems posed by their alcoholism, of the measures taken by the organisation to limit damage to its members and itself, and of the extent of damage done. Once again, if nothing else, the shoddy quality of the ANC/SACP exile operation comes to light. It appears through the characteristic form of personal tragedy, masked by rhetoric from an organisation that is more symbol than substance. Nationalist and stalinist phrases blunted sensitivity to real needs, real patriots were hunted down as 'enemy agents' while real enemy agents urged on the hunt. The deaths of these two senior figures of the exile show that the ANC operation in exile, to which so much blood and life was sacrificed, was in large part a tragedy in the form of *opera bouffe* — a clowning with real needs. It was this perception, and its truth, that produced the mutiny of almost the entire ANC trained forces in Angola, a perception punished by the high-ups with torture and executions. The prison camp was the expression of an ideology of suppression and denial.

That mutiny, the gravest crisis of the exile, was the moment of truth for the ANC, the moment at which fictions took absolute hold. For penetration by the skilled, ruthless, well-resourced security managers of the South African state, there could not have been a more suitable culture than that of lmbokodo, through which the ANC was seized by an ideologically-driven security mania. As in Goya's painting of Chronos devouring his children, iMbokodo devoured the best, most able and most dedicated of the generation of 1976. This was a coup for MI. The ANC provided it with this prize.

The ANC security department was MI's most viable route of penetration into the ANC in exile. Mouthing of vehement rhetoric was the appropriate way to get into iMbokodo, and to advance in rank. Nothing was easier for a trained agent to mimic. In a bureaucratic, hierarchical organisation in which real opinions and feelings were driven under ground, the advantage lay with the individual who could most successfully lead a double life. In this sense, little was learnt by the ANC/SACP from the experience of penetration by state intelligence of the underground inside South Africa in the early 1960s.[8]

In this nest of sadism and special privilege, individuals took leave of their senses, as well as ordinary human feeling. An example: during training by the Stasi in the former German Democratic Republic, teenage iMbokodo recruits were taken on tours of Nazi extermination camps where they were shown lampshades made of Jews' skins and other delights. They returned to Angola, Zambia and Tanzania, psyched up by their Stasi controllers to believe that this would be their own fate if critics of the ANC/SACP line gained authority (personal communication). This was an appalling perversion of the death camps by their then supervisors. The result was naturally a further perversion. These young people, who had been abused in this fashion, told the victims they tortured: 'We are not sadists; we are doing this in defence of the struggle.' Or, in words they learnt from the former ANC commissar and SACP leader, Andrew Masondo:[9] 'We are waging war, not playing war.'

These were the semiotics of torture. This specific ideological milieu of the ANC, and especially of iMbokodo, provided cover to the spies of MI.

THE KITSON AFFAIR

One of the shameful episodes of the exile was the hounding in London by Smith, Meli and others of David Kitson, a former leader of Umkhonto weSizwe who had been a member of the Communist Party of South Africa since 1940. Like other white members of the CPSA, Kitson had fought in the South African army during World War Two.[10] This prior military experience by white members of the Communist Party played a crucial part in the formation of Umkhonto weSizwe. It gave the ANC a decided edge in military organisation over the rival efforts of the Pan Africanist Congress, which had minimal military experience or scientific technology to draw on when it embarked on violence in the early 1960s.

Having qualified as an engineer at Natal University after the war, Kitson had worked as a draughtsman in an aeronautical engineering firm in Britain. An ardent stalinist, he joined the technical workers' trade union in Britain, the Draughtsmen's and Allied Technicians' Association, later the Technical and Ancillary Staffs Association (TASS), which was controlled by members of the Communist Party of Great Britain. He won a scholarship to Ruskin College, Oxford, funded by his union.

In 1959, Dave Kitson and his wife Norma returned separately to South Africa, where both worked in the SACP underground. After the arrest of the first High Command of Umkhonto in Rivonia (a Johannesburg suburb) in 1963, Kitson became one of four members of the second High Command. Arrested, interrogated and tried in 1964 along with Wilton Mkwayi, Mac Maharaj, Laloo Chiba and John Matthews, he was sentenced to 20 years in prison, which he served in full. Kitson's union, TASS, played a major part in the campaign for his release, prominently placing his name and South African racist conditions before its members.

Norma Kitson, who had carried out secret printing work for Umkhonto in Johannesburg during the Rivonia Trial, left for London after Dave Kitson's arrest and campaigned in Britain as a member of the ANC for his release, for his transfer away from a prison basement in which Kitson had become very ill, and for the release of all political prisoners. Norma and her children were central in the formation of the City of London section of the Anti-Apartheid Movement (AAM), which advocated a strategy of non-stop picketing of the South African embassy in London, situated in one of the most central and most visible sites in London, alongside Trafalgar Square.

After his release from prison, Kitson rejoined his family in London and participated in the picketing of the South African embassy. By this time, City Group and Norma Kitson had been instructed by the London leadership of the SACP, the ANC, and the AAM to abandon their strategy of the non-stop picket, principally, it seems, because of disquiet on the part of the leadership of these organisations that possible disorder on the picket in such a central London location might jeopardise their own relationship to the British establishment. When David Kitson refused an instruction from two senior members of the SACP in London to make a public denunciation of the political campaigning strategy of his wife, both of them were then expelled from the SACP, and suspended from the London ANC in November 1984. City Group was expelled from the AAM the following February.

Leaders of TASS now broke their promise, made in 1969 while David Kitson was one-quarter way through his prison sentence, to fund David in a fellowship at Ruskin College for life, following his release from prison. He had tutored in statistics at Ruskin for a year. The leadership of TASS now ordered Kitson to obey the ANC, or lose his Ruskin post. This amounted to an order by leaders of a British trade union that a South African stalwart of the struggle against apartheid, who had completed 20 years in prison, should denounce his wife, who had loyally stood by him throughout his imprisonment, or lose his source of employment. He indignantly refused.[11] Kitson was then informed in the same week by the ANC London office that his suspension would continue and by TASS that his funding to teach at Ruskin in Oxford had been withdrawn. A major part in this sordid affair was played by Solly Smith, who behaved like a hatchet man.[12] This squalid conflict was manipulated by MI, working through Smith and Meli, and assisted by the methods of control within the AAM and TASS. Such was the treatment — in London — of a prison hero of the SACP and the ANC, a person utterly uncritical of the Soviet Union and, in his own words, a 'Mandela man'.[13]

A PERSON ABOVE SUSPICION

The ANC spokesperson who confirmed that Smith had been a spy stated that his death needed investigation. After Smith's fears for his life, he said, his death was 'suspicious' (*Weekly Mail*, 28 May 1993). If the ANC is serious about these suspicions, it should publish a truthful report on the deaths of its operatives in Zambia in 1988 and 1989, in addition to making a complete public inventory of all its information concerning Smith and Meli, in London and elsewhere. At the time of the spy-mania in Zambia, completely innocent former members of the ANC — critics of iMbokodo — were condemned for bombings, drug smuggling and other offences, in full knowledge that the charges were nonsense, and beaten up and imprisoned by iMbokodo, with the connivance of the Zambian state.[14] As with its response to the criticism of the young security officials in Lusaka in 1980, with the discontent of the troops in Angola in 1984, in the dispute with the Kitsons in the mid-1980s and in the response of *Sechaba* to the revelations in *Africa Confidential* in 1988, this was the normal response of the ANC to any threat to its central ideological apparatus.

Honest accounting is the least that is owed by the ANC to its members. Without full disclosure, and an end to suppression and denial, it is impossible to know whether a trail of murders of leading officials has spread from Zambia to South Africa.[15]

The uncertainty itself constitutes a poisoning of public life.

The revelations about Smith and Meli make it all the more essential that there should be candid and public accounting for murky episodes from the past, including the Kitson affair. The guardians must be held to account.

REFERENCES

1. Francis Meli, *South Africa Belongs to Us. A History of the ANC*, James Currey, 1989.
2. Stephen Ellis and Tsepo Sechaba, *Comrades against Apartheid: The ANC and the South African Communist Party in Exile*, James Currey, 1992, p 7.
3. Meli's book was published in London after these revelations.
4. This climate of unease and dissension in the security department in Lusaka in 1980 is referred to by Bandile Ketelo et al, 'A Miscarriage of Democracy: The ANC Security Department in the 1984 Mutiny in Umkhonto weSizwe', *Searchlight South Africa* No. 5 (July 1990), pp. 39–40 — see pp. 13–14 in this book.
5. Ibid. p 45 — see p 19 in this book.
6. Meli's generation at Fort Hare in the early 1960s provided an important nucleus of younger ANC and SACP leaders in the exile, with a deeply stalinist ideological make-up. Others in this cadre, besides Sigxashe, were Chris Hani and Stanley Mabizela. The leading influence on their development at Fort Hare was Govan Mbeki, then leader (in Port Elizabeth) of the best ANC and SACP branches in the country.

   A major split took place with one of their former Fort Hare colleagues, Thami Mhlambiso, after the Morogoro conference of the ANC in 1969. Mhlambiso had been a leader of the National Union of South African Students while at Fort Hare, a head of the ANC Youth and Students section in London in the mid-1960s and became ANC representative at the UN. He was expelled from the ANC in 1975 as one of the so-called 'Gang of Eight' who opposed the increasing influence of the SACP in the leadership of the ANC. Dismissed as

ANC representative at the UN, Mhlambiso faced strenuous but unsuccessful efforts by Thabo Mbeki (Govan's son, then a leading international spokesperson for the ANC) to have him dismissed from a UN salaried post.

7. In its issue of October 1988, *Sechaba* responded to revelations published in the London news-sheet *Africa Confidential* with an editorial headed: 'Whom does Africa Confidential serve?' It denounced recent articles that gave a 'gloomy, if not a horrifying and frightening picture' of conditions in the ANC in exile. Articles which portrayed the ANC as 'a mafia-type organisation' were 'more like distorted intelligence reports than serious journalism'. *Sechaba* made the characteristic response, when the exile conduct of the ANC was brought up for discussion: 'Who is *Africa Confidential* working for?'

   This followed two detailed articles in previous issues of *Africa Confidential*, one of which referred to the role of Chris Hani — then army commissar — in 'Putting down the 1984 mutiny in the ANC training camps in Angola' (Vol. 29, No. 16, 12 August 1988). This was probably the first reference to the dread secret at the heart of the ANC in exile. *Africa Confidential* was not deterred. In December 1988 it provided specific and accurate reference to imprisonment by the security department of the ANC's research director, Pallo Jordan, in June 1983 (Vol. 29, No. 24).

   This was probably the first public reference to the ANC's imprisonment of members for political dissent since publication of similar information by the British left-wing newspaper *Black Dwarf* in the late 1960s. Details were confirmed by Jordan in 1992 in evidence to the ANC commission of inquiry headed by Advocate Thembile Skweyiya (see *SSA* No. 10, 'The ANC Camps: An Audit of Three Years, 1990–93', p 16 — see p 72 in this book), and again in evidence this year [written in 1993] to the commission headed by Dr Sam Motsuenyane (*Star*, Johannesburg, 20 May 1993). While *Sechaba* under Meli's editorship concealed abuses, *Africa Confidential* was for two crucial years the sole reliable source of information about the victims of iMbokodo.

   Meli was a major figure in the management of information (and disinformation) by the ANC. His relation to Boakye-Djan suggests the problem of who ultimately was in charge of this system of manipulation of minds and of the media. One could rephrase the question: Whom did *Sechaba* serve?

8. *Author's note, 2009*: This perception derives from the author's experience of the penetration of the illegal SACP in Johannesburg in the early Sixties by a secret police agent, Gerard Ludi, later author of *Operation Q-018* (Nasionale Boekhandel, Cape Town, 1969), Ludi's autobiographical account of this operation.

9. *Author's note, 2009*: subsequently a Lt General in the SANDF.

10. *Author's note, 2009*: White members of the CPSA nearly all joined the South African forces only after Germany invaded the Soviet Union, in June 1941. During the Nazi invasion of Poland, Norway, the Netherlands, Belgium and France, and the Battle of Britain, prior to the invasion of the Soviet Union, military resistance to German imperialism was opposed by the CPSA as constituting an 'imperialist war'.

11. According to Norma Kitson 'The Anti-Apartheid Movement was controlled by the chevra' (Norma Kitson, *Where Sixpence Lives*, Hogarth Press, London, 1987, p 262). Chevra means Comrades, but as used here was a friend's abbreviation for the *Chevra Kadisha* (the Jewish burial society) when referring to a small group inside the SACP in London. She quotes this friend as saying:

    > If anyone starts any activity that is not under their control, they "bury" them — immobilise them, or manoeuvre them out of the solidarity movement .... The

> chevra hold sway over the London ANC, and have influence over the Anti-Apartheid Movement and David's trade union, TASS. They're a very small, powerful group over here — mainly middle-class whites who left South Africa before the going really got tough.... Those who criticise the chevra are called "Trotskyist" or "ultraleft" — words used as insults that have no relation to their real meanings.... Those who wish to expose them are in danger of being accused of siding with the South African regime, of being called anti-communist or enemies of the movement. So most keep quiet. (pp. 214–16)

Ironically, through Smith and Meli, MI had detailed access to the thinking, decisions and manoeuvres of 'the chevra'.

The Kitson affair illuminates the high degree of success of stalinist manipulation of public perceptions in Britain and South Africa. Among the many South African exiles in Britain, there was abysmal support for the right of David Kitson to retain his funding from TASS, except for a very small number of his former political comrades from prison in Pretoria. Even here, though, past loyalties were sundered. Kitson was barred from attending a gathering of exiles held in the mid-1980s at the north London home of the subsequent ANC MP, Ben Turok, with whom he had been in prison in Pretoria, at the insistence of another of Kitson's prison companions, the SACP leader Fred Carneson (who served five years, by comparison with Kitson's twenty). Guests were kept ignorant of this pre-arranged and shaming exclusion: even the guest of honour, Harold Strachan, their prison colleague, then on a visit to London.

12. Ibid., pp. 286, 312, 317.
13. *Author's note,* 2009: After the exposure of Smith and Meli, Norma and David Kitson were 'reinstated' in the ANC. By that time David Kitson's post at Ruskin College had been made redundant, and he did not return, following his forced departure.

    Norma Kitson died in Harare, Zimbabwe, on 12 June 2002. Their experience in London in the Eighties had caused her and David to choose to live there rather than in South Africa after the ANC and other organisations had been unbanned in 1990, despite their lifetimes' commitment to political change in South Africa. The author's obituary of Norma Kitson in the *Independent*, London (14 June 2002), was reprinted by the *Sunday Independent* in South Africa on 15 June 2002 in an adapted version, under the author's name, which nevertheless succeeded in editing out all reference to the Kitsons' troubles in London. David Kitson lives in a retirement home in Johannesburg.
14. See Trewhela, 'A Can of Worms in Lusaka: The Imprisonment of Hubert Sipho Mbeje', *SSA* No. 9 (August 1992).
15. This might include the murder of Joe Gqabi, the ANC chief representative in Harare, in July 1981. He was one of the very few senior ANC leaders who sympathised with the demands of the troops in Angola for greater openness and accountability (Ketelo et al, p 38). He told a visitor a few weeks before his murder that he feared for his life from within the ANC (personal communication from Norma Kitson). Participants in the mutiny in Angola considered his murder to have been 'an inside job'.

    Author's note, 2009: For all these concerns, there is no doubt that Gqabi's assassination was the work of the South African Military Intelligence. One of his assassins, Major Gray Branfield, an operative both of the Rhodesian police and later of South African MI, was shot dead in battle as a security contractor in Iraq in 2004.

8 *The Problem of Communism in Southern Africa**

Bram Fischer's and Geoffrey Cox's journey into the Soviet heart of darkness

On 2nd April 2008 one of the greatest British journalists of the last century died in England, aged nearly 98: a man whose life throws the light of truth on a central problem of the political culture of southern Africa, the problem of Communism. This problem of Communism is in turn central to the dictatorship in Zimbabwe, the sordid farce of its electoral system, collusion with this dictatorship by the government of South Africa under President Thabo Mbeki and the humiliating spectacle of the leaders of the Southern African Development Community in a phalanx of agreement with President Robert Mugabe: their old and young grey heads as fixed and corpse-like as the Politburo of Soviet Communist Party lined up on Lenin's tomb in Moscow in the days of yore.

This political culture was set in place in southern Africa primarily by white people, not by black people. It is one of the shining virtues of the life of Sir Geoffrey Cox that he provided clear and truthful witness to the Big Lie on which this culture was founded, tangled up as it is in a brave, heroic contribution to the ending of apartheid. Two lives are joined here, as if fused at the hip: Sir Geoffrey Cox (1910–2008), the founder of modern television news journalism in Britain (a beacon of integrity, by contrast with the permanently shameful role of the South African Broadcasting Corporation), and Bram Fischer QC (1908–1975), chairman of the illegal South African Communist Party and principal defence counsel in the Rivonia Trial in which Nelson Mandela and his colleagues were sentenced to life imprisonment in 1964, who died as a political prisoner nine years into a life sentence in South Africa, more than thirty years before Cox.

Fischer's courage is rightly celebrated in South Africa today at the Bram Fischer Library in the Legal Resources Centre in Johannesburg, and in its annual Bram Fischer Memorial Lecture, first delivered in June 1995 by then President

*This first appeared on the `www.politicsweb.co.za` website, 16 April 2008.

Mandela, Fischer's colleague in the formation of Umkhonto weSizwe, the military wing of the SACP and the African National Congress.

As the writer of this article, I had a personal connection with Bram and the problem of Communism in southern Africa, since I was secretly the editor in Johannesburg of the underground journal of Umkhonto, *Freedom Fighter*, while Fischer led the defence of the Rivonia accused; I was then Bram's co-accused in a trial of white members of the SACP in 1964–65, from which Bram absconded in an attempt to hold together the shattered fragments of the ANC/SACP resistance to apartheid at a time of fierce repression; and I then shared a cell with him for some months in Local Prison in Pretoria, after his re-arrest, conviction and sentence for sabotage in 1966. Bram contracted cancer while in prison and died a hero of the resistance. His life and fate, like that of Ruth First, his SACP colleague who was assassinated by the security police in 1982, remains an emblem — one of many — of the non-racial political opposition to the racist state that culminated ultimately in the present government in South Africa.

The exemplary side of this contribution is widely recognised and celebrated. For 14 years it has not been difficult for South Africa to honour those who took the brave, often lonely and sometimes fatal path of people like Mandela, Fischer, Ruth First and Govan Mbeki, the father of President Mbeki. What is more difficult is for the problems of this heritage to be clarified. This is where the life of Geoffrey Cox provides a unique and invaluable guide.

Bram and Geoffrey Cox (who was born and grew up in New Zealand) arrived as Rhodes scholars at Oxford University in England in 1931. The following summer, in June and July 1932, they travelled together with three student colleagues on a four-week journey to the Soviet Union, organised by the state-run Soviet travel agency, Intourist. Their journey took them through the heartland of the famine in the Ukraine caused by Stalin's policy of forced collectivisation of agriculture, a catastrophe now replicated in Zimbabwe by the whim of President Mugabe, and endorsed and sanitised by Mbeki and the SADC. This state-enforced famine in the Soviet Union brought about the death of millions and gave a massive stimulus to the Gulag: the state-enforced system of slave labour and working to death, most horribly in the frozen goldfields at Kolyma in eastern Siberia, where millions of famine victims were deported under armed guard, to work and die.

This was at a time when contract labour by black mineworkers was at the base of South Africa's position as the biggest gold producer in the world, while working to death at Kolyma brought the Soviet Union to second place: two despotic systems of labour in the production of gold, one by far the more absolute in its destructive result to the worker.

The journey of Cox and Fischer has been described by Cox himself in a volume of autobiography, *Eyewitness: A Memoir of Europe in the Thirties* (University of Otago Press, New Zealand, 1999), and by Fischer's biographer, Stephen Clingman, chair of the department of English at the University of Massachusetts, Amherst, in the United States (*Bram Fischer, Afrikaner Revolutionary*, David Philip, Cape Town; Mayibuye Books, Bellville; University of Massachusetts Press, 1998). The journey took them along a fault-line of the 20th century, a moral fault-line in the witness to truth which notoriously divided the journalism of the young British writer Malcolm Muggeridge (who reported on his own experiences while travelling in the Ukraine in the *Manchester Guardian* on 25, 27 and 28 March 1933) from fellow-travellers such as Walter Duranty, correspondent of the *New York Times* in Moscow, and 'Stalin's apologist' (as described in the title of his biography by S.J. Taylor), who covered it up.

Cox and Fischer were similarly divided. Their common experience and polarised responses provide insight into the best qualities of British moral witness to the events of Europe of the last century, as well as to persisting long-term problems in the politics of southern Africa, where the governments of South Africa and Zimbabwe owe intellectual sources to the Stalin regime. The two books carry the same photograph of Cox and Fischer together in the Ukraine.

In his book, Cox recalls Bram as a 'short, cheerful, self-possessed man, who had for me the additional virtue of having played scrum half for the Orange Free State against the All Blacks'. What they witnessed on their journey through the Ukraine, part of it by paddle steamer down the Volga, was the 'collapse of agricultural production as farming was collectivised, a process which was then under way, particularly in the Ukraine.' It was a journey 'which was to provide us with first-hand evidence of this profound event'.

They found 'peasant Russia on the move, in a massive, unexplained migration'. At wharfs along the Volga were huge crowds of peasants carrying bundles on their backs, 'ready to stampede for the gangplank. ... As stampede followed stampede, one of the Rhodesian Rhodes Scholars [their companions] said: 'They are just like kaffirs' ... We were witnessing — though we had no idea of it then — the shock waves of that process [of collectivisation], as dispossessed peasants and their families sought refuge in other parts of the country.'

At Samara (later re-named Kuybyshev), they came across 'a long column of peasants, old big-bearded men in patched clothes and straw gaiters, being marched towards the landing stage, guarded by Red Army soldiers wearing high-peaked cloth caps with a red star on the front and carrying rifles with long sword bayonets. ... Reluctantly the guides agreed that they were peasants being taken off to prison camps "for sabotaging the communal property of the new co-operatives in their village." It was a rare glimpse of the realities of collectivisation.'

Bram, Cox and the other Oxford students 'filled the time by arguing about what we had seen, debating whether Soviet communism offered an answer. ... In that summer of 1932 the Great Depression reached its deepest point.' While alert to major achievements (he remained a Labour voter in Britain until 1959), Cox was sensitive however to a 'sense of constant strain, of wary uneasiness, indeed of fear. It was something I came to know later in Nazi Germany and in Fascist Italy' (where he worked later as a journalist). He noted the 'constant awareness that only one point of view was allowed expression, and the wary, guarded manner in which the Russians with whom we came into contact dealt not with us, but with each other. ... Somehow the place did not feel right, and certainly did not feel happy. I was forced inescapably to the view that the Soviet system we had seen in those July days of 1932 did not offer an acceptable answer....'

Cox's understanding was confirmed in Oxford in 1935 when he came across a novel by Muggeridge, *Winter in Moscow*, which made clear to him that 'we had glimpsed a huge and hideous reality.' Above all he appreciated Muggeridge's depiction of the paranoia of the Soviet commissar of those days: in Muggeridge's words, 'enemies at work everywhere; secret underground enemies corroding the Dictatorship of the Proletariat; enemies in the Party, perhaps even in the Polit Buro; enemies all around him night and day, intriguing, sabotaging' — enemies to be ruthlessly crushed. It is a portrait of a mindset now all too familiar in southern Africa.

As Fischer's very capable biographer notes, however, 'Bram's views did not change when he read Malcolm Muggeridge as his friend Geoffrey Cox's did, but it was not just a question of relative credulity. In the Soviet Union, both then and as he looked back, he saw a way of dealing with South Africa's problems and issues...' (Clingman, p. 86). After leaving the Soviet Union, having witnessed what Muggeridge later described as an 'organised famine', Bram wrote a ten-page letter to his father in Afrikaans, in which, as Clingman says, 'his spirit was still largely buoyant. ... Bram evidently agreed with much of what he had been hearing and reading. ... In that light, wrote Bram, there could be no doubt of the advantages of communism.'

In the light of the organised famine and repression now taking place in Zimbabwe, Bram's response to his and Cox's Soviet experience makes chilling reading. As Clingman continues, Bram 'knew that most of the harvest had failed. He was also aware of repression in other areas: the Communist Party, with its 'famed Gay-Pay-Oo' (OGPU, predecessor to the KGB), exercised total control. But, said Bram, according to communist philosophy this was a necessary historical stage, and taking into account both the ideals and the difficulties of the system one could see that it was "the only method whereby a world communist existence could be brought into being"' (pp. 82–83).

At that stage, the worst of Stalin's purges and the Gulag system still lay ahead. More chilling still, given the role of the SACP in the modern history of southern Africa, was Bram's stand in a subsequent episode of moral denialism, with direct relation to the opposed choices made by him and Cox. The story was recorded by Clingman in an interview with Joel Mervis, former editor of the *Sunday Times* in Johannesburg, and an old school-friend of Bram. At a dinner party held by Mervis at his house in Johannesburg, probably in 1940, in the period of the Stalin–Hitler Pact following the occupation of Poland, the 'guest of honour was Malcolm Muggeridge, who had written with such effect on the horrors of collectivisation during the early 1930s (persuading Bram's friend Geoffrey Cox, but not Bram himself, of the excesses of stalinism), and who was now visiting Johannesburg, staying at Mervis's house.'

Bram and Muggeridge had a 'three-hour stand-up debate on the question of Bram's commitment to Russia and his attitude to the war, while some thirty other guests looked on in silent and awed fascination. ... Bram's position was that, without giving any credit to Hitler, he was not prepared to fight in any capitalist war [which was how stalinists then described Hitler's invasion of France and the Low Countries, and Germany's preparation for the invasion of Britain — PT]. On the question of the show trials, he maintained that the accused had had a defence, that they had confessed, that all the rest was Western propaganda. ... Later, when Germany invaded the Soviet Union, Bram was all for fighting the war.' (p 150)

Advocacy of terroristic state behaviour has a long history in southern Africa.

9 *The ANC: Fifteen Wasted Years**

A TRIBUTE TO KOŁAKOWSKI: THE BALANCE SHEET OF ANC GOVERNMENT

Fifteen wasted years: this must be the balance sheet of the African National Congress as the unchallenged party of government.

In terms of the great mass of South Africa's citizens, whom it purports to represent, and who have presented it with one mandate after another to act as their representative, it has failed — by any reasonable test.

No party ever came to government with such an overwhelming mandate from the people, and with such immense goodwill internationally. Few dissipated that trust so convincingly.

Not that the ANC as the single majoritarian party of government, politically, did not from the beginning face immense challenges in terms of society, economy and culture. This was a given, the bottom line. The centuries-old divisions in the society along the line of race, its stratospheric polarisation between extremes of wealth and poverty, the inherited deadweight of mass illiteracy and sub-literacy, abysmal conditions in housing, healthcare, sanitation: these and many others were the challenges set to the ANC government in 1994, as daunting as they would have been to any other party in South Africa, or the world, for that matter. No easy walk to freedom, and human betterment, indeed.

The question is, what did the ANC do with this gift of state power, for which it had yearned for almost a century, and for which so many of its followers had made great sacrifices. Here one has to say that at best its achievements have been modest. Often they have been pitiful. In crucial matters they have been disastrous, as would be accounted by honest reckoning in any society.

By my own judgement, its most terrible failure has been in education.

This was one variable, in my view, which the ANC government could and should have seized upon from the beginning, and said to the whole society: 'We have limited resources, there are great competing needs, but this above all — with dedication and good sense and common effort — can raise up and

*This first appeared on the www.politicsweb.co.za website, 24 July 2009.

prepare for the future a new generation that will be better fitted to solve the country's problems than ourselves.'

The society could have been asked to sacrifice some more for its children, so that South Africa could have been transformed in as short a time as possible into a high-skilled and more highly cultured society, at the same time as its old economic foundation in a mass of unskilled and semi-skilled labour had become increasingly redundant, in a world of globalised economy. The greatest possible resources, and the greatest possible assemblage of teaching skills and idealism, could have gone towards this mission, which would have drawn upon and enhanced the most profound aspirations of the society, and harvested great international support.

Its institutions of first-world quality in third-level education and its pockets of international-standard excellence in primary and secondary education could have been drawn upon as resources in raising up the lower depths. A planned, sober, determined effort stretching across the whole of the society, founded on a true respect for education and the mind and soul of the human person, could have done this.

Instead... the materialistic scramble for personal wealth, at any price. The rancour, the power-play, the strutting about of Great Men (and a few women), the arrogance of office, the delusions. The false gods. Style, instead of substance. Fifteen wasted years.

I thought about this when reading the obituary of a philosopher who died last week, a man born in 1927, the year in which the ANC president of that time, Josiah Gumede, made the first visit by any ANC member — the first of many such — to the Soviet Union, that great sunken wreck of so many South African political aspirations.

Leszek Kołakowski was born in Poland, a country that knew well the feel of foreign occupation, which during his lifetime — during his childhood and youth — suffered its most terrible Calvary at the hands of both Germany and Russia, its historic oppressors, situated to its west and east. Like a good number of young Poles of his generation, he was grateful when the Russians (who had invaded his country in tandem with the Germans at the beginning of the Second World War) chased out the Germans towards the war's end, and made themselves its new masters. He became a marxist, and joined the Polish Communist youth organisation. Why not?

Well, he found out why not. Kołakowski's journey of consciousness up until his death last week ran parallel to the ascent of the South African Communist Party to a never-before reached eminence and power in the state.

The failure of the ANC government — in which there has **never not** been a string of ministries in the hands of serving or former members of the CP — can be examined in the light of Kołakowski's diligent, lifelong re-examination of his own former Communist Party conscience.

Author of the three-volume *Main Currents of Marxism: Its Rise, Growth and Dissolution* (1978), published after he had fled his native country, Kołakowski has home truths to tell about the men of power who led Russia onto the rocks, and who have helped guide South Africa into the swamp.

In this thoroughgoing study, he characterised marxism as 'the greatest fantasy of our century… [which] began in a Promethean humanism and culminated in the monstrous tyranny of Stalin'. A fantasy that still strides the narrow world like the living dead at the southern tip of Africa, after having been buried almost everywhere else. A visit to Moscow in 1950, when the General Secretary was still doing his work, had opened his eyes to what he would later describe as 'the enormity of material and spiritual desolation caused by the Stalinist system.' The great bulk of South African luminaries were still to make their sacred pilgrimage thither….

Written more than 50 years ago, his 72 definitions of *What Socialism is Not* — banned in Poland, but widely read underground — contained words that still buzz in the ear in South Africa today. 'Socialism is not: a society in which one man is in trouble for saying what he thinks while another is well-off because he does not say what he has on his mind; a society in which a man lives better if he doesn't have any thoughts of his own at all; a state which has more spies than nurses and more people in prison than in hospital; a state in which the philosophers and writers always say the same as the generals and ministers — but always after they've said it…'

He was particularly scathing about the nice, left-liberal apologists for marxist regimes, who argued that 'economic progress' in communist countries or the necessities of the National Democratic Revolution somehow justified a lack of political freedom: 'This lack of freedom is presented as though it were a temporary shortage. Reports along these lines give the impression of being unprejudiced. In reality they are not simply false, they are utterly misleading. Not that nothing has changed in these countries, nor that there have been no improvements in economic efficiency, but because political slavery is built into the tissue of society in the Communist countries as its absolute condition of life.' He dismissed modern manifestations of marxism , as in the SACP, COSATU and the ANC today, as 'merely a repertoire of slogans serving to organise various interests'.

It could not be better put. After 15 years of squandered government, a reading of Kołakowski is as good a curative as any for the South African disease of Radical Chic.

Salute to an honest thinker.

10 *Obituary: Tebello Motapanyane (1955–2006)**

TEBELLO MOTAPANYANE, one of the brightest and best of the children of Soweto of the '76 generation, died in abject poverty in Johannesburg General Hospital last month, 'shunted to the periphery,' as he put it, 'to starve.'

Thirty years previously he had been a leader of the Soweto school students' revolt, when he and other pupils organised a mass march of children in school uniform through Soweto on 16th June 1976 to protest against the decision of the apartheid government to impose Afrikaans as the medium of education in three school subjects.

When the police responded with profligate shooting of the children, revolt spread through the schools, factories and townships of South Africa. Despite a huge toll in casualties, the children of Soweto — Motapanyane one of the foremost among them — rejuvenated energies crushed by the police repression of the early Sixties, revived a spirit of combativity and prepared the downfall of apartheid 14 years later.

Soweto knows his name. It is in all the books about June 16th and on all the government's commemorative websites. It was recalled last June when President Thabo Mbeki marched through Soweto at the head of the official state commemoration of the students' revolt. The first black vice-admiral of the South African Navy spoke at his funeral two weeks ago.

DIED IN POVERTY

Yet he died in poverty, his wife of two decades still not granted citizenship of the country to which he dedicated his life, and his children struggling for school fees, refused a grant from the Mandela Children's Fund. His house at 7214 Vilakazi Street, Orlando West — where tourists come to see where Nelson

*This first appeared as *A Death in South Africa: Tebello Motapanyane* (1955-2006) on the `ever-fasternews.com` website, 5 January 2007.

Mandela and Archbishop Desmond Tutu used to live, the street in which he was born and grew up — is almost bare of furniture.

The story of Tebello Motapanyane's life and death is a story of contemporary South Africa, with its cruel highs and lows. An unusually trenchant article last April in the Johannesburg newspaper, the *Sowetan*, characterised his life and declining health as: 'Hero's hopes betrayed.'

When the crisis year of 1976 arrived, a year in which President Mbeki and so many in the cabinet had already been long out of the country, Motapanyane was elected secretary-general of a nation-wide organisation, the South African Students Movement (SASM). He had been expelled from Orlando High School two years earlier because of his political activities, and was then a senior student at Naledi High: the school which carries the honour of having been the first to march on June 16th.

As the middle of June approached, he was elected chairman of the Action Committee of SASM which prepared and organised the march. He chaired the first meeting of the Soweto Students Representative Council, which grew out of the Action Committee, and which gave leadership in the following months of struggle and terror, before being succeeded by his colleague from Morris Isaacson High School, Tsietsi Mashinini.

LEADERS OF THE REVOLT

In the words of the historian, the late Dr Baruch Hirson, in his book *Year of Fire, Year of Ash* (banned under the apartheid regime, following Baruch's nine years in prison), 'it was the SASM which provided much of the leadership, SASM that called the crucial demonstration for 16 June 1976, and SASM which created the Soweto Students Representative Council (SSRC) from which leaders of the Revolt were drawn.' The leadership of SASM at that time in Soweto was principally Motapanyane.

His interview 'How June 16 demo was planned' in the ANC exile journal *Sechaba*, published in 1977, is a seminal first-person account, now a standard reference in scholarly studies of the period. He worked directly in exile with the former political prisoner Alan Brooks (subsequently a leading organiser of the Anti-Apartheid Movement in London) in preparation of another major study of June 16th, *Whirlwind before the Storm*, co-authored by Brooks and Jeremy Brickhill, and published by the International Defence and Aid Fund in London in 1980.

Having escaped the country following the police terror — first to Lesotho and then Mozambique — he like so many others of that time joined the ANC army Umkhonto weSizwe in exile, and was sent to East Germany for military training as platoon commissar for his unit, having earlier worked for the Intelligence Department of the ANC in Lesotho.

His qualities of leadership were further recognised at ANC headquarters in Lusaka when he was appointed deputy head of the Youth League in 1977, with responsibility for liaison with the Organisation of African Unity and the United Nations. He travelled in several European countries mobilising support for the ANC's objectives, before returning to Africa. In Swaziland, where he had been delegated by the ANC to work in the Internal Reconstruction Unit in 1979, he met his wife, Jabu Shongwe (now Mamakgotla Motapanyane).

WHY DID HE ASK: 'WHO GOVERNS?'?

How then did this star of the '76 generation, who had organised the march in Soweto alongside Tsietsi Mashinini and Murphy Morobe, and risen to the heights of deputy head of the ANC Youth League in Lusaka, working alongside Oliver Tambo, come to his grave saying that contemporary South Africa does not remotely resemble the country which he and others fought to establish?

'Who governs?' he asked. That question, so sharply posed, in my view is the reason why his family is in poverty, why Mamakgotla (Jabu) despite more than ten years residence in Soweto and marriage to a hero of the South African struggle is still without citizenship, and why Motapanyane himself could not afford the medicines and treatment for his diabetes that could have given him extra years of life.

Who governs? Motapanyane answered this question in the negative. In an interview with the British author Carol Lee in 2004, published last year in South Africa in her book *A Child Called Freedom* (Century) — a book that is now a memorial to Motapanyane, and available in bookshops in South Africa — he stated: 'Here, in South Africa, our people do not choose a representative. The MPs are appointed from above, so they are not independent and the community cannot challenge them.'

Motapanyane's argument was that the promise of the Freedom Charter — that 'The people shall govern' — was left meaningless under the present electoral system. Without providing for a significant majority of constituency-based MPs, voters under the present party-list system had no means of holding their elected representatives to account. Despite the decades-long struggle for the vote, central values and objectives of the struggle had not yet been realised.

NOTORIOUS 'IRAN' PRISON

The same logic led this champion of youthful revolt into the notorious 'Iran' prison run by the ANC in exile for its own dissenting members in Luanda in Angola, where he was tortured by members of his own organisation. Finding himself in exile in a top-down political organisation structured similarly to its major funder, the Soviet Union, Motapanyane's critical and democratic spirit nurtured on the events of '76 made him powerful enemies in the older generation of exile apparatchiks.

For his misery in detention and in exile, Motapanyane blamed above all Andrew Masondo — political activist of the Fifties and Sixties generation, Robben Island veteran, one of the architects of the ANC's system of prison camps in exile for its own members, principal of the Solomon Mahlangu Freedom College at Mazimbu in Tanzania (where he was accused of abusing his position of authority) and lieutenant-general in the South African National Defence Force.

In this clash of generations and clash of values, Motapanyane suffered for his beliefs, both abroad and at home. And for this his children too are to suffer, for the deeds of their parent.

A biblical harshness has fallen on this man's house. We are covered in shame.

PART B

Namibia & Zimbabwe

11 *A Namibian Horror: Swapo's Prisons in Angola**

In November 1989 two persons associated with *Searchlight South Africa* were introduced to, and interviewed, two former prisoners of the South West Africa People's Organisation, in London. Impressed by the story they heard, and convinced of its veracity, they wrote the following account. As we explain at the end of this article, we have considered all the problems associated with telling the story and are convinced that justice can only be served by giving it the space it deserves. If we had kept silent we would be little more than accomplices to the perpetrators of outrageous and heinous crimes.

SILENCE OF THE GRAVES

There are people, some of them socialists, who welcome the exposure of crimes in the stalinist regimes of eastern Europe but insist that the crimes of the leadership of the South West Africa People's Organisation (SWAPO) against its own members in Angola and elsewhere remain concealed.

They justify this on the grounds that SWAPO fought the South African military in Namibia in a very long guerrilla war and at a terrible cost in casualties, and that South Africa — bearing in mind its overwhelming economic superiority, and SWAPO's failure to win a single region within Namibia by force of arms — must continue to remain a power in the land. This ignores the appalling scope of SWAPO atrocities continuing right up till the end of 1988, involving further hundreds of prisoners still unaccounted for. It ignores also SWAPO's subjection in and out of the Constituent Assembly to the capitalist interests lying at the heart of the old regime: predatory mineral-stripping by multinational and South African mining capital, capitalist farming on the grand scale by a small number of white farmers, the state-within-a-state of the Oppenheimer diamond interests centred on Oranjemund.

To this is added South Africa's continuing occupation of Namibia's main port at Walvis Bay, which remains a heavily fortified South African military base on Namibian soil. To put the matter in terms of Cuba (and thus in terms

---

*First published in *Searchlight South Africa* Vol. 1, No. 4 (February 1990), pp. 78–94.

very comprehensible to SWAPO's security officials), it is as if the US had continued to hold not the base at Guantánamo but instead Havana harbour. Namibia has become independent neither of capital nor of South Africa's military power.

To reach this negligible result, SWAPO's war against its own members reached extraordinary dimensions. We print in this issue an interview with two sisters, Ndamona and Panduleni Kali, both committed to the same ideals with which they joined SWAPO inside Namibia while at school 14 years ago.

They were arrested in Cuba in 1984 while studying on SWAPO scholarships, flown to Angola under armed Cuban guard, handed over to SWAPO in Luanda, tortured repeatedly on an absurd pretext by the SWAPO security apparatus and imprisoned in holes in the ground for five years. They were released in 1989 in the transfer of political prisoners arranged by the United Nations as part of the global Namibian settlement.

We have received a number of documents prepared mainly by the Political Consultative Council of Ex-SWAPO Detainees (PCC) and the Parents' Committee, organizations which have fought bravely to establish the truth about the imprisoned, tortured and murdered SWAPO fighters, when a deafening silence reigned everywhere else. These documents include lists of hundreds of names (still incomplete) of SWAPO fighters known by the returned prisoners to have been held in numerous prisons, lists of prisoners known to have been murdered or died in the hands of their SWAPO jailers, and a list of names of those immediately responsible.

From the interview with the Kali sisters it is clear that during official inspections of the prisons, the top SWAPO political leadership— Nujoma, Mueshihange, Garoeb, Toivo ya Toivo — were confronted face to face by the prisoners with the facts of torture and extraction of false confessions on several occasions: and did nothing. There is no escaping the complicity of the entire political leadership of SWAPO, especially Nujoma as president, over a very long period. These individuals have no place in any except a government of criminals and must be held to account.

AN INTERNATIONAL INQUIRY

We support the PCC's call for an independent international commission of inquiry to uncover the facts, let the consequences be what they may. If the inquiry concludes that all the SWAPO prisoners — or a majority, or even a large minority of them — were South African spies, so be it. There is no other way southern and central Africa can begin to be made safe for democratic politics. This abscess infects the politics of the whole subcontinent. Without fully establishing the truth about these horrors associated not just with the 'liberation movements' but specifically with the name of Marx — we shudder to report that SWAPO's torture headquarters was named the Karl Marx Reception Centre in Lubango — there can be no really democratic politics in the region, let alone socialism.

The momentous events in eastern Europe and the Soviet Union — in states which armed, funded and above all trained the SWAPO torture-machine — cannot be cut off by the length of the continent from the struggles to create a free, democratic, prosperous and socialist society in southern Africa. The people of Namibia have the same interest as the tens of millions who seek to put an end to stalinism and undemocratic politics in Europe, and in China.

SWAPO's spy-mania has left a terrible legacy in the region, not only in the presence inside Namibia of scores of brutalized torturers and guards in the clique around the leaders of the majority party. In this huge territory with its pitifully small population (only one and a half million), the low level of development of manufacturing industry leaves the army and police in a very strong position to organize society. The question uppermost in the minds of many in Namibia is clearly: Will the torturers of SWAPO get their hands on the Namibian police and military? For many, that could be a death sentence. As it is, SWAPO's legacy is a daily life of fear immediately reimposed on the returned prisoners, with videos of their false confessions circulated by SWAPO in their home areas even before their arrival, like some kind of stalinist obscenity. Fighters against imperialism are daily threatened with lynching by gangs stirred up by their former jailers, and their families are threatened and bullied.

The legacy remains in other ways too. As Max du Preez of the South African journal *Vrye Weekblad* has pointed out, SWAPO's spy-mania had three leading elements: a powerful tribal consciousness on the part of the mainly Ovambo-speaking old guard around Nujoma, grouped especially in the Kwanyama sub-tribe; a very deep seated anti-intellectualism; and a contempt for democracy, in an organization which is not known for elected congresses and whose politburo and central committee are self-perpetuating (29 September 1989). To this we would add the consequences of SWAPO's growing stalinization in the Brezhnev years, especially after the Cuba/MPLA victory in Angola in 1975.

The successive changes at the top of the USSR after Brezhnev's death altered nothing in SWAPO's methodology of rule. *Vrye Weekblad* reports in the same issue, for instance, the arrest and almost certain murder in Angola at the end of 1988 of Josef Hendricks, 18, known as 'Comrade Axab', the vice chairman of the Namibia National Students' Organisation (NANSO), only months after a SWAPO journal *The Namibian Worker* had described him as a hero. He had escaped to Angola while on bail on a charge of incitement. Returning fellow-prisoners from Angola say he was hauled out of an underground cell and never seen again after threatening to tell what had happened to him. As Du Preez writes,

> The brutal truth of the drama of the last few years is that anyone who could read or write well in SWAPO became victims of the 'cleansing process', especially if they were not Ovambos. Especially students and graduates went down [translated].

Du Preez takes himself to task for not having investigated more vigorously the disappearance of several of his former friends in the SWAPO leadership. He makes the observation that SWAPO's measures against its own members have done more than Pretoria and the South African military over many years to destabilize the delicate tribal inter-relations in the country. He writes: The Ovambo-versus–the-rest sentiment is now sharper than I have ever experienced it in the eleven years in which I have actively covered Namibia as a reporter' [translated]. By comparison, the South African-supported Democratic Turnhalle Alliance (DTA), which SWAPO for years excoriated as tribalist, had emerged in this connection, if in no other, as 'little angels'.

This is borne out by the results in the subsequent elections to the Constituent Assembly in early November. SWAPO won over 90 percent of the votes in rural Ovamboland, and the largest total of any party in the three urban areas in the centre and south where there are big concentrations of Ovambo migrant workers (Windhoek, Swakopmund, Lüderitz). This provided SWAPO with 57 percent of the total vote throughout the country, and 41 of the 72 seats in the Constituent Assembly. SWAPO's vote corresponds roughly to the proportion of Ovambo-speakers in the society. The non-Ovambo-speaking peoples in their entirety rejected SWAPO. Yet it was not always thus. While large numbers of the prison victims have non-Ovambo names, all at one time enthusiastically committed themselves to supporting SWAPO with the same naive good faith as Comrade Axab.

DESCENT INTO THE PIT

The process of internal fracture within SWAPO will need much further study, but a provisional interpretation can be offered here. Following an episode in the 1960s when the Tanzanian army was called in by SWAPO to put down critics in its military training base at Kongwa, there were two crucial periods accelerating SWAPO's descent to barbarism. The first was in the mid-1970s, when a storm of student struggles in Namibia — following the general strike of 1971 — coincided with the development of the black consciousness current in South Africa which culminated in the Soweto students' demonstration and massacre in June 1976. The black consciousness politics of that period set aside the former racially segregated divisions between the people designated in South Africa as African, Coloured and Indian enshrined in the old Congress alliance. Its effect within Namibia, especially among the youth, was to propel a large number of non-Ovambo speakers into SWAPO, which had been formed in 1960 out of the Ovamboland People's Organisation, led by Nujoma.

In the same years, the collapse of the Portuguese empire compelled SWAPO to reverse its alliances in Angola. Having fought previously alongside the UNITA guerrilla army of Jonas Savimbi, the SWAPO leaders now adapted to the Cuban/MPLA regime that won the civil war in Angola following the incursion by South African/CIA/mercenary forces. The new regime in Angola, dependent on the USSR, intensified moves within SWAPO towards stalinism that conflicted with the demands for democracy among its younger members, who called for a new constitution and convocation of the SWAPO congress. On this occasion, SWAPO called out the Zambian army against its own members, more than twenty of whom are listed by the Parents' Committee as having last been seen alive in Zambia in 1976/78.

The second crucial descent (literally) into the pit took place in 1983/84, when the security apparatus under Solomon 'Jesus' Hawala — head of security and deputy army commander — carried out a purge of the military leadership. Peter Eneas Nanyemba, SWAPO's secretary of defence, died in 1983 in southern Angola, allegedly in a car accident. He was a member of SWAPO's old guard, an organizer of the fish cannery workers at Walvis Bay on behalf of SWAPO's predecessor, the Ovambo People's Organisation, as far back as 1959 (Herbstein et al, p 6). According to Johannes Gaomab (see below), Nanyemba was 'busy replacing members of the old guard in the military hierarchy. He was trying to replace illiterates with literates...'

Hawala claimed that Nanyemba's policy favoured only southern Namibians. In fact Nanyemba usually chose young, urban and educated men. The old guard ignored the fact there were many Ovambos among them. Educated Ovambos were considered decultured — *Mbutidis* (or weeds between the true corn). It seems that:

> Nanyemba's reshuffle offended many Kwanyamas (the largest Ovambo sub-group). So Jesus aligned himself with the Kwanyamas and encouraged them to perceive Nanyemba and the educated group as a threat... [Without

> Nanyemba's protection after his death] the educated officials in party and army were purged as Jesus pleased. (*Weekly Mail*, 5 October 1989)

At the time, leading South African nationalist leaders in exile (who knew Nanyemba) believed he had been murdered. Shortly before his death, Nanyemba and two of his closest colleagues in the leadership of the People's Liberation Army of Namibia (PLAN) had released a number of SWAPO prisoners against the opposition of the security apparatus, headed by Hawala.

After Nanyemba's death, these two colleagues — Tauno Hatuikulipi and Bennie Petrus — were arrested by Hawala's men and died in prison, probably murdered after torture. Hatuikulipi was a former director of the Windhoek Christian Centre (the predecessor of the Council of Churches in Namibia — CCN) and a member of the SWAPO central committee and military council. His death was not made public until six months later, when he was branded as an enemy agent who had committed suicide by swallowing poison from a capsule hidden in a tooth.

In the same period, one of the most successful of PLAN's military commanders inside Namibia, Johannes Mie Gaomab ('Comrade Mistake'), was recalled from the field as commander of the southern sector in March 1984, arrested, tortured, made to 'confess' in GPU fashion and kept imprisoned until his release and return to Namibia last July. Gaomab, who had been decorated by both the Cuban and East German armies, was a friend of Petrus (*Independent*, 29 September 1989).

> In the event eight members of the Central Committee of which two were members of its political bureau were also seized... On the part of PLAN the arrest swept [away] the Chief of Personnel, the Chief of Military Intelligence, his Deputy, and the Chief of Protocol at the DHQ and numerous other officers and combatants. ('A Report')

The lunacy of the spy-mania may be appreciated from the fact that even Nujoma's wife Kowambo was held as a suspect, together with her sister and her brother (a member of the SWAPO central committee). The parallels in the history of stalinism are obvious: in the purge of the military, the paranoid destruction of leaders' families (see *20 Letters to a Friend*, by Stalin's daughter Svetlana Alliluyeva), the method of fabrication of 'confessions' (described in *On Trial* by Artur London, a victim of the Czech show trial of 1951 and former deputy foreign minister) and the spiriting away of foreign students, as happened to Chinese trotskyists in Moscow at the end of 1929, described by Wang Fan-hsi [Fanxi] in his book *Chinese Revolutionary*.

A TURN TO THE LEFT

What is further important about the SWAPO prison tortures is the range of official bourgeois institutions that knew what SWAPO was doing, and kept quiet; or were told, and did not investigate. The affair perpetuates the worst elements of the Popular Front politics of the 1930s when socialists and others found it expedient to remain silent over the destruction of all groups opposed to the tactics of the USSR during the Spanish civil war. Particularly culpable in Namibia are the United Nations and the churches. We can expect nothing from the ANC or the SACP, nor apparently from the organizations that claim to stand to the left of this unholy alliance.

At a press conference in Windhoek on 7 July 1989 organized by the Parents' Committee and by detainees released by SWAPO, a former leader of the SWAPO youth, Erica Beukes, whose brother Walter Thiro was murdered in the camps, stated:

> Since 1985, or 1984, we continually sent letters and telexes to Dr de Cuéllar [the UN Secretary General], we phoned the UNHCR [High Commissioner for Refugees] in Zambia, but nothing came of it until last week, at the return of these detainees...

According to Phil ya Nangoloh, the chairman of the press conference, a delegation of the Parents' Committee met with UNHCR as recently as 20 April 1989 and was told 'that there were no human rights violations in those SWAPO camps'. Ya Nangoloh accused the CCN of having also denied the allegations. He said the Parents' Committee had contacted the Lutheran World Federation (LWF) in 1987, but 'unfortunately [their] response...was negative'. After being invited to Angola by Nujoma to inspect the SWAPO camps, he said, the LWF reported that it 'could not find any human rights violations in those camps'. In addition, the British government had knowledge of SWAPO's practices from at least as early as 1985, when it granted asylum to former SWAPO members. Like the claims of the SWAPO prisoners themselves, it is vital that these and other matters be checked by a painstaking inquiry.

The return of the prisoners has now brought about a small though marked turn to the left, especially in non-Ovambo-speaking areas. Revulsion against SWAPO's practices has radicalized politics in Namibia. This is focused on a small group around Erica Beukes, which launched the Workers Revolutionary Party (WRP) on May Day 1989. The WRP campaigned in the recent elections within an umbrella organization, the United Democratic Front, which secured four seats and the third biggest total of votes after SWAPO and the DTA. SWAPO is now under attack from a vocal extra-parliamentary opposition that brands its programme and actions as a stalinist betrayal to imperialist interests, and seeks a socialist revolution in Namibia and South Africa. A demonstration outside the legislature was organized by the WRP on the day the assembly began, denouncing the SWAPO murders.

Three points need to be made about this group. First, it is politically dependent on the orientation, method and history of a British trotskyist group, the Workers Revolutionary Party, which before 1985 was under the stalinoid hands of Gerry Healy and others. The British WRP has made no independent study of the social conditions in Namibia, but has now found access for its politics in southern Africa. In giving support to the former prisoners of SWAPO we must make it clear that we are in no way associated with the WRP or its political perspective. Second, the international campaign to publicize SWAPO's crimes against its own members is now principally the work of the British and the Namibian WRP. Other left-wing groups in Britain shied from this task. Third, the turn to the left among sections of students and workers in non-Ovambo-speaking areas presents a very complex phenomenon, with a bearing on conditions in South Africa. On the one hand, unlike in eastern Europe, the revelations of stalinist crimes has not affected the attraction to the left. On the other hand, the form of politics of the WRP in Britain and the hasty and unconsidered way in which a programme of demands has been put together give serious grounds for concern. These and other matters relating to Namibia cannot be explored here and will be considered in a future issue. The fact that the main nationalist party in a country so closely tied to South Africa should already be so discredited, even before any public negotiations have begun over South Africa — where the working class occupies the pivotal place in the region — is a new element in a very swiftly changing scene.

Swapo's Prisons in Angola

We print the following edited and abridged interview with Ndamona and Panduleni Kali, twin sisters from Namibia. Until their return to Namibia in July 1989, they each spent five years in SWAPO prisons in Angola.

Following interviews with other ex-SWAPO prisoners, the London *Independent* concluded that there were 'hundreds, perhaps thousands, of bemused victims' of SWAPO's security apparatus (18 September 1989). Discussions are taking place to set up an independent international commission of inquiry to establish the truth of what took place in SWAPO's prisons.

Born to Ovambo-speaking parents in 1958, the twins attended the Martin Luther High School in Omaruru (north of Windhoek) from 1974 to 1978. At school they took part in political activity in the Namibian Black Students' Organisation (NABSO). In 1978 the political situation was tense and, harassed by the police, they left the country for Angola to join the military wing of SWAPO, the People's Liberation Army of Namibia (PLAN). In 1979 they received military training at the Tobias Hainyeko camp. Ndamona was then sent to the USSR, Panduleni to Cuba. Both studied Lenin, Marx and Engels: Ndamona at the Komsomol in Moscow, Panduleni with the Federation of Cuban Women. After completing her course in the USSR, Ndamona returned to SWAPO bases in Angola and was then sent to join Panduleni at the University of Camagüey (in Cuba) where they both studied economics. Ndamona was a leader of the SWAPO youth at the university, Panduleni a leader of the women's council.

Ndamona: Our recall to Angola was very dramatic. One day in November 1984 the man at the head of the foreign students at the university told us that we had to sign some papers from SWAPO. A strange woman ordered us to go with her to a little office we had never seen before at the university. She ordered one of us to leave. We refused to separate, and when we tried to leave together we were violently pushed inside by Cuban security men who were outside the door. The woman ordered us to undress: everything off. She gave us no explanation and after examining our clothes she put on hand gloves and examined us internally. After we dressed, the men came in and when we asked why this was being done to us they said, 'You'll be given the explanation if you deserve it'.

Panduleni: Later in Angola we learned that the main accusation against female comrades was that they were supposed to be carrying poisoned blades in their private parts.

Ndamona: Then I was taken back to the hostel. Everything of ours was already packed and I was asked to separate the university's books from our personal books. All the foreign students were rushing to see what was happening. The security men told them not to communicate with me. The woman responsible for the foreigners told me this was a question of state security and even she did not know. When one of the security men bent down I could see the pistol in his trousers, and it was clear to me that I was dealing with the state security.

When I was taken back to the little office, Panduleni and I and a [Namibian] man [also under arrest] were driven by car to a building with 'State Security' written on it. We asked them what we had done wrong on Cuban soil but no answer was provided. The security men changed into full uniform. We were handcuffed. Then we demanded to be handed over to our office, to our representative of SWAPO. They said, 'Well, you'll see where you're going to end up'.

We drove from Camagüey to Havana, handcuffed for ten hours. We were taken to the State Security again, made to undress and checked internally. We were locked in a cell. Very early in the morning we banged on the door demanding to see the senior officer on duty. At last we were granted that privilege and we demanded to see our representative of SWAPO. We were told that in an hour we would see him, and we were happy that we would be able to report to the SWAPO official how the Cubans were treating us, not knowing the essence of everything. After an hour this man came, and we were taken separately to see him. We each told him we were very astonished that Cuban security should treat us in this way. Why had they handcuffed us, why had we been put in prison, what crime had we committed on Cuban soil? 'Well', he said, 'no, no, that was just a mistake, they were not really supposed to treat you in that way. You are just being called to Angola to clear up a very little matter, a small matter, and then you will come back'. We said we didn't even have clothes, only the clothes on our bodies. He said, 'No, that's not a problem, you'll be back within a week'. With those words we were led away to the cell again.

We stayed in that cell for four days. Early the next morning we were taken out of the cell and met with two more male comrades, so there were three now. While in prison we had been joined by three more female comrades. We were now eight in number. It was the 12th of November, 1984. We were told to go into a minibus, and we noticed that one leg of [each of] the male comrades was in plaster [of paris] so as to make movement difficult. In that minibus there were eight to ten security men, and we were escorted to the airport with heavy military vehicles including anti-personnel carriers. On the plane, we always had to ask for permission from security guards before going to the toilet. Plastic knives were removed after meal times. Arriving in Luanda, we were again given over to the Cubans at the airport who put us in separate cells. After approximately an hour we were handed over to the SWAPO people.

Then followed a journey in a sealed truck. At a post in the bush one man was taken away and the remaining seven stayed there for a couple of days. One night the remaining two male comrades were removed, and the women were very worried. When they later saw the two men, the plaster had been removed from their legs but they had been handcuffed behind their backs to a big log.

We got into a truck at sunset and found two people inside covered with blankets, one screaming. From their screams we realized those were the two comrades. They were saying 'please loosen my handcuffs, my blood circulation is becoming very difficult.' This was met with cynical laughter from the SWAPO security guards. The cuffs were loosened during the day, but at about six o'clock the handcuffs were tightened behind their backs. We all slept in a big tent and these two comrades could hardly sleep, they could scream the whole night from the pain on their wrists. A few nights later we came at night-time to the Karl Marx Reception Centre belonging to SWAPO at Lubango, in the south of Angola. We were separated from the male comrades. I could not tell you what the centre looked like. I could only tell you specifically of three rooms: the one I was sleeping in, the office and the torturing chamber. We were not allowed out during the day, and had to go to the toilet at only two times, before sunrise and after sunset.

Panduleni and I were separated, only to meet again after two years. The day after we arrived I was told to write my autobiography. Then I was taken to a room where I spent three months in solitary confinement. I was called out from my cell at 2.30 in the morning and went into the office, where there were about six to eight men. I was told to sit flat on the floor and they asked me to repeat my autobiography, this time orally. I repeated it and they told me that I had left out something very important. I couldn't guess what it was and I told them that I didn't think I had left out anything important. I was told to go and think. After a couple of minutes I was told to come back. They told me to repeat my autobiography and at the end they said, 'You didn't add anything'. I said I didn't have anything to add.

They said, 'Stand up and go with this man'. I was told to follow a man with a lantern. It was very dark and the man said, 'Listen, if there is anything to tell, tell me now, and I will go and tell them, before anything can happen to you'. I told him there was nothing I knew that I had left out. I went into an under-ground room. There were two [upright] poles with a horizontal pole. I was told to sit down. The whole gang arrived and they said, 'Tell us what you have deliberately left out of your autobiography'. I said I had left out nothing and they told me to undress. They tied my hands and feet. My hands were tied to one end of the horizontal pole and my legs were fastened to the other end. My stomach faced down and my spine was curved. I had terrible pains in my back because of that position. As if this pain was not enough, they started beating me with sticks. I was beaten, I screamed and a woman guard came in and said my screams could be heard outside. A cloth was pushed into my mouth. They said, 'Tell what you have been hiding'.

When I said I was hiding nothing, the beating continued.

I fainted and was taken off. I don't know for how many minutes I lay there on the floor. When I regained consciousness I was told to dress myself, but I could only do it with difficulty. Again I was beaten and told, 'Make it quick'. They have combat names: Kawaya, Teenie, Katalionga, Santiago, Castro, BK and Poli. Some we had known in Cuba.

The next day at the same hour, at 2 a.m., I was taken again to the same place. They said, 'Are you ready to talk now?' They said they were going to work with me properly because I was unwilling to cooperate. I was tied in the same position and beaten up again. After a time they said: 'Now we are going to give you a clue. When, where and by whom were you recruited to work for the enemy?' To these questions I gave a negative answer, and told them I was never recruited by the enemy and I've never had any mission of infiltration into SWAPO. I was beaten again. They said, 'We've just to work with you like the enemy and you know what we do to the enemy. If they are fighting with South Africa, we kill them. Now, you are going to be killed'. I said, 'You are going to kill me, but remember that you are going to kill a comrade and not an enemy.'

They said, 'Now, are you ready to talk?' I said no. They said, 'Well, we'll just have to kill you.' This worked on my nerves. With this emotion I went back. Every boot in front of my door meant death to me. I just thought, this is the person who is going to take me out and eliminate me. It was terrible. That was the type of psychological torture I had.

After three months I left the Karl Marx Reception Centre and was taken to another notorious camp, Etale. There I was told that if I had managed to get away alive from the Karl Marx Centre, there, I would never get away alive. So they started off again with their torturing. Here, they took two sticks, tied them together at one end, inserted my head between the two sticks, and tied the other end with my head between the sticks. With that pain in my neck, two to three started beating, one with a stick, another with tyre rubber. I endured the pain. They also took the string of a bow, loosened one end and tied my finger in it, and then tied up the loose end so that that string would be fastening until it gets on to my bone. I lost the function of the finger for about two months, it was kind of dead, I try to massage it. I've never experienced such pain in my life, even from sticks.

After four months of resistance in that camp trying to prove my innocence I was transferred to Tobias Hainyeko camp, or Shoombe's camp. There, since it was near the military training centre, I was told that they only dealt with military people. They said that they would deal with me militarily, so that I would talk. I went through torture. After a year I decided, no, I would have to make up a false story since even some of the interrogators approached me saying, 'There were people here who came resisting like you, and they died. Those who were clever made up a story and they survived'. So I just decided that, well, I will make up a story, and since the motto of the organization is 'Freedom, Solidarity and Justice', I strongly believed that justice will prevail one day and I will prove my innocence.

So I made up a story, giving them a lot of impossible information to make it easier for them to find out that this person was only forced through interrogation, she is really not guilty, she is innocent. The dates I said I was being trained by the enemy coincided, for example, with the dates when I was at school. But I've come to realize that SWAPO was not interested in making a thorough investigation into the matter, and this was never found out. I confessed on 1st December 1985, and on 18 December 1986 was transferred again to another jail called Minya Base. There I met Panduleni after two years of separation. We were placed in dug-outs, holes deep in the ground about six metres square and covered with corrugated iron. We had to get into some of them with a ladder, others down steps, and they were damp.

Panduleni: I persisted under the torture for eight months. There was no alternative, I had just to make up a story, so I said I had been trained in Nyobo by two Boers living there in a high building with 'South African Military Training' written on the wall. I put the time when I was still at school. I thought they would find out and free me because no white people live at Nyobo, and there are no big buildings there. But I stayed in that dungeon for five years.

Generally dug-outs were normal for the war situation but they were only used for emergencies, not for sleeping in. We were in them all the time. The men who were guarding us, the 'loyal sons of SWAPO', slept in ordinary rooms. There was a small layer of bricks at the top of the hole to serve as windows. We covered ourselves with empty rice bags, sleeping on boxes. In one corner there was the toilet, and we were so overcrowded that the last person had to sleep only a few centimetres from the toilet. There was no fresh air. The dug-out served as hospital, dining room, toilet and even in one case as maternity room.

We were kept completely uninformed, we were not even allowed to read SWAPO bulletins, everything that was happening was a big secret. We could only tell of the coming of visits [by SWAPO leaders] from the behaviour of the commandants.

We were visited by Sam Nujoma, the president of SWAPO, on 21st April 1986. Before the arrival of the president we were visited on 4th April by Solomon

Hawala, the chief of security of SWAPO, and Dimo Amaambo, the army commander. Amaambo is the top military leader of PLAN and Hawala is supposed to be deputy commander of PLAN. We were told to gather under a big tree, and 'Jesus' Hawala introduced us to Dimo saying, 'Those are the traitors of the nation, who have betrayed the Namibian nation'. He said that some of the 'females' — that was the general term for us, the 'females' — had come with blades hidden in our bodies and had killed many combatants of PLAN. And very much surprising, the response of Dimo was, 'I wish I can see these blades, I've never seen anything like that'. That was the response of the army commander in 1986, and yet many females have been arrested right from 1980, 1982, with this main accusation of having blades.

My impression was that Dimo Amaambo did not really believe in these blades, but he didn't say anything more. Then on 21st April the president came. He was accompanied by Peter Sheehama (recently the representative of SWAPO in Cuba, later Minister of Safety and Security), Nahas Angula [currently Prime Minister of Namibia — PT], Peter Mueshihange [a former SWAPO secretary for defence] and of course Solomon Hawala was there. We were put in parade formation, in rows. Among other things, Nujoma said that we were enemy agents, that we came with poisons to kill the combatants of PLAN, some of us even tested our poisons, we put them in the water and food of PLAN combatants, and these people died. He promised that they would fight more than ever before to liberate Namibia, and to take us to our mothers and fathers, and we would be paraded at a revolutionary square where they were going to hoist their flag and the nation would decide what to do with us.

Nujoma was told by us that we were never enemy agents, that we were forced by torture to confess: Theresa Basson was one who intervened, and Magdalena Goagoses was another. They both told Nujoma that people were forced to make false confessions, and it was even put clear to him that some of the interrogators gave people advice to make false confessions to save their lives. There was no reaction from the side of the president, he left.

Nujoma came back a second time to Minya Base in March 1987. By then Ndamona and I were together. He was told the very same thing, by Ilona Amakutua and Sarie Eises. Marta Angula also spoke. Emma Kambangula went to the extent of undressing herself to show the scars of interrogations, and also to show that she had had an operation while very young, on her back. She had been operated on in South Africa, and had later gone to the GDR for medical treatment. When she was arrested, SWAPO security claimed she had a radio communication in her back. She tried to demonstrate to the president that that was a lie. Nujoma said nothing, he didn't mention any investigation, nothing.

Ndamona: He said, 'I've heard', that's all.

Panduleni: One girl said, 'The moment you turn your back, we'll be beaten. You must tell these people not to beat us any more'. The only response was 'I heard'.

On 10 January 1989 we had another visit, from the SWAPO administrative secretary, Moses Garoeb. His main mission was to tell us that the leadership of SWAPO had decided we would be released. He said that on 1 April, the UNTAG forces were going to take over in Namibia under Article 435. He informed us that there would be no second dungeon for us in Namibia. When he said there would be no second dungeon for us, by implication that means death. He said Namibia was going to be free, we were going to find the Boers, including those who had sent us to infiltrate SWAPO.

After Garoeb left, a video team visited the camp. At that time there were about a hundred women in the camp and about twenty men. We received no visit from the Red Cross. Only the women were videoed. If you see these videos, it appears that the people being interviewed are really speaking from the depths of their hearts, but we were intimidated into sitting for the video. We were told, 'If you don't confess, you'll face another situation'. Those who did not appear before the video did not arrive in Namibia. We were told later in the UN High Commissioner for Refugees camp in Lubango that Gerhard Tjozongoro, who had been held at Mungakwiyu, had not returned. Only security men were present at the interview, many who had tortured us. The interviewer was Peter Nambundunga, the chief of logistics of PLAN, wearing military dress.

Ndamona: On the video I said I couldn't remember my confession. I said I had forgotten the year I had been recruited. A SWAPO security man called Bongi said, 'You will be reminded'. The video would stop, and a security man with the text of our confessions would give information to the interviewer. In a second video we took the oath of allegiance not to work again with the enemy and to report all enemy activities to SWAPO. We were filmed signing the oath of allegiance to SWAPO.

After signing the oath we were taken to another camp on 12 May, called Production Unit. We were supposed to be free, but it was a semi-prison and we couldn't go to visit other camps. A regular visitor to Production was SWAPO's secretary-general, Andimba Herman Toivo ya Toivo. We as prisoners had hope in that man. He was the only and last man in the SWAPO leadership who could understand our position. We said, 'Comrade Toivo ya Toivo, you're the only man in the SWAPO leadership that our hopes rely on, since you languished on Robben Island for 16 years. You know what torture can make you do'.

He said: 'The truth lies in your own hearts. Here is a declaration from SWAPO. You have two options. One, you accept you are forgiven, you go back to the ranks and your files will be closed.' We said we wanted our files to be kept open, so that we could be judged by the nation. We wanted the leadership of SWAPO to know we are innocent. Then we could forgive and forget, we could accept it as a mistake of the revolution. But Toivo ya Toivo gave us no positive answer. He said, 'Option two, you remain enemy agents. Then SWAPO will arrange for you to be transferred to representatives of South Africa in Namibia, and your files will remain open and active'. We said we had no interest in being handed to a representative of South Africa, we had done nothing to bring assistance to the enemy. We had never betrayed the nation either in thought, word or deed. We were patriots of the nation, and we wanted our problem to be treated as a SWAPO problem, within SWAPO. We did not want to go out of SWAPO.

After that we were visited by UNTAG forces, and by international journalists from West Germany, France, Angola, Cuba and Namibia. Toivo ya Toivo introduced us to the international journalists as traitors who had betrayed the nation, they had been forgiven, now they were going to go back to Namibia. We found ourselves in an awkward situation. We went to the Cuban journalists and said that we had never been enemy agents, and that we want to clean our names. A few days later we handed ourselves over to the Angolan government, and on 4th July we arrived back by UN plane in Namibia.

The videos were already circulating in Namibia, saying that we are enemy agents. We had no option except to clear our names. We had to stay in Windhoek, we could not stay in our home town, Lüderitz. It was a very sad picture when we went to visit our mum in hospital in Lüderitz. She was very sick, paralyzed after a second stroke. Whenever we visited her at the hospital it was always thrown at us that we were enemy agents. The hospital staff were starting to neglect her. One woman at the hospital referred to her as if she were not human, saying, '*Sy kan nog vrek*'. [*Vrek* is a term in Afrikaans used for the death of animals.]

One evening we visited our mum and we saw a group of youngsters near the hospital, and we could see that they were waiting for us to go home in the evening. We had to ask for a lift home, and on our way home we could see that they were planning to ambush us. So we stopped seeing our mother in the evenings, only in the afternoons, and we asked if she could be transferred to Windhoek, as she was deteriorating. She passed away on 10 September. We last saw her on Saturday the ninth. That Sunday, people shouted at us, 'Puppets!' and 'SWAPO will win and you'll get it!'

I still get the feeling that if it were not for this enemy agent thing, my mother would have lived. We still don't know how many members of my family will suffer. The children of our two sisters at Lüderitz come home from school crying, the other children say 'Your aunties are enemy agents and and are responsible for the death of many people'.

Searchlight South Africa asked the Kali sisters why they thought all this had happened to them.

Ndamona: You have to go back to the history of SWAPO. In 1976 SWAPO showed its undemocratic, dictatorial nature. At that time some youth demanded more democracy in the movement. They wanted a congress to elect new leaders. The response was their imprisonment, with the help of the host countries, Zambia and Tanzania. Our imprisonment was a consequence of this unresolved crisis.

SWAPO does not understand a person who has a different opinion. While we were in Cuba I was a leader of the youth and Panduleni was a leader of the women's council. We had a problem with some of the SWAPO students, so we visited Nahas Angula [SWAPO's education secretary] but our move was taken as a criticism. We said that the SWAPO students on the Island of Youth didn't have clothes. Cuba has economic problems, and as foreigners we didn't have ration tickets. We said to Angula that SWAPO had to treat Cuba as any other settlement, but he said SWAPO could not send bundles of clothes to Cuba, and that we were lucky to be there. So at the school the students didn't get clothes.

Also, Panduleni and I were studying economics at the University of Camagüey, and of course we were doing maths. So we said we needed calculators. We were told there was only one calculator in the whole of SWAPO, in Angola, in the finance department. SWAPO couldn't supply us with any.

Panduleni: For them, everything is a threat. Our main aim is to make the world know what was happening inside SWAPO. All these crimes against the Namibian people in the name of the Namibian people have been kept a secret. We feel it is our duty to make these things known to the international community, so that friends of Namibia can help us by pushing for an Independent Commission of Inquiry to clean our names, to bring these atrocities to light and to let the blame be put where it lies.

Ndamona: Some people who say they are friends of SWAPO call this demand for an international commission of inquiry a right-wing plot. In 1976, when SWAPO arrested freedom fighters, letters were written to the Anti-Apartheid Movement, but they were ignored.

Panduleni: There are still SWAPO prisoners in Angola, we know who they are. The Political Consultative Council of Ex-SWAPO Detainees and the Parents' Committee [which have campaigned for the freeing of the prisoners] spoke to the Red Cross and the UN. The UN set up a commission but without including any ex-detainees, although we know where the different jails are. The UN said they would not share responsibility with anybody. The UN said people had been repatriated and had been registered in Windhoek, but we know they have not come back. People like me are losing trust in the UN.

Panduleni: In the middle of 1984 the SWAPO students in Cuba were brought on parade at the Hendrik Witbooi school on the Island of Youth and told that Tauno had committed suicide while under interrogation as an enemy agent, using poison carried in a tooth. His death was kept a complete secret from the exiles, and was revealed only after six months.

A few months later came their own arrest. The security apparatus under Hawala was in all probability trained by the KGB: this is a further matter for investigation. The 'Report to the Namibian People' also mentions a visit to SWAPO prisons in Angola of a Soviet prosecutor in 1983, and the arrest and deportation to Angola of a SWAPO student by the Bulgarian security police in 1986. Nujoma, Toivo ya Toivo, Hawala and others now head the majority party in Namibia after the November elections for the constituent assembly. The formation of an independent commission of inquiry is urgently necessary, first of all to protect the lives of former SWAPO prisoners both in Angola and Namibia, and equally to establish the historical truth.

SOURCES

1. Alliluyeva, Svetlana (1968), 20 *Letters to a Friend*, World Books.
2. Herbstein, Denis and Evenson, John (1989), *The Devils are Among Us: The War for Namibia*, Zed.
3. London, Artur (1970), *On Trial*, Macdonald.
4. Wang, Fan-hsi (1980), *Chinese Revolutionary. Memoirs 1919–49*, OUP.

DOCUMENTS

1. 'A Report to the Namibian People. Historical account of the SWAPO Spy drama'.
2. People Missing or Detained by SWAPO Listed by Region of Origin', 'Murdered by SWAPO' (two lists), 'List of SWAPO's Gestapo who Tortured Innocent Namibians on

behalf of the SWAPO Leadership', all issued by the Political Consultative Council of Ex-SWAPO Detainees, Windhoek, July 1989.

3. Text of Press Conference by the Parents' Committee and the Detainees Released by SWAPO, Windhoek, 7 July 1989.
4. *Verkiesing '89*, Windhoek (text of election programmes).

NEWSPAPERS

Windhoek Observer, *The Worker*, published by the WRP, (Namibia); *Vrye Weekblad*, *Weeky Mail* (South Africa); *The Independent* (London).

Postscript

The full weight of SWAPO's 22 years of war against the occupying South African power bore down on the half-million rural population in Ovamboland in Namibia's northern border. The sheer horror of South Africa's reign of terror operating without any restraint is catalogued in the book by Denis Herbstein and John Evenson, *The Devils are Among Us: The War for Namibia* (Zed, 1989). Military and police terror ensured that only those corrupted or broken by state violence would fail to support SWAPO, which was regarded by the vast majority of the population as its defenders. What these authors fail to investigate with the same journalistic thoroughness was the degree to which the barbarism of the South African regime was reflected also in the hierarchy of its SWAPO opponents.

We have thought carefully about publishing the above interviews. We are aware that the first major revelations of SWAPO atrocities were made by a right-wing organization, The International Society for Human Rights, based in West Germany. However we consider that this makes it all the more essential that as a socialist journal we do our own research and reach our own conclusions on a matter of vital concern.

Our readers will judge for themselves. After the pulling down of the stalinist regimes in eastern Europe, we believe even more firmly that exposure of crimes against any section of the people is an essential task of every socialist. Concealment can only aid reaction — and has nothing in common with our commitment to socialism.

12 *Swapo and the Churches: An International Scandal**

Swapo has the right to protect her people from those who are collaborating with the enemy ... Yours in Jesus Christ.
— Dr Abisai Shejavali, General Secretary of the Council of Churches in Namibia.[1]

The illegal occupation of Namibia has been facilitated by Namibians who have collaborated with South Africa and have been traitors to the cause of a free Namibia. Yet Swapo is willing to accommodate these people in a free Namibia and forgive their misguided behaviour.
— Report of the World Council of Churches, May 1988.[2]

So it goes.
— Kurt Vonnegut, *Slaughterhouse-Five*.

THE PROBLEMS OF THE TEXT

On 14 November 1989, Pluto Press published *Church and Liberation in Namibia* (CALIN), edited by Peter Katjavivi, Per Frostin and Kaire Mbuende. The book contains a number of documents on the relation between the churches and political conditions in Namibia, from 1958 to 1988, with individual essays by each of the editors and three others. David Theo Goldberg, assistant professor at the School of Justice Studies at Arizona State University, has described the book as 'crucial for anyone wanting to comprehend the role of the church in the promotion and realization of Namibian independence'. (*Southern African Review of Books*, Jan/Feb 1991).

Goldberg's review is characteristic of the ignorance combined with tunnel vision of the international liberal/left establishment relating to southern Africa. The book in fact makes it impossible to comprehend the role of the churches in one of the most important episodes in the recent history of southern Africa: the cycle of wholesale arrests, torture, imprisonment and murder of SWAPO members on the orders of their own leaders, dating from at least 1976 until the release of survivors in May 1989. The emergence of SWAPO's prisoners from

*First published in *Searchlight South Africa* Vol. 2, No. 3 (July 1991), pp. 65–88.

their dungeons took place six months before publication of CALIN and more than 18 months before Goldberg's opaque review.

The complicity of the churches — their refusal to speak out, and the sanitary screen they provided to the torturers — is continued in this book, which serves to perpetuate the offence. Like the churches, the editors of the book are culpable. Their book is a knowing deception, offered to readers at the moment when the truth could no longer be concealed. To throw light on what the book obscures, I append, at the end of this article, two letters from innumerable texts available to the editors, which they omitted to publish. These stand in criticism of the book and, more important by far, of the whole spectrum of official Christianity

The foremost editor, Peter Katjavivi, author of *A History of Resistance in Namibia* (1988), is described in a biographical note as 'Namibia's leading historian'. (p v) He is currently Vice-Chancellor at the university in Windhoek, and is also a member of the National Assembly. For many years he was a leading representative in Western Europe and the US of SWAPO, during its long guerrilla war against the South African regime. Frostin is a Swedish academic and theologian. Mbuende, who holds a PhD from the University of Lund, is described in the book as a leading SWAPO activist since the 1970s. In 1989 he was a reader at the Institute of Future Studies, Stockholm. The editors represent the historical working together of SWAPO and the Christian churches, the subject — from very different perspectives — of CALIN.

BLACK THEOLOGY AND THE PITS

SWAPO's purges of its members have been described in 'A Namibian Horror', an interview with Panduleni and Ndamona Kali published in *Searchlight South Africa* No. 4, February 1990 (pp. 140–158 in this book), and in Trewhela 1990/91 — Chapter 13 in this book. It is characteristic of the cover-up disseminated by the nationalist parties, the churches, the liberals, the stalinist states and the left internationally — including nearly all the trotskyist sects — that CALIN should be prefaced by additional clouds of incense in the form of a preface by one of the pillars of black theology in South Africa, Rev. Nyameko Barney Pityana, director of the Programme to Combat Racism of the World Council of Churches (WCC), based in Geneva. In the period of the formation of the black consciousness movement in South Africa in the late 1960s, Pityana was secretary-general of the South African Students Organisation (SASO) when Steve Biko was its first president. It was Pityana's view in the early 1970s that 'a study of Black Theology is a study of black consciousness or self-awareness'.

(Pityana, p 58) The quality of his awareness may be judged from his encomium on the relation of SWAPO to the Christian virtues. 'The church is the life and soul of the people of Namibia', he declares:

> In times of sorrow, of struggle and in times of joy, Namibians have known their church leaders to stand alongside them.
>
> ... SWAPO pioneered the programme of providing chaplaincies among Namibians in exile. The SWAPO leadership petitioned the church to ordain some among their number who would symbolize the presence of the church among them as they struggle for liberation. Such was the foresight of the SWAPO leadership and their insight into the needs of the Namibians in the diaspora... The SWAPO team of chaplains has direct access to the President of SWAPO, Dr Sam Nujoma, who is ready to listen to the needs of his people. (pp. viii–ix)

This intimate and subservient relation of a team of priests to the leadership of a nationalist political party, with its own army, secret police, prisons and torturers, throws an interesting light on the New Testament text that distinguishes between the obligations owed by Christians to God and Caesar. It is precisely this identity between nationalist politics and religion that Pityana, following the practice of SWAPO and the Christian churches, seeks to idealize and promote in his laudatory comments on the Council of Churches in Namibia (CCN), a kind of popular front of Christianity in Namibia.

The development of the CCN — set up in 1978 — was for Pityana a 'very significant step'. It meant that

> through CCN, Namibians maintained a unity of perception of the social reality of Namibia. Not only was it being demonstrated that there was no dichotomy between the gospel and politics but it was shown by the example in CCN projects and staff who were active in the liberatory movement either as SWANU [South West Africa National Union, the smaller nationalist movement in Namibia — PT] or SWAPO. (p x)

The word about 'no dichotomy' between the churches and SWAPO became flesh in SWAPO's torture pits, as the churches in Namibia and internationally turned their eyes from the maimed body of the victim and like the priest and Levite strode past on the other side of the road. Or, like Pilate, washed their hands and delivered sentence. Or, like the Sanhedrin, called for exemplary justice to be delivered on the heads of those who, in the words of Dr Shejavali, quoted above, were 'collaborating with the enemy'. SWAPO members who succumbed to its internal purges were victims of a totalitarian 'unity of perception' (in Pityana's phrase) between the nationalist leaders, the independent African states, the stalinist bloc and the churches. Their experience illuminates with a garish light the nature of world society in the three decades before the crack-up of the Berlin Wall.

It is Pityana's opinion that 'under CCN, Namibians were liberated to experiment, dream and have visions about the future of their country'. He states that during this period 'a distinctive theology of Namibia could be said to have emerged'. Between the candy floss of the priests and the torture chambers of SWAPO lies a distinctive theology of complicity. One recalls Pityana's comment from his days in SASO that the 'first step' was to 'make the Black man see himself, to pump life into his empty shell; to infuse him with pride and dignity, to remind him of his complicity in the crime of allowing himself to be misused and therefore letting evil reign supreme in the country of his birth'. (quoted in Hirson, p 110)

A SPECIAL RELATIONSHIP

Pityana's preface gives an adequate reflection of the character of the book as a whole, supposed by him to offer insight into the 'soul of Namibia' (whatever that might be). (p xi) His preface is dated Geneva, June 1989. By this time, about two hundred SWAPO members detained in the region of Lubango in southern Angola had already been released from the pits in which they had been held. Agence France-Presse reported the first meeting between journalists and the released prisoners, still held under SWAPO guard, on 27 May 1989. The AFP correspondent, Marie Joannidis, reported: 'One after another the ex-prisoners undress to show marks and scars — most of which are old — left by torture.' (*Call Them Spies*, hereafter referred to as CTS, p 87) On 9 June, a freelance photographer, John Liebenberg, reported in the pro-SWAPO weekly, *The Namibian*, published in Windhoek, that he had met many detainees held by SWAPO who had apparently been subjected to 'severe beatings, rape, mental torture and extreme deprivation'. There is no reference to any such reports in Rev. Pityana's preface of June 1989.

The introduction to the book by its editors Katjavivi, Frostin and Mbuende is dated July 1989. On 4 July, a planeload of about 150 former prisoners of SWAPO arrived back in Namibia at Oseri Kari camp, immediately followed by extensive reports in the international media of their allegations of torture. Outside southern Africa, reports appeared in the *New York City Tribune* (5 July), the *Daily Telegraph* (London, 5 July), the *Independent* (London, 5 July), the *Frankfurter Allgemeine Zeitung* (7 July) and the *Neue Zürcher Zeitung* (Switzerland, where Pityana was based, 7 July). There is no reference to these reports of torture and imprisonment in the introduction to *Church and Liberation in*

Namibia, despite the editors' warm references to SWAPO and 'Namibia's own experience and contribution to liberation theology'. (p xvi)

In his essay on 'The Role of the Church in the Struggle for Independence', Katjavivi speaks delicately of a 'special relationship' between the churches and the nationalist movement in Namibia, noting that some individual church leaders held 'key posts' in SWAPO. (pp. 25, 3) One that he mentions is Dr Zephania Kameeta, vice-president of the Evangelical Lutheran Church in SWA/Namibia (Rhenish Mission, known by the initials ELK), whose poems and other writings are quoted extensively throughout the book. Rev. Kameeta is an executive committee member of SWAPO. Another pastor, the Rev. Hendrik Witbooi of the African Methodist Episcopal Church (AME), is vice-president of SWAPO. Daniel Tjongarero, who is not a priest but was director of the communications department of the CCN at the time of publication of the book, was also at the same time SWAPO's deputy national chairman. The overlap between SWAPO, the leadership of individual churches in Namibia and the executive of the CCN was a primary fact of Namibian national life throughout the period of the purges.

THE CHRISTIANIZING OF A HORROR

In a more crudely conceived essay entitled 'Church and Class Struggle in Namibia', Mbuende drops pearls of wisdom. For example:

> We are living in the epoch of imperialism, the highest stage of capitalism. Therefore, our crisis is the imperialist crisis and our problem is imperialism and capitalist exploitation. (p 43)

For Mbuende, nationalism as a 'non-class ideology' could be used to 'articulate the interests of the bourgeoisie in one historical setting and those of the working class in another setting'. (p 41) He develops the fantastic conception of a future 'third church, which will be proletarian' (in opposition to the old missionary-colonial church and the current 'petty-bourgeois' reformist church with its bourgeois ideological basis), and of a future struggle in which 'only the proletarian church will be able to succeed'. (p 45) For him, the church is 'linked to SWAPO and other popular forces by the struggle against foreign domination' (p 40), a struggle which somehow through SWAPO will 'lead to the building of socialism and not capitalism'. (p 44) The notion of internationalism is alien to Dr Mbuende in this heady atmosphere of millenarian futurology. The suggestion of this Christianiser of leftist rhetoric is that in some way SWAPO was a party of socialism.

The essay by Frostin is a paean to a 'holistic' theology of liberation. The writer appears to be unaware that a leading proponent of the philosophy of holism was the former South African Prime Minister, Jan Smuts, who made a serious attempt at the holistic incorporation of Namibia (then South West Africa) into South Africa in the 1940s. Frostin polemicises against a 'dualistic theology', by which he means one in which religion is compartmentalised away from political and social life: again unaware of the 'dualism' by which the issue of SWAPO's torture system is evaded by SWAPO's supporters. It is not my province to judge between the clerical proponents of abstention or participation in political causes. What is noteworthy, however, is that Frostin's essay is specifically critical of the 'dualistic understanding' of a statement issued in the early 1970s by a conference of pastors of the German Evangelical Lutheran Church (DELK), published in a work edited by Pastor Siegfried Gröth, of the Vereinigte Evangelische Mission (VEM) based in Wuppertal in Germany. (Gröth, 1972) In this statement, DELK was explicitly hostile to political action that 'obviously oversteps the bounds of the church's competence'. (CALIN, p 53)

ENTER PASTOR GRÖTH

Gröth had been adviser on southern African affairs to the VEM since 1961, and was prevented from entering Namibia by the South African regime from 1971 to 1987. In the early 1970s he was asked by the two black Lutheran churches in Namibia (ELK and the Evangelical Lutheran Church in Namibia — ELCIN) to tend to the spiritual needs of the refugees, especially in Zambia and Botswana. Significantly, Gröth was the only priest of note who attempted to save the SWAPO detainees in the purges of the 1980s. The problematical character of his intervention is discussed later in this review. Familiarity with the work of Gröth is shown in CALIN not only by Frostin but also by Emma and Zedekia Mujoro, principal at the Lutheran Theological College at Otjimbingwe in central Namibia, in an essay 'Namibian Liberation Theology and the Future'. Yet CALIN preserves scrupulous silence on the central place of Gröth in the relation of the churches to the spy drama.

Gröth spoke and wrote extensively to his many church contacts about the horrors taking place in the SWAPO camps, to no avail. In a letter to a Namibian priest in July 1985 he wrote that his visit to SWAPO exiles in Zambia in March 1985 was the 'most difficult trip to Africa for me since more than twenty years.'[3] Shortly afterwards Gröth suffered a breakdown in Zimbabwe brought on by his discovery of what was taking place in SWAPO. He returned to Wuppertal on 13 May 1985, where he gave a full account of the purges to Rev. Kameeta, Mujoro's predecessor at the Theological College. Gröth's letter continued:

> [I] had the chance to discuss this serious issue with Brother Kameeta. I informed him about the emergency situation in Zambia and Angola and mentioned the names of my friends and brothers who are in such a dangerous situation ... I told Brother Kameeta that responsible Christians and SWAPO-members are appealing to the churches for their support and help. (CTS, p 42)

Gröth also urged the matter on Pastor Hendrik Frederik, the Preses (president) of the ELK, at a confidential talk on 14 June, and with Bishop Kleopas Dumeni, head of the Evangelical Lutheran Ovambo-Kavango Church (ELOK). Between them these two churches have over half a million members, an enormous moral force in a population of less than a million and a half. As Gröth confirmed in a letter to the director of Amnesty International: 'They know about the present difficult developments in Zambia and Angola'. (17 September 1985. CTS, p 43) Yet despite representing through their churches the majority of blacks in Namibia, whether individually or collectively, the church leaders Kameeta, Frederik and Dumeni did nothing. Yet for Pityana, it is Kameeta through his eucharistic prayers and verse who best represents the 'distinctive theology' and the 'soul of Namibia'. (pp. x, xi)

THE SCANDAL IN THE CCN

At the time of publication of CALIN, the CCN represented the following churches:

- Evangelical Lutheran Church in SWA/Namibia — ELK
- Evangelical Lutheran Church in Namibia — ELCIN, formerly ELOK
- Anglican Church in Namibia
- African Methodist Episcopal Church
- United Congregational Church in Southern Africa
- Roman Catholic Church
- Methodist Church in Southern Africa
- Evangelical Reformed Church in Africa.

The German Evangelical Lutheran Church withdrew from the CCN in 1987, on the grounds that the body was too politicized. DELK's membership, which was exclusively white, expressed the strongest reservations about church identification with the political struggle in Namibia in the early 1970s. These reservations appeared in the book edited by Gröth in 1972.

The highest policy-making body within the CCN is the general meeting of church representatives, convening every second year. Between these meetings the executive committee governs the CCN as a whole and is responsible for policy implementation. All church members are represented on the executive committee. When CALIN was published, the president of the executive committee was Bishop Hendrik Frederik, whom Gröth had met on 14 June 1985. The vice-presidents were Sister Irmgart, OSB, of the Roman Catholic Church, and the Rev. Matti Amadhila, assistant to Bishop Dumeni (whom Gröth had also approached).

The chief official of the executive was its general secretary, Dr Shejavali. He acted throughout the purges as chief hatchetman of official Christianity in Namibia. His former associate general secretary, Vezera Kandetu, contributes a brief essay to CALIN on 'The Work of the Council of Churches in Namibia' in which there is no word on the grimmer side to the work of the CCN, or on the character or conduct of his immediate superior, Dr Shejavali. With the coming of independence in March 1990, Kandetu ascended unto government as assistant to the new deputy Minister of Information and Broadcasting, Daniel Tjongarero, also late of the CCN. So it goes.

PILATE IN AFRICA

Two episodes irreparably stain the record of the CCN, which courageously offered assistance to the huge numbers of victims of the South African regime. The first was the murder of a former director of the Christian Centre in Windhoek, the predecessor of the CCN, about which church leaders and the CCN kept silent. As reported in *Searchlight South Africa* No. 6, the director of the Christian Centre in the 1970s, Tauno Hatuikulipi, was murdered in Angola, apparently in January 1984, on orders of fellow members of the SWAPO central committee. After arrest, trial and constant harassment by the South African regime in Namibia, Hatuikulipi had escaped to join the SWAPO political and military leadership in Angola, but clashed with the security apparatus when it set out to express its dominance over the military. A report by the Committee of Parents — formed in 1985 to attempt to defend SWAPO's victims in exile — noted that Hatuikulipi's wife, Magdalena, who had remained in Windhoek, was

> kept in the dark by the internal leadership about the fate of her husband. In May, 1984, she was still cheering the SWAPO delegation, which left for the [Lusaka Conference] Conference [at which delegates from Namibia learnt at first hand for the first time of the terrors abroad]. A few weeks later a friend informed her about her husband's murder. She confronted the internal leader-

ship who admitted that he was dead but they claimed that he had committed suicide. She is left with five children.[4]

Neither the CCN nor the churches protested the murder of Hatuikulipi, their own former top-level representative, and direct predecessor to Shejavali. The Committee of Parents described the reaction that followed inside Namibia, as delegates to the Lusaka Conference conference brought back accounts of the atrocities abroad.

> Parents went up in arms. They chose the most logical thing to do under the circumstances. They went to the church leadership to affect at least moral intervention into the maltreatment of their children...
>
> But the expectations turned out a painful nonetheless revealing experience. They found that in exercising their trust in the institutions which for generations they had considered their friends, they had instead created violent enemies. Priest and pastor slandered them, called them agents and destroyers and accused them of spreading malicious rumour. (ibid)

After keeping their campaign out of public scrutiny for a year and a half 'to give the spiritual leaders and their supporters the chance to mitigate the SWAPO tragedy' — the disillusioned relatives set up the Committee of Parents in Windhoek in March 1985 to campaign directly on their own behalf. This led to the second specific instance of clerical connivance with the SWAPO torture machine: the dismissal from the CCN of two active members of the Committee of Parents, under the ever-beneficent hand of Dr Shejavali.

FROM THE CHURCHES TO THE PARENTS

At the beginning of 1985, Erica Beukes, an activist in the SWAPO Youth League during its most militant period in the mid-1970s, worked for the CCN in Windhoek as head of the health section in its development department. Her brother, Walter Thiro, one of SWAPO's prison victims, died painfully in a SWAPO labour camp at Kwanza Sul in southern Angola. On hearing of her brother's imprisonment, Erica approached the local priest, Pastor Nakamela, for assistance. He in turn consulted Rev. Kameeta. Rather than take up this matter, despite his position as one of the leading churchmen in Namibia, Kameeta referred the petitioners to Nico Bessinger, SWAPO's foreign relations secretary: a truly Pilate-like referral to Caesar.

Having no confidence in Bessinger, Erica Beukes arranged to see the most respected of all SWAPO leaders, Andimba Toivo ya Toivo, who had himself been tortured by the South African police and imprisoned on Robben Island for 16 years. She met Toivo in August 1984 and

> expressed her concern on behalf of her family for the safety of her brother. She told him that they had received information that he was languishing in jail in Angola, and she expressed grave criticism of the leadership of SWAPO. He thanked her for the trust the family had shown to approach him on so grave a charge. But, he pointed out that the South African regime had launched a concerted propaganda campaign against SWAPO to discredit the movement.... He could not promise to free her brother, but would investigate the matter and report back. He did not return.[5]

It was after meeting Ya Toivo, and still feeling relatively reassured, that Erica Beukes and her immediate superior in the CCN, the director of its development department, Attie Beukes (no relation to Erica), toured Europe in February 1985 to raise funds for the work of the CCN. They met church leaders and supporters of the struggle against the South African regime who gave them disquieting news of the purges in Angola and Zambia. Namibian refugees gave them copies of letters to church leaders and pleaded with them to do something when they returned to Namibia.

> Some requested them to again try to move the church leadership to action. Others were sceptical, reasoning that they were fully informed about the reign of terror unleashed by the SWAPO leadership. The latter turned out to be right. (ibid)

On 21 March, the same day that they returned to Namibia, Attie Beukes, Erica and Erica's sister Bertha Yon met with Bishop Frederik to press for action. Attie and Erica approached him both as individuals and as officials of the CCN, on whose behalf they had travelled to Europe. They later met Pastor Kristof Shuya, general secretary of the United Evangelical Lutheran Church of South West Africa (VELKSWA). Attie Beukes also informed Bishop Bonifatius Haushiku, head of the Roman Catholic Church in Namibia, and then reported to Dr Shejavali, his immediate superior in the CCN. Mr Beukes 'stressed the urgency for the church leadership to convene a meeting to plan action. But, no-one would commit himself to such a course of action'. (ibid) The response of the Namibian activists to this dereliction by the churches was to set up the Committee of Parents.

THE CHURCH MILITANT

On 2 June the Committee of Parents delivered a memorandum to the church leadership: it received no reply. A month later, a delegation from the Committee met with Bishop James Kauluma, head of the Anglican Church in Namibia, in an attempt to get action on the proposed meeting. The bishop's response was forthright. He was incredulous at

> the insolence of the committee to level charges at a respected leadership. He refused to take part in further discussion about the topic. He suggested that the committee should take up the matter with the SWAPO leadership, because it had nothing to do with the church leadership. He charged that the women reacted without factual information, but he refused to read the letters offered to him by the delegation. (ibid)

The Committee, represented by 24 delegates, finally met with the church leaders on 9 September, almost six months after the first approach to Bishop Frederik. The churches were represented by Bishop Frederik (ELK), Dr Shejavali (CCN), Bishop Dumeni (ELOK, now called ELCIN), Pastor Matti Amadhila (assistant to Dumeni in ELOK), Bishop Haushiku (RCC), Father Nordkamp (RCC) and Pastor Prinz (Methodist Church). The Committee made a full report and Bishop Frederik showed he was aware of the testimony of Pastor Gröth, but the meeting closed without any definite commitment from the church leaders. A bland and meaningless letter followed from Dr Shejavali on 19 September, thanking the parents for the meeting and concluding: 'May God bless you all'.

That September, Attie Beukes went to Geneva as director of the development department of the CCN for a conference with donor agencies. In Europe, he met some of the support groups and Namibian refugees, and returned home with further information about the purge victims. He also met Pastor Gröth, who was unwilling for the information in his files to be made public.[6] Coinciding with Beukes's visit, the Committee sent letters to support groups of SWAPO in Europe (the Namibia Support Committee, the Namibia Association), to church bodies (World Council of Churches, Lutheran World Federation, British Council of Churches, Vereinigte Evangelische Mission, Swedish Free Church, United Church of Canada), to the UN secretary-general, to the SWAPO president (Nujoma) and to the presidents of Cuba, Angola and Zambia: the countries most directly in authority in the zones where SWAPO held its prison camps. Evasive replies were received from the church bodies and silence from the UN secretary-general, on behalf of the world authority that had recognised SWAPO as 'sole and authentic representative' of the people of Namibia.

Matters came to a head in the early months of 1986. The Committee decided to send a delegation to the UN secretary-general, Javier Pérez de Cuéllar, to be led by Stella-Maria Boois (whose son Ben Boois was a SWAPO prisoner) and Erica Beukes. They asked the VEM in Germany — Gröth's mission — for financial help with travel expenses, but were refused, apparently at the urging of Namibian church leaders. As a result, the delegation was unable to set off.

Then on 16 February 1986, the SWAPO leaders Theo-Ben Gurirab (foreign relations secretary, now Minister of Foreign Affairs) and Hidipo Hamutenya (secretary for information, now Minister for Information and Broadcasting) issued a statement at a press conference in London declaring that SWAPO was holding as prisoners at least 100 members who were South African government spies. It declared that the spy network had first been detected in December 1983, and had penetrated both political and military wings of the movement abroad. Gurirab made it clear that the statement was a response to reports circulating in Namibia and Europe that SWAPO was involved in 'fascist' activities against Namibian refugees. (CTS, p 48).[7] Alleged confessions on video tape accompanied the press conference.

On 13 March 1986, less than a month after SWAPO had admitted that it was holding many prisoners — in fact many more than a hundred — Attie Beukes and Erica Beukes received a firm response from the collective guardian of the Christian soul in Namibia, the CCN. They were informed by Dr Shejavali that they had been dismissed from their jobs, with immediate effect. The letter to Erica Beukes stated:

> The decision to terminate your employment with the Council of Churches in Namibia was reached only after careful consideration of your leading role in the 'committee of parents' and the various statements issued and published on behalf of that committee 'care of the Council of Churches in Namibia'.
>
> This Council is most perturbed about the way you have chosen to represent the serious allegations made by that committee. It regards the attack on the credibility of 'local pastors and priests' in a very serious light, unwarranted and uncalled for. The statements issued on behalf of that committee, coming, as it is, from an employee of the Council of Churches in Namibia, contains very serious allegations, inter alia, in regard to the role of the Churches and it's [sic] commitment to upholding basic human rights...
>
> It is in these circumstance that the Council had no choice but to terminate your employment.[8]

The decision was confirmed by the executive committee of the CCN, meeting on 17 March. In a letter from the legal firm of Lorentz and Bone of 18 March, Attie Beukes was ordered to hand over the keys of his office as well as all documents and correspondence, 'against the background of recent developments which have brought about serious tension between you and other senior office bearers' of the CCN.[9]

Attie Beukes and Erica Beukes refused to comply with these instructions, until the CCN obtained a legal injunction issued by the South African-appointed court. Soon afterwards, Oxfam in Britain summarily stopped funds to a teaching project (the Science and Mathematics Programme) in Katutura township in Windhoek with which Erica Beukes was connected. The project was then evicted from its teaching premises, which were taken over by the CCN.

The worthy Kandetu, writing in CALIN on the work of the CCN (his then employer, prior to the SWAPO government), says not a word about this sordid affair. The omission is characteristic of the book as a whole. Kandetu does, however, blandly report that the 'Faith, Justice and Society Cluster' of the CCN serves to provide advice and information to the Namibian people 'on their rights, privileges and responsibilities before the law'. (p 210)

FROM THE BIBLE TO THE WITCH-HUNT

Two months after the sacking of Attie Beukes and Erica Beukes, leaflets were circulated in the townships of Windhoek, written in Afrikaans and headed '*Verraiers van Suid-Afrika in Swapo Geledere*' ('South African Traitors in the SWAPO Membership'). In tone reminiscent of Germany in the 1930s, the leaflet concluded with the slogan: '*Swapo is die Volk... Die Volk is Swapo*'. The leaflet was issued by SWAPO as a direct threat to leading members of the Committee of Parents ('*Ouerskomitee*'), seven of whom — including Erica Beukes, her husband Hewat, Attie Beukes and Stella-Maria Boois — were listed by name as among a 'whole group of traitors that South Africa has apparently planted within the leadership corps and activists of SWAPO, both within Namibia and abroad'. (translated) Suspicions were voiced going back to 1977. These 'puppets or spies of South Africa' were accused of having given information to their 'bosses', resulting in South African military attacks and massacres at SWAPO camps in Angola such as Kassinga and 'Vietnam'. Many of these spies, it stated, had already been caught and were being 'held under the supervision of SWAPO' ('*aangehou onder die toesig van Swapo*'). The Committee of Parents was accused of having sent letters and telegrams to world leaders stating that SWAPO had arrested their children without justification and that women were mistreated in SWAPO camps. A direct and very menacing attack was made on Stella-Maria Boois: 'she herself and her son [held by SWAPO in its pits in Angola] are South African spies'. The leaflet incited the instincts of the lynch mob with a further chilling call:

> *Irrespective of whether they are friends, relatives or mere compatriots*
> — STAY AWAY FROM SOUTH AFRICA'S POISON!

Weg met Maria Boois! (Away with Maria Boois!)
Weg met Stella Gaes!
Weg met Talitha Smith!
Weg met Attie Beukes!
Weg met Hewat Beukes!
Weg met Erica Beukes!
Weg met Paul Vleermuis![10]

Three months later, on 31 August 1986, the house of Erica and Hewat Beukes was mysteriously fire-bombed and gutted. Fortunately, neither they nor their children were injured.

None of this history relating to the CCN and its victims appears in CALIN. One would be entitled to wonder whether this terroristic SWAPO leaflet was itself not the work of the dirty tricks department of the South African military occupation forces, if identical sentiments had not been expressed a year later in a letter published in the *Windhoek Observer* on 30 May 1987 by a leading SWAPO member, the advocate Anton Lubowski (assassinated in Windhoek in 1989). There Lubowski dismissed allegations of the kind put forward by the Committee of Parents as 'false propaganda that is being spread by puppets, collaborators and spies'. The holding of SWAPO's alleged one hundred 'spies, collaborators and puppets' (i.e., people identical to the members of the Committee of Parents) was vigorously defended, in the firm expectation that 'we will be catching even more in the not too distant future'. Lubowski concluded his letter, addressed to Erica Beukes, by accusing her of being a 'person who has committed the worst crime against the freedom of your countrymen imaginable'. (CTS, pp. 71–72) It is hard to penetrate the psychopathology of such sentiments, in which the authentic tone of the SWAPO spy drama is expressed.

THE SANCTIFICATION OF TORTURE

In the same month that Lubowski's menacing letter was published in the *Windhoek Observer*, the nationalist movements of southern Africa, including SWAPO, met in what the World Council of Churches describes as an 'historic dialogue' with international church leaders in Lusaka, Zambia. (CALIN, p 199) The meeting culminated in the 'Lusaka Statement' which inter alia expressed recognition of SWAPO by the WCC as 'sole and authentic representative of the people of Namibia', the formulation adopted by the United Nations. In its own words, the 'WCC adopted the Lusaka Statement as its own'.[11]

For all practical purposes, the standpoint of the churches was that of Advocate Lubowski and the authors of the SWAPO leaflet distributed in Windhoek in May 1986. Despite the mass of evidence about SWAPO's purges — which now included a book, including 92 pages of documents, some from Pastor Gröth, published in Namibia in 1986 by Erica and Hewat Beukes and Attie Beukes, called *Namibia, A Struggle Betrayed* — the Africa Secretary of the British Council of Churches, the Rev. Brian Brown, made a submission to a hearing of the WCC in Washington DC on 3 May 1988 that 'both church and SWAPO are people's movements ... partners in opposition to the South African occupation'. It was not true to say that 'the church is SWAPO and SWAPO is the church'; a more accurate description was that 'the "people" are SWAPO and the "people" are the church'. Nicely, he declared that the churches 'endorse SWAPO's purposes, if not all of its methods'. The Christian churches, in Brown's words, had 'become an integral and important part of SWAPO'. (CALIN, pp. 188–90) With these semi-totalitarian semantics, the men of God sprinkled incense on the torture pit. Without any hint of qualification relating to SWAPO's own admission that it held large numbers of members as prisoners, despite the testimony of Gröth and the appeals of the Committee of Parents, the WCC reported formally in tones worthy of a stalinist regime. It stated that

> The illegal occupation of Namibia has been facilitated by Namibians who have collaborated with South Africa and have been traitors to the cause of a free Namibia. Yet SWAPO is willing to accommodate these people in a free Namibia and forgive their misguided behaviour. (CALIN, p 202)

Not only did the churches uncritically promote this Orwellian Newspeak, the editors and publishers of CALIN more than a year later were content to reprint this kind of language without comment. The WCC was recommended by its Washington hearings to call upon the governments of the world to 'provide all necessary forms of support to SWAPO...' (p 203) This enthusiastic endorsement of SWAPO followed a visit to SWAPO's camps in Angola in December 1987 by one of the WCC's sister organizations, the Lutheran World Federation (LWF), based like the WCC in Geneva. As Gröth reported, in 1989 after the release of SWAPO's detainees, the visit followed a 'very painful discussion' within member churches of the LWF in response to the appeal of the Committee of Parents in Namibia. While in Geneva, the SWAPO president, Nujoma, invited the LWF to send a fact-finding delegation to Angola to investigate the charges of human rights abuses.

After months of preparation, a six-person delegation spent five days in Angola and reported on 29 March 1988. The visit was a fiasco. The churchmen were predictably shown merely what SWAPO wished them to see and were not allowed access to the prisoners themselves. Their report was circumspect, stressing that because of lack of time and preparation the delegation could not satisfactorily complete the task with which it had been entrusted. This did not prevent the LWF secretary-general, Gunnar Staalsett, from declaring a month later in the bulletin *Lutherische Welt-Information* (No. 14/88 of 14 April 1988) that allegations of human rights abuses in the SWAPO settlements were unfounded and that the work of the Committee of Parents was 'part of the ongoing South African propaganda war aimed at discrediting the liberation movement'. Staalsett's bizarre act of disinformation appeared in the bulletin under the heading: 'Angola: No indication of SWAPO violations', expressing a very different emphasis from the one actually recorded by the delegates. (Gröth in CTS, pp. 35–36)

A second LWF delegation led by Staalsett had met SWAPO representatives in Angola only the month before, among them the Catholic Bishop Haushiku and Pastor Shuya of VELKSWA, both of whom had been briefed by Attie Beukes as far back as March 1985. The LWF's visits turned the authority of the churches even more terribly against the detainees. This is how, in the late twentieth century, on the eve of the collapse of the regimes of eastern Europe, world public opinion was manipulated and managed on the issue of Namibia.

A GUILTY SECRET

There is a passage in CALIN which directly connives at sanctification of the SWAPO prison system. It appears in a summary of reports from a delegation of Namibian churchmen to political and church leaders in ten countries of western Europe (including the Vatican) and the United States, presented at an evaluation meeting in Frankfurt, Germany, on 4–5 December 1986. The visits of the delegation had taken place over the previous ten days. Coming after the work of Attie Beukes and Erica Beukes for the CCN in western Europe in 1985, the SWAPO statement about holding 100 'spies' of February 1986 and the sacking of Attie Beukes and Erica Beukes in March 1986, this interconfessional mission was characterized by explicit bad faith. The delegation met top government and church leaders, and functioned unashamedly as a fund raiser for SWAPO. Under the hymnal rubric 'We are Slaves of Hope', the delegates in their report record their concern with Mammon. Different types of support were welcomed by the Namibians 'as long as it was channelled through the churches, the Council of Churches in Namibia, or the South West Africa People's Organisation (SWAPO)'. They reported that Sweden had 'promised a substantial raise in its financial support to SWAPO'. (pp. 185–86)

In London, the Namibian delegation attended an ecumenical meeting at Bloomsbury Baptist Church, at which there was 'evidence of good knowledge of the Namibian situation' among the church-related action groups, and at which solidarity was expressed with SWAPO. Yet the question of SWAPO's prisons, so far from Bloomsbury, was posed to this cosy gathering. The delegation reported evasively:

> Outside, the church members of the International Society for Human Rights (ISHR) held a protest at the delegation's visit and the presence of SWAPO representatives. Delegation considered this protest to be inspired by South Africa to defame SWAPO and the churches.... (p 172)

The focus of the ISHR protest, omitted by the church leaders in their laundered report, was the purges in SWAPO and the fate of its prison victims. It is not necessary to endorse the political perspective of the ISHR to acknowledge that its reportage on the detainee issue in SWAPO has been factual. As in the sacking of Attie Beukes and Erica Beukes, the Namibian Christian leaders in their report chose to mask a system of gross abuses by defaming those who reported it.[12]

In reproducing the report of the Namibian church delegation, the editors of CALIN connived with the churches by failing to explain the context of the protest by the ISHR at Bloomsbury, despite having published a number of footnotes to elucidate the document. The uninformed reader is not permitted to grasp the context of the protest by the ISHR or the issue at stake, while those in the know are strengthened in their effort to conceal the truth. A dishonest piece of mis-reportage is made worse by editorial complicity.

Today there are signs that the churches have gently begun to wean themselves from their previous uncritical embrace of SWAPO, and a tiny trickle of funds has gone to projects aimed at helping SWAPO's former torture victims. (letter from Erica Beukes, April 1991) The Rev. Brian Brown is no longer with the British Council of Churches. But the murky past remains well shrouded, especially through books such as CALIN. All this is in sharp contrast to the work of Rev. Salatiel Ailonga, the only cleric to come out of this episode — including even Gröth — with his humanity and his honour fully unimpaired.

A WITNESS TO HUMANITY

Ailonga was a Namibian refugee, based in Zambia, the first clergyman to go into exile. At the beginning of the SWAPO spy mania in the mid-1970s he was compelled to flee to Finland after he drew attention to SWAPO's crimes against its own members. As could be expected, Ailonga is a non-person to the editors of CALIN. His name does not appear at all. Writing from Finland on May 24 1977, Ailonga took advantage of the fact that his bishop, Leonard Auala, was in Dar es Salaam attending a meeting of the Lutheran World Federation. (Auala was the predecessor to Bishop Dumeni, with whom Pastor Gröth and the Committee of Parents pleaded in vain for assistance in 1985). While Bishop Auala was in Dar es Salaam, the government of Tanzania was holding eleven former leaders of SWAPO in prison without trial or the benefit of habeas corpus, at the behest of the SWAPO leadership and the government of Zambia. Those in prison — critical of corruption in high places in SWAPO, its lack of democracy and the participation of SWAPO armed forces in the war in Angola alongside the South African army — had been arrested in Zambia in April 1976 along with over a thousand trained fighters and members of the SWAPO Youth League, and threatened with mass executions by the SWAPO president, Nujoma.[13]

Giving details about torture and shootings at the Zambian army's concentration camp at Mboroma, Ailonga appealed to Bishop Auala to visit the detainees, among whom were several well-known members of his church. Auala, who died in 1982, had made a bold stand along with Moderator Paul Gowaseb of the ELK in a major document of resistance to the South African regime of 30 June 1971. Read aloud in every black Lutheran assembly the following Sunday, the statement — written by students at the Lutheran seminary at Otjimbingwe, endorsed by the boards of ELOK and ELK and signed by Auala and Gowaseb — stated that the South African regime in Namibia had 'failed to take cognisance of Human Rights', that black people in Namibia were continuously being 'slighted and intimidated in their daily lives' and were not free.[14]

The slighting and intimidation of SWAPO's exile members by its leaders, and the unfreedom of SWAPO's internal critics in the prisons of Tanzania, failed to register with Auala and his delegation. He did not respond to Ailonga's plea, It was left to the exiled Anglican bishop of Damaraland, Colin Winter, to administer to the spiritual needs of the eleven jailed dissident leaders. The church leaders preserved silence on their guilty knowledge. As Gröth reported in a memorandum written after the arrival back in Namibia of SWAPO detainees in July 1989,

> Very little of the SWAPO conflict of 1976 was publicized. In the upper echelons of the Namibian churches, it was indeed never officially discussed. The Namibian churches' emerging solidarity with SWAPO and its liberation struggle since the early seventies made them avoid discussion on the issue of violations of human rights by the exiled SWAPO. (CTS, p 34)

Yet the question of publicizing the abuses of the 1980s was very problematical for Gröth himself.

THE PASSION OF PASTOR GRÖTH

Gröth's intervention, its conditions and limits posed a moral and theological dilemma to the German churches as sharp as any since Hitler's time: more specifically, to the Lutheran tradition, and in particular to the oppositional current brought together in 1934 as the Confessing Church (*die bekennende Kirche*). I am not here discussing the fall of such as Kameeta, Hendrik, Auala and Dumeni beneath the highest moment in the Lutheran tradition, and even beneath their own standpoint, expressed by Bishop Auala in his talk with the South African Prime Minister B.J. Vorster on 18 August 1971 as a 'burning thirst for human rights'. (quoted in 'Report' by Siegfried Gröth, CTS, p 34) The distinctiveness of cultural life in Namibia, especially compared with South Africa, consists very largely in its being drenched in religious consciousness, above all that of the Lutheran churches of northern Europe. Thus the seamless interweaving of politics and religion in Namibia, and between Namibian politics and northern European religion. Especially in the 1980s, the moral character of the Protestant churches of northern Europe — mainly German and Lutheran — was hammered on a Namibian anvil. The theological context of the questioning on Namibia was very well known in Germany, and thus to the pastors of the VEM (to which Gröth belongs), since its parameters were those of their own theological education. This German education centred largely on the teaching, influence, and life and death of Pastor Dietrich Bonhoeffer, hanged by the SS in the concentration camp at Flossenbürg on 9 April 1945.

It is not without significance that Bonhoeffer — gagged, banned, imprisoned and finally executed by the Nazis — acted at one time in the early 1930s as secretary to the Youth Commission of the World Alliance for International Friendship through the Churches, and of the Universal Christian Council for Life and Work, two early ecumenical organizations which led after World War II to the founding of the WCC. At the height of the war, as an emissary of the German resistance, Bonhoeffer delivered messages in Geneva to Visser 't Hooft, later the first General Secretary of the WCC. Through its relation to Bonhoeffer and also after the war to Pastor Martin Niemöller — imprisoned for eight years under Hitler — the WCC passed judgement on itself in the 1980s by its silence on the detainees in SWAPO's pits. At the war's end, Niemöller became president of the Lutheran Evangelical Church's Office for Foreign Relations, and was present when the WCC was formed in Amsterdam in 1948. The

WCC's response to SWAPO in Angola calls to mind Niemöller's self-critique of his early response to the Nazi terror, the three words: 'I was silent'.

Gröth gave voice to this crisis of the German Christian conscience, which required him to be measured by its own standard. Through his breakdown and through his efforts to mediate through the churches, but also through his refusal to take the step of public opposition to the purges in Zambia and Angola, Gröth drew a line rejected by Bonhoeffer between a purely religious act and a worldly one. After an intensely bitter dispute between himself and Attie Beukes in Germany in September/October 1985, over whether or not he should make his files public, Gröth preserved silence even after Attie Beukes and Erica Beukes were dismissed by the NCC in March 1986. His moral authority was thrown publicly on the side of SWAPO's prison victims only after they were already released from the pits, and had returned to Namibia. Gröth's testimony was then published in Germany as *Menschenrechtsverletzungen in der Exil-Swapo* (Human Rights Violations in SWAPO in Exile) on 18 September 1989, and reproduced as Gröth's 'Report' in CTS (October 1989) There he states:

> It was not possible for the Namibian churches to exercise any noteworthy influence on the issue of the violation of human rights. In the joint liberation struggle, the clerics responsible in Namibia relied on what the SWAPO representatives told them.

This is contradicted by Gröth's own representations to those same churchmen, from 1985 to 1989. He continues:

> It remains incomprehensible how the exiled SWAPO succeeded in violating human rights for more than ten years ... SWAPO could arrest people or be responsible for their disappearance without it being seriously discussed at an international level, in the church, or in the ecumenical domain.
>
> In Namibia itself, even in the churches, it was impossible to officially and publicly address the facts of the case concerning torture by SWAPO. [Yet this was done by the Committee of Parents, and by the publication of *Namibia, A Struggle Betrayed* — PT.] Amongst international bodies, this topic was taboo. The international community, as well as the churches, were overcome with a lameness, a powerlessness, that is difficult to explain.

Gröth states that after the return of SWAPO's prison victims, he had been confronted as pastor for Namibian refugees with the question: 'Why are you only making this public now? And what made you treat the violation of human rights by SWAPO as a purely internal and confidential matter to the church?' (CTS, p 39) His reply in his own defence, printed in CTS, is that firstly, he did not wish to 'create problems for the families in Namibia' with whom he was in contact; secondly, he 'did not want to speak out publicly' because in his view it was 'more important to negotiate on these difficult issues with the leaders concerned'; and thirdly, that he was afraid that what he had to say would be 'abused for propaganda purposes, that the South African propagandists would get hold of it', even in Germany. (ibid)

Taken in themselves, these are reasonable criteria, but unsatisfying. Effectively the churches in Namibia, the WCC, the British Council of Churches and the VEM, with Gröth as its crucial representative, were *non*-confessing religious bodies. In Bonhoeffer's terms, they preferred the 'cheap grace' of conventional left-nationalist liberation theology to the 'costly grace' of active commitment to their own professed principles. Gröth's powerlessness stemmed from his self-confinement to the 'inwardness' that Bonhoeffer found inadequate in his prison letter of 30 April 1940, by contrast with Bonhoeffer's conception (following Hegel on the social nature of humanity) of the need for outward action and relationship with others. Gröth's Gethsemane, his theology of the cross, found its suffering figure in the torture pits at Lubango. Bonhoeffer had argued that the Christian was called on to participate in the 'suffering of God in the life of the world'. (Letter of 18 July 1944, in Bonhoeffer, p 13) In the last resort, Gröth retired into religion and left the worldly defence of humanity — and the calumny — to others.

FIRST AND LAST WORD

In the exceptionally difficult campaign to reveal the truth about SWAPO's purges and to rescue the victims, the most courageous individuals were the small group in Namibia around Erica Beukes, Attie Beukes and Stella-Maria Boois. The last word on the complicity of the churches, continued in CALIN, belongs to Ailonga. He has the place of honour because of his humanity and his prescience and because his was also practically the first word to be raised on behalf of the victims. He was fearful, he wrote to Auala, that all the thousand members of SWAPO then still held in detention in Zambia in May 1977

> may be lost within a short time and never return to Namibia. But there are thousands of families, friends and relatives of these people, and their voice will be demanding an explanation. What will the answer of the church be? ... If you as leaders of the church in Namibia will fail to go with love into this question in SWAPO, which is a small group, how will you be able to cope with problems which will arise on a much larger basis within a free Namibia, be it under the leadership of SWAPO or someone else? (CTS, p 40)

In the following years, until the detainees crept from their dungeons in May 1989 like the prison wraiths in *Fidelio,* the churches in Namibia and internationally gave their answer. It is one of the scandals of the twentieth century. SWAPO's prison system, preserved from investigation by complicity of the churches, will be endured in its effects for many years in the social life of southern Africa and in the personal lives of its victims. The volume under review is the product of a shameful history.

REFERENCES

1. Dr Abisai Shejavali, General Secretary of the Council of Churches in Namibia, in a letter on the subject of SWAPO's detainees to Mr Koshy, 23 December 1985, in *Call Them Spies* (CTS), p 47. CTS was published in October 1989 by Motinga, an ex-SWAPO detainee and former commander in SWAPO's military frees, and Basson, a former senior officer in the South African Defence Force . It is probable that Basson's connections with the South African Defence Force made publication possible. It is exclusively a book of documents.
2. In CALIN, p 202.
3. Letter to Reverend Paul Isaak in Chicago, 8 July 1985, CTS, p 42. Isaak's brother Sam had been detained by SWAPO.
4. Report by Committee of Parents, April 1987. In CTS, p 63.
5. Ibid, p 64.
6. The manner in which this became available to Beukes awaits its own telling.
7. Deputy to Hamutenya in the new ministry of information and broadcasting is Tjongarero, formerly director of the communications department of the CCN, assisted by Kandetu, former associate general secretary of the CCN and author of the brief essay on the CCN in CALIN. In Namibia, saintliness is the surest road to power and place. The spokesperson for labour camps is assisted by public relations officers for the Almighty.
8. Photocopy of letter in possession of author.
9. Photocopy of letter in possession of author.
10. Leaflet in possession of author.
11. Report of the World Council of Churches, Washington Hearings on Namibia, 2–4 May, 1988. In CALIN, p 199.
12. Because of the standpoint of the ISHR on Mozambique, Angola and Nicaragua, Erica Beukes and Attie Beukes later worked separately, still under the name of the Committee of Parents. Those like Stella-Maria Boois worked under the name of the Parents' Committee.
13. For a detailed history of the SWAPO spy-drama of 1976 see Trewhela (1990/91) — Chapter 13 in this book.
14. In Herbstein and Evenson, p 54.

BIBLIOGRAPHY

1. Nico Basson and Ben Motinga (eds) (1989), *Call Them Spies: A Documentary Account of the Namibian Spy Drama*, African Communications Projects, Windhoek.
2. Erica Beukes, Hewat Beukes and Attie Beukes (1986), *Namibia, A Struggle Betrayed*, Rehoboth, Namibia.

3. Paul Trewhela (1990), 'A Namibian Horror', *Searchlight South Africa* No. 4, February.
4. Dietrich Bonhoeffer, ed Eberhard Bethge (1959), *Letters and Papers from Prison*, Fontana.
5. S. Gröth, et al (1972), *Kirchliches Handeln oder politische Aktion? Modell Südwesafrika*, Wuppertal.
6. Baruch Hirson (1979), *Year of Fire, Year of Ash*, Zed.
7. Denis Herbstein and John Evenson (1989), *The Devils are Among Us: The War for Namibia*, Zed.
8. Independent Group (1987), *Swapo: The 1976 Anti-Corruption Rebellion*, Windhoek.
9. Panduleni and Ndamona Kali (1990), 'Swapo's Prisons in Angola', *Searchlight South Africa* No. 4.
10. Peter Katjavivi (1988), *A History of Resistance in Namibia*, UNESCO/James Currey.
11. N. Pityana (1974), 'What is Black Consciousness?' in Basil Moore (ed), *The Challenge of Black Theology in South Africa*, John Knox Press, Atlanta, Georgia.
12. Paul Trewhela (1990/91), 'The Kissinger–Vorster–Kaunda Détente: Genesis of the SWAPO "Spy-Drama"', Parts I and II, *Searchlight South Africa* Nos 5 and 6.

DOCUMENTS

Document 1

Letter from Reverend Salatiel Ailonga, a Namibian pastor, then a refugee in Finland after having fled from SWAPO in Zambia, to Bishop Leonard Auala of the Evangelical Lutheran Ovambo-Kavango Church (ELOK), 24 May 1977. Auala was the senior figure in Ailonga's church. He was then attending a conference of the Lutheran World Federation (LWF) in Dar es Salaam, Tanzania, at the head of a Namibian church delegation. The letter refers to SWAPO's suppression in 1976 of resistance to its collaboration with the South African army in the war in Angola. For the background, see Paul Trewhela (1990/91).

Dear Bishop Auala,

As you know, since 1976 there was a conflict among the Namibians in Zambia. This led to many leading members in SWAPO and my Chaplaincy being imprisoned on the request of SWAPO's leadership. First, eleven leading members of the Party and Youth League, then forty-eight from the front, talking on behalf of the soldiers, and later on over one thousand Namibians disappeared. In the wake of this I had to leave Zambia and since June 1976 I have been staying in Finland.

Now you have the opportunity of being in Dar es Salaam, Tanzania, where eleven of the imprisoned are being held. They are said to be in the following places:

- Immanuel Engombe, Zakaria Shikomba, Andreas Nuukuawo and Martin Taaneni, who at the present is seriously ill, are in Keko Women's Prison, Dar.
- Filemon Moongo and Johannes (Jimmy) Ampala in Mtwara Prison (?).
- Keshii Pelao Nathanael, Ruben Shangula, Tabora Prison (?).
- Andreas Shipanga and Solomon Mifima, Isanga Prison, Dodoma.

I request for you to look for a possible way to see these people, because some of them are said to be seriously ill. It is a good luck for you that Zambia is close to Tanzania and it would be well if you would try to go there to see the people in Buloma [Mboroma — PT] camp North of Lusaka, who are reported to be dying because of lack of food and medicine.

According to the proofs and my knowledge, this is not a purely political case or internal SWAPO affair. It is a case concerning the well being of the Namibians and their human rights, which touches the church and its responsibility to a great extent. The imprisoned in Tanzania and Zambia are members of all churches, including Lutherans, Anglicans and Roman Catholics.

The reason for the imprisonment is not yet known to the world, and there is no legal ground to hold people without trial. This needs to be said with all seriousness even at the present meeting [of the LWF in Dar es Salaam — PT], looking for the justice and dignity and liberation of the human being as a whole. If there should be any fault or crime, not all the thousand could be held responsible. There is a reliable report that at Buloma camp in August last year many people were shot at, many were wounded and some died, among them Frans Nangutuuala and Naftali Lilya.

In matters like these, which may have the most serious effect for the future, the church should not be silent. All these thousand may be lost within a short time and never return to Namibia. But there are thousand of families, friends and relatives of these people, and their voice will be demanding an explanation. What will the answer of the church be? I would say that in every leadership, church or state, the leaders have to be led and shown the truth without fear or partiality. That shows not enmity, but love for the leaders you correct, because you care about what he is doing. If you as leaders of the church in Namibia will fail to go with love into the question in SWAPO, which is a small group, how will you be able to cope with problems which will arise on a much larger basis within a free Namibia, be it under the leadership of SWAPO or someone else?

I request you in all humility to take this matter seriously and prevent more vain bloodshed. I attach some proofs of personal statements and written letters to support the information above, showing the very serious state of many Namibians outside our country.

(signed) *Salatiel Ailonga*

Copies:
Dr Lukas de Vries, Pres. ELC,
Rev. Albertus Maasdorp, Assist. Secr. Gen., LWF,
Prof Mikko Juva, Chairman LWF.

Printed in CTS, p. 40. First published in *Namibia, A Struggle Betrayed*, 1986. Also in *Swapo: The 1976 Anti-Corrptlon Rebellion*, Windhoek, 1987, a pamphlet issued by the 'Independent Group' and edited by Hewat Beukes. De Vries later joined the pro-South African interim government as a deputy minister. Juva and Maasdorp were leading world officials of the LWF. The *Times of Namibia* reported accurately on 6 October 1989 that Namibia's 'most prominent and well respected churchmen' had been well informed about the plight of SWAPO detainees abroad since 1977 but had 'failed to inform the nation of this tragedy and preferred to remain silent'. It is plain from this letter that the same applies to the LWF.

Author's note, August 2009: Frans Nangutuuala was the brother of Johannes Nangutuuala, the principal leader of the Namibian contract workers' strike of December 1971–March 1972 which first shook the South African apartheid regime in Namibia to its foundations. In August 1973 Johannes Nangutuuala suffered public flagellation by 21 strokes on his naked body, carried out by the authorities of this barbarous regime; Frans suffered 17 strokes. Barbarous as this was, SWAPO's subsequent sentence on Frans Nangutuuala was even more terrible, and absolute.

Document 2
Letter from Rev. Siegfried Gröth in Germany to Rev. Paul Isaak in Chicago, 8 July 1985, informing Isaak of the imprisonment in Angola of his brother Samuel Isaak, a SWAPO member.

Dear Brother,

After such a long delay I am now able to write to you. In the meantime I hope you have received the letter of Mrs Sohn, my secretary, made at May 18, 1985. The reason of my long silence is a very serious illness. After my three weeks' stay in Zambia among the Namibian refugees I had a break-down in Harare, the capital of Zimbabwe. In the middle of May I returned to Germany, accompanied by my wife who came to Zimbabwe to my support. But here again I had to go to a hospital for further treatment. Since last week I started slowly my work in the office.

First of all I have to say to you: This was the most difficult trip to Africa for me since more than twenty years. I arrived in Lusaka on March 19 and made immediately the experience that there was a very dangerous situation among the Namibians in Exile. I was confronted with an atmosphere of fear and mistrust, hopelessness and despair. Some of my good friends and brothers in Christ I could not find, among them your brother and Thomas. As far as I know, a lot of SWAPO-members disappeared and were brought from Zambia to Angola. As I heard in a lot of confidential talks with old friends among SWAPO, these brothers are accused to be spies of South Africa. They must be in detention after internal SWAPO-trials.

On March 4 hundred of SWAPO-members were invited by SWAPO-leaders to the Namibia Institute of the United Nations in Lusaka [in a report written after the return of the prison victims to Namibia, Gröth gives the number of people present on this grisly occasion as 'more than 400', CTS, p34]. From the afternoon up to one o'clock in midnight the invited people had to watch video tapes which were shown to them. On these tapes Namibians were confessing about South African actions among SWAPO people in Zambia and Angola. According to the confessing Namibians they were recruited as spies for South Africa. Two key-persons in this trial were Samuel Thomas and Benny Boois. Boois and Sam and maybe others were confessing that a lot of SWAPO-members became spies for South Africa. Among the names which were mentioned is your brother. As I heard from close friends who are still SWAPO-members he had to go from Zambia to Angola and is now detained. This happened after the video-tape was shown in the time between March 12 and 20, according to the information of a close friend to me.

Dear Brother, when I got these informations during my stay in Lusaka it was a shock for me which I shall never forget. I could not believe what I heard again and again from my brothers in Christ and good friends. As you know your brother is a very close friend to me since years and we had all the years when we met in Lusaka a spiritual fellowship and became more and more brothers in Christ and close friends. We had a relationship and friendship of trust and brotherhood. And, as you know, I'm close to your family, to you, and I remember with great thankfulness your father who was one of the first pastors of the Evangelical Lutheran Church in Namibia. I am personally convinced that your brother is not a South African spy. All the years when we met I made the experience that he was a loyal member of SWAPO. Therefore he left his family and his country years ago and therefore he was willing to accept the difficulties and sufferings of a life in exile. He was very much concerned to make his studies in order to be a responsible member of a new and free Namibia in future. And Sam was also a responsible and committed Christian who was willing to suffer as a disciple of his Lord. And finally he was concerned about his family in Namibia. These three loyalties were important for your brother Sam and my friend. I'm saying this as the pastor and shepherd of Sam with whom I had a close relationship by faith and friendship.

I was asked by responsible Christians and SWAPO-members in Zambia to contact representatives of the Evangelical Lutheran Church in Namibia. I was asked by them to inform brothers of the Namibian churches so that they know about the critical situation of the Namibians in Exile. Our brothers in Zambia are convinced that there is such a great crisis in Zambia and Angola among SWAPO that churches in Namibia have to give their support and advice. Otherwise it could get worse and worse for the Namibians in Exile. This cry for help from Namibian churches came to me as a pastor who is asked by Namibian churches to take spiritual care among the Namibians in Exile in Zambia.

On May 15 I had a confidential talk with Rev. Zephaniah Kameeta in my house in Wuppertal. I returned from Africa on May 13 and had the chance to discuss this serious issue with Brother Kameeta. I informed him about the emergency situation in Zambia and Angola and mentioned the names of my friends and brothers who are in such a dangerous situation. I also mentioned names of your brother and Samuel Thomas. I told Brother Kameeta that responsible Christians and SWAPO-members are appealing to the churches for their support and help. I hope very much that Brother Kameeta as Vice-president of ELC will do his best and I trust in him. I also had confidential talks with Pastor Hendrik Frederik, the Preses of the ELC on June 14 in my house. I informed him as the President of the Church about these dangerous developments and the needs of friends and brothers in Zambia and Angola. And the consequence of the experience in Zambia was my break-down in Harare some days later. But I'm also convinced that our Lord Jesus Christ is our only Saviour and Good Shepherd. Since my visit in Zambia I'm praying daily for my brothers and sisters in Angola and Zambia who are suffering and have to go through the valleys of despair and darkness. I don't know what exactly is happening with Sam and the others in Angola. The Lord knows and he is taking care of them. This is my conviction. All the years that Sam and myself were listening to the Good News that Jesus Christ is our only Saviour and good shepherd. And I am convinced that the Lord is also the good Shepherd of your brother who is in such a difficult and dangerous situation.

I'm writing this with great sorrow as somebody who is also suffering because of the situation in Angola and Zambia among our friends there. May our Lord give you strength and hope! Let us pray to him that he will save your brother and my friend and the others! And let us pray for your mother and your whole family! In my daily prayers I am very much with all of you.

This is a very personal and confidential letter to you. Your family and other families are affected by these events. But also the churches in Namibia are affected and have to take care of those who are struggling for survival, hope and faith.

I would be very grateful if you could respond as quickly as possible to my letter. I'm waiting for your reply. And if I get any new information I shall write to you as soon as possible. I would like to greet you very heartily with the word of Our Lord Jesus Christ which has strengthened and encouraged me during the last weeks: 'I will not leave you alone; I will come back to you'. (John, 14, 18)

Your brother in Christ,

(signed) *Siegfried Gröth.*

Printed in CTS, p 42. Samuel Thomas is the brother-in-law of SWAPO's vice-president, the Rev. Hendrik Witbooi. Such an illustrious relative by marriage did not save him from the purge. He returned to Namibia from SWAPO's underground prisons on 4 July 1989, along with the bulk of his fellow victims.

13 *The Kissinger–Vorster–Kaunda Détente**

The agents of the South African regime and imperialists have been rooted out of our movement and the Central Committee carried out a systematic purge of all the traitors.
— Sam Nujoma, 5 August 1976.[1]

A RELIGIOUS EXPERIENCE

Independence day in Namibia on 21st March was welcomed by the international media in a mood of rapture. It was a variety of religious experience. As the rites of passage took place in Windhoek on the 30th anniversary of the massacres at Sharpeville and Langa in South Africa, the social and political relations within Namibia underwent a mystical transfiguration.

The past was to be forgotten. Reconciliation was all. Namibia was 'free' (*Guardian*), the outcome was a 'United Nations triumph' (*Independent*), Sam Nujoma the new president was 'a kind man' (*Independent on Sunday*) — all British newspapers. The tone of wonder appeared at its most elevated in the *Observer*, owned by Tiny Rowland's Lonrho corporation. Under the headline 'Namibia set to become Africa's model state,' its correspondent in Windhoek, the South African journalist Allister Sparks, declared: 'there is an atmosphere now of something quite unbelievable and almost magical happening.'

It was 'almost too good to be true.' Namibia had the prospect of becoming 'the continent's most genuinely democratic and economically viable country,' with 'black Africa's only authentic multi-party system.' The miracle in Windhoek acquired not merely continental but universal significance: 'The whole world, it seems, wants to celebrate this deliciously unexpected event.' Similar compliments on the 'birth of democratic Namibia' were expressed by Glenys Kinnock of the Labour Party and by David Steel, former leader of the Liberal

*First published in two parts in *Searchlight South Africa* Vol. 2, No. 1 (July 1990), pp. 69–86, and Vol. 2, No. 2 (January 1991), pp. 42–58 as 'The Kissinger–Vorster–Kaunda Détente: Genesis of the SWAPO "Spy-Drama"'.

Party, in a letter to the British press. To these spiritual chords were added the choirs of cash registers jingling and not principally either for Windhoek's hoteliers and the bed-and-breakfast industry. In the words of the *Observer*, of 18 March,

> The mood among businessmen is bullish. 'It ranges from cautiously optimistic to very optimistic', says Ude Freuse, who runs a consultative forum that brings government and business leaders together. 'SWAPO [the South West Africa People's Organisation] has been de-demonized and now businessmen see that it is opening new doors to the world for them.'

To this could be added the comment of the US financial pundit Eliot Janeway, published in the British press on the eve of Namibia's independence: 'South Africa is the gateway to black Africa, which is the new market about to explode in the world' (*Guardian*, 20 March). Seldom have the ecstasies of faith ascended to heaven so purely from the cash nexus.

THE CASE OF ANDREAS SHIPANGA

The whole affair was characterized by the grotesque. In the fairy tale, Beauty fell in love with the Beast (actually a handsome prince), but in the case of SWAPO it is something bestial that is celebrated as beautiful. Under conditions of permanent terror inflicted by the South African regime in Namibia, SWAPO in exile was shaped by a history of purges of its members during the 1980s which reached lunatic proportions. Over this period over a thousand SWAPO members were purged in southern Angola: tortured, forced to confess to fabricated charges of being South African spies, imprisoned in pits in the ground for up to seven years, executed at will, and very frequently worked, starved or beaten to death. One man who returned to Windhoek with other ex-SWAPO prisoners in July last year lost seven brothers in this way. Even President Nujoma's wife was arrested at one point. Some of the best-known heroes of the Namibian resistance were murdered and defamed, in addition to a host of others.

Searchlight South Africa No. 4 was the first (and perhaps still is the only) South African political journal to make the cause of the ex-SWAPO detainees its own, to report extensively on the 'spy-drama' of the 1980s, to interview its victims and to call for an independent international inquiry, as the former detainees themselves demand. (See the statement of the Political Consultative Council of Ex-SWAPO Detainees [PCC] in this issue).

Former SWAPO prisoners now in Namibia are convinced that very many of their fellows who have not returned continue to be held by SWAPO elsewhere in Africa, if they have not already been murdered. Their return is the PCC's first demand. *Searchlight South Africa* undertook to return to the question of SWAPO's prisons, and this guided the research resulting in this article. Both the original material on SWAPO's prisons and the present article were written in the knowledge that similar atrocities had happened in ANC camps, and that the question of SWAPO was an acid test for politics in South Africa. The publication of the first, extended, first-hand account by former ANC members of their experiences at the hands of the ANC's jailers and torturers, appearing in the London *Sunday Correspondent* on 8 April, followed by the ex-ANC members' 'Open Letter to Nelson Mandela' of 14 April (see pp. 43–45 in this book), completely vindicated this perspective.

The present article investigates the historical forces that propelled SWAPO towards its cycle of tortures and executions, and locates them in complex interrelations of global and regional politics of the mid-1970s, focused on the civil war in Angola. This was not the beginning of SWAPO's descent to barbarism, as former SWAPO prisoners see it. They report an early rebellion by members of SWAPO's military wing at Kongwa in Tanzania in the 1960s, put down by the Tanzanian army on behalf of SWAPO's leaders. Very little is known about this event. According to ex-SWAPO prisoners, the Kongwa rebellion 'has never been fully discussed even at the highest levels of the organization. To this date, a veil of secrecy prevails over it' ('A Report to the Namibian People'). It is not yet possible to appraise its significance for SWAPO's future evolution.

The present article, however, does present the first comprehensive picture of conditions in the 1970s that determined SWAPO's fatal course: towards eating its own children. It is a matter that requires a great deal of further research. Yet already a picture emerges of one of the great hidden scandals of southern Africa, centred on political and military collaboration of SWAPO's top leaders with the South African government and with UNITA when Angola was invaded by the South African army in September/October 1975. Several of the leaders of SWAPO most active in the events of that time now head the government of Namibia, including the president, Nujoma, the Minister of Defence, Peter Mueshihange, and the Minister of Security, Peter Sheehama.

SWAPO's collaboration with the South African government expressed itself perversely, and in a manner that reversed the real relationships, in the so-called 'Shipanga affair' of 1976. The episode is named after Andreas Shipanga, SWAPO's former secretary for information, born in 1931 to a rural family in Ovamboland in northern Namibia. After working in Ovamboland, in Angola, on the gold mines of the Witwatersrand and in Rhodesia, he went to Cape

Town in the 1957 where he was an early member of SWAPO's parent body, the Ovamboland People's Congress (OPC). In the early 1960s he was one of SWAPO's leaders in Cape Town, and also a member of the Yu Chui Chan Club, a small discussion group with members drawn from several political organizations who shared a common interest in theories of guerrilla warfare.[2] The club was a product of the times: of the all-pervasive conviction after the Sharpeville shootings, that only violence could remove the regimes that ruled in southern Africa.

In June 1963, YCC Club members in Cape Town were arrested and jailed. Among these, Dr Neville Alexander — now [1990] a leader of the Cape Action League — and Elizabeth van den Heever spent more than 15 years in prison. Shipanga escaped arrest and returned to Namibia. At the same time, another Namibian associated with the YCC Club, Dr Kenneth Abrahams, was saved from arrest by local people in his native Rehoboth in central Namibia. Shipanga and Abrahams escaped to Botswana (then Bechuanaland, still under British control), along with two of Abrahams' rescuers, Paul Smit and Hermanus Christoffel Beukes, one of the first Namibians to petition the United Nations. There the four men were kidnapped by South African police, subjected to a ferocious beating and smuggled back. Abrahams was flown to Cape Town, the others imprisoned in Namibia. After heated demands from the British government, the South African government was compelled to return the four men to Bechuanaland.

Shipanga then joined other SWAPO leaders in exile. SWAPO had opened its first mission in Dar es Salaam in 1961, with missions in Cairo in 1962 and Algeria in 1963. Its future course was decided with the setting up of the African Liberation Committee of the Organisation of African Unity (OAU) in May 1963, which channelled funds from member states to nationalist parties that took up arms against the white regimes in their countries. This was decisive for SWAPO, since its main rival in Namibia — the South West African National Union (SWANU), with support originally among Herero speakers — did not get funding from the OAU because it did not take up the gun.

The first batch of SWAPO members arrived for military training in Cairo in 1964. The first guerrillas then entered Ovamboland in the early months of 1966, crossing through Zambia into the Caprivi Strip from their headquarters in Tanzania, and, after a period of preparation, began attacks on police posts. SWAPO marks 26 August 1966 as the launch of its armed struggle, the date when South African police attacked a guerrilla training camp. Mass arrests, tortures, very long periods of imprisonment, killings and a military/police reign of terror now became the rule especially in northern Namibia, as SWAPO fought the South African state in arms. The huge cost in lives of this war is the permanent background to the SWAPO spy-drama.

THE DEMAND FOR A CONGRESS

SWAPO's first two national congresses were held within Namibia in 1961 and 1963, but after the turn to arms the third congress was held at Tanga, in Tanzania, from 26 December 1969 to 3 January 1970. No further congress was held during the next six years. Since the demand for a fourth national congress was central to the internal crisis in SWAPO between 1974 and 1976, a knowledge of SWAPO's organizational structure at this period becomes important. Shipanga (appointed to the national executive committee as secretary for information at the third congress) describes SWAPO's formal structure at this time as follows:

> The National Congress is the supreme policy-making body of SWAPO, bringing together people from… the military, the National Executive Committee, and humble cell members from inside Namibia. The resolutions passed by the Congress determine principles and policies and guide the work of all members.
>
> …the Congress also elects, and where necessary suspends, members of the two other main national structures, the National Executive Committee and the Central Committee. In 1974–75 the National Executive was composed of sixteen members selected from the Central Committee and was responsible for the day-to-day execution of SWAPO policy, ensuring that the resolutions of the Congress were carried out by all organs of SWAPO, including the military…
>
> The Central Committee, with 35 members, was the watchdog of the National Executive: it was meant to oversee its work and make recommendations to it, and all important decisions of the National Executive required the approval of the Central Committee. (Armstrong, p 99)

Between 1974 and 1976, however, SWAPO's internal workings became enmeshed in a vast international and sub-continental imbroglio. By the time Shipanga joined the national executive, SWAPO had become the personal fiefdom of a small number of top leaders including two from the days of the OPC: the president, Sam Nujoma, and the secretary for defence, Peter Eneas Nanyemba.[3] They disregarded SWAPO's constitution, using the National Executive Committee as a fortress against the whole organization. At the time of the internal crisis of 1974–76, according to Shipanga, something like a state of siege existed in SWAPO. He states:

> Since the Tanga Congress not even the Central Committee had met. The

> situation was totally unhealthy, because power was concentrated in the Executive Committee, and the military wing, PLAN [the People's Liberation Army of Namibia], had no representation on the Executive, only in the Central Committee. (op. cit., p 100)

For militants in the front line fighting the South African state — both within PLAN (waging its military campaign mainly from Zambian bases) and in the SWAPO Youth League, active politically both inside and outside Namibia, this was unacceptable. It became increasingly insufferable during 1974. As Shipanga reports, the Tanga congress had resolved 'unanimously' that the next national congress would be called at the end of five years, in December 1974. Shipanga says that he constantly urged the Executive that a steering committee be appointed to prepare the 1974 congress.

> Nujoma and Nanyemba kept saying no, there was no need for a Congress. In 1973 they said the same thing. Then, after the military coup in Lisbon, on 25 April 1974, came the sudden collapse of Portugal's African empire. (ibid)

The coup propelled SWAPO, with its undemocratic and unconstitutional internal regime, into the vortex of great power politics, completely destabilizing relations between members and leaders of the organization. Unable to cope in a revolutionary manner with the powerful currents set loose in central and southern Africa by the developments of 1974, SWAPO was pulled into a fatal downward spiral of repression and falsification.

THE SLIDE INTO THE ABYSS

At the time of the Portuguese career officers' coup, there were three separate nationalist movements in Angola, each with its own military cadre and specific ethnic base. In the north-east, the National Front for the Liberation of Angola (FNLA), led by Holden Roberto, had organized an uprising on the coffee plantations in March 1961. Based in neighbouring Zaire, and corruptly bound up with the Zairean elite, it rested on Angola's third biggest ethnic grouping, the Bakongo people.

In the capital Luanda, situated in the north-west on the coast, the major organization was the Popular Movement for the Liberation of Angola (MPLA). It had participated in an urban insurrection in Luanda against Portuguese rule in February 1961. After a period of intense factional strife and dormancy before the coup in Portugal, it was to emerge triumphant from the anti-Portuguese struggle and the subsequent civil war, aided by massive supplies of Soviet heavy arms and the deployment of thousands of Cuban troops, as well as

Cuban administrative, teaching and medical personnel. MPLA politics were determined by the association of its major leader, Dr Agostinho Neto, with the rigid stalinism of the Portuguese Communist Party during long years of exile (and many of imprisonment) in Portugal. Its base was the workers in the *muceques* (hill slums) of Luanda, the intellectuals, the relatively less oppressed urban *mestico* (or mixed race) population, and the second most numerous of the tribal groupings in Angola, the Mbundu, living in the eastern hinterland of Luanda.

The largest ethnic grouping in the country, the Ovimbundu, formed the mass base for the third of Angola's nationalist parties, the National Union for the Total Liberation of Angola (UNITA). The Ovimbundu occupied the central region of Angola, along the Benguela Railway running east-west from Zambia through southern Zaire to the port at Lobito. The founder and leader of UNITA, Dr Jonas Savimbi (a graduate of the University of Lausanne, with a thesis on the Yalta conference), was previously foreign secretary of the FNLA but broke from it in 1964, condemning it as tribalist and incompetent. At this point the Chinese government, seeking a base distinct from the Soviet-backed MPLA after the Sino-Soviet split, provided Savimbi and eleven followers with military training in China in 1965–66. It is not irrelevant to the future development of SWAPO that UNITA's 'Chinese Eleven' were smuggled back into Angola by SWAPO, located first in Tanzania and then in Zambia (Bridgland, pp. 67–71).

In January 1975, ten months after the coup in Portugal, the three organizations signed a declaration of unity at Alvor in Portugal. Independence was to follow on 11 November, after elections in October for a constituent assembly. The elections never happened. No one party had support across the whole country, and a combination of international great power politics and internal antagonisms propelled them to civil war. Between June and August 1974, the FNLA based in Zaire received arms from China and Romania, as well as military instructors from China. From July 1974 the United States, unofficially through the CIA, and from January 1975 officially through the '40 Committee' of the National Security Council, provided the FNLA with large sums of money, which was used to finance an attempted coup. Then, in late August 1974, the USSR sent huge quantities of weapons to the MPLA and in December a big contingent of MPLA officers left for the USSR for intensive military training. The scene was set.

Followers of Agostinho Neto — the leading grouping of the MPLA — attacked members of a rival faction led by Daniel Chipenda in Luanda in February 1975, killing fifteen. Chipenda and his followers fled from Luanda and joined the FNLA, bringing about 3,000 soldiers. The next month, swollen and super-confident with its CIA funds, the FNLA carried out its attempted coup in Luanda; it was driven out by the MPLA in July after massive killings on both sides. In June, MPLA troops massacred UNITA members in the suburb of Pica-Pau in Luanda, compelling UNITA to withdraw to central Angola where its support was concentrated. Savimbi then flew to Zambia for discussions with President Kenneth Kaunda, and shortly afterwards, on 4 August, after MPLA troops fired on Savimbi's jet at Silva Porto, UNITA entered the civil war against the MPLA.

In July, US President Gerald Ford authorized $14M for covert supply of arms to the FNLA and UNITA; and on 20 August the chief of the CIA task force in Angola, John Stockwell, arrived in UNITA territory on a visit of inspection, dressed as a priest, having previously joined the FNLA's march on Luanda from the north. Information on the US operation comes mainly from Stockwell, a veteran of operations in Vietnam, Zaire and Burundi, who broke with 'the company' in December 1976 and published a book on his role.

In September and October 1975, nearly a thousand Cuban troops arrived by sea to bolster the MPLA. It was they that decisively turned the tide against the FNLA when a second assault was launched on Luanda in November 1975, supported by two regular battalions of the Zairean army, aimed at capturing the capital before independence day, 11 November. The FNLA was routed, never again to appear as a factor in Angolan affairs. Between June 1974 and September 1975 Angola became a cockpit of the superpowers. The mass supply of Soviet war materiel (tanks, armoured cars, trucks, helicopters, MIG-21 jet fighters, rocket launchers, small arms plus the 122mm cannon), together with the Cuban expeditionary force — between 1,100 to 4,000 troops by November 1975, rising to 12,000 by January 1976 — decided the first phase of the Angolan war in favour of the MPLA, in addition to the important factor of popular support in the capital, Luanda. This produced a paroxysm throughout the sub-continent, with profound and grotesque effects on SWAPO.

THE DÉTENTE SCENARIO

What decided SWAPO's evolution in 1974–76 was the response of the government of Zambia to the war in Angola. SWAPO had its military bases in Zambia, and was directly accountable to President Kaunda and his army. The Zambian regime was thrown into panic by the war. The country had become independent in October 1964 under the leadership of the United National Independence Party (UNIP), headed by Kaunda, and governed since 1973 as a one-party state.[4] After the Unilateral Declaration of Independence (UDI) by the Smith regime in Rhodesia in November 1965, Zambia was the most 'frontline' of all the frontline states. Its economy, dependent on the mining of a single product, copper, remained in the hands of the Anglo American Corporation (based in South Africa) and Lonrho, based in Britain. Landlocked, and with a border with Angola of 1,300 kilometres, all its exports and 95 per cent of its imports at the time of independence travelled east and west through the railway systems of Mozambique and Angola, or south through Rhodesia and South Africa. Access to the coast by the shortest route, through Rhodesia to Beira in Mozambique, was cut off after UDI. By the time of the civil war in Angola, Zambia depended heavily on the Benguela Railway, taking copper from the Copperbelt through southern Zaire, and westward through central Angola to the port of Lobito. Clear passage for Zambia's main export along the Benguela Railway was a chief concern of Kaunda throughout the war. This was made even more urgent by the end of 1974, when a fall in the price of copper, brought about by the international recession, left the Zambian economy in a perilous condition.

The combination of world recession and civil war in Angola made Zambia all the more dependent economically on South Africa. While his army raced towards Luanda, the South African Minister of Economic Affairs visited Lusaka in October 1975 to arrange an export credit deal worth a quarter of Zambia's annual imports: the Kaunda regime was desperate for hard currency. South Africa was believed to have become Zambia's most important foreign supplier (*Economist*, 20 December 1975). Official talk of a boycott of South African goods was dropped, a regular air freight service began between Johannesburg and Lusaka, and there were rumours that South Africa had agreed to finance Zambia's soaring bill for oil (which had increased nearly threefold between 1973 and 1974).

At the same time, Zambia depended for its electricity supply on the Kariba dam, the turbines and switchgear for which lay on the Rhodesian side of the Zambezi river. As David Martin and Phyllis Johnson point out in their study of the war in Zimbabwe,[5] this left Zambia a 'hostage state', at the mercy of the Rhodesian government which 'could cut off electricity at any time, blacking out Lusaka and the Copper Belt, and flooding the mines when the pumps ceased working' (1981, p 130).

Very shortly after independence, Kaunda's government had given permission to Zimbabwean guerrillas to build bases in Zambia for action against the Smith regime. Less than two years later, guerrillas from the two main nationalist parties, the Zimbabwe African People's Union (ZAPU) and the Zimbabwe African National Union (ZANU), which had split from ZAPU in

1963, crossed the Zambezi to prepare for military activity inside Rhodesia, which began seriously in April 1966. In October 1966, the Zambian authorities permitted SWAPO guerrillas, trained in Ghana and Egypt, to set up military camps for action in Namibia, striking through the Caprivi Strip. At this stage Kaunda's government favoured the MPLA in Angola. Host to guerrillas against white-ruled territories on three of its frontiers — in Mozambique to the east, Rhodesia and Namibia to the south, and Angola to the west — the Zambian government attempted to balance contradictory interests, with its political imperatives at odds with its immediate economic needs.

Soon after UDI, Kaunda had sought and got assurances of increased access for trade from the Portuguese dictator, Dr Salazar. Because of these ties with Portugal, and with Lord Colyton, chairman of Tanganyika Concessions (owner of the Benguela Railway), Kaunda was approached by representatives of the Portuguese military in Mozambique to act as a mediator towards the end of 1973, shortly before the coup in Portugal. Kaunda was warned that the regime was about to collapse (Martin and Johnson, 1981, p 127). Early in 1974 he briefed Rowland about his contacts with the Portuguese military (but neglected to inform Frelimo, the nationalist movement fighting in Mozambique).

Through Rowland and Dr Marquard de Villiers, a South African director of Lonrho, Kaunda's information was passed on to the South African Prime Minister B.J. Vorster in Pretoria on 29 March. De Villiers again met Vorster, together with General Hendrik van den Bergh, the head of the South African Bureau of State Security (BOSS), the day before the coup in Portugal. According to Martin and Johnson, 'Lonrho's intention from the outset was to bring Kaunda and Vorster together' (1981, p 129), and it succeeded famously. The subsequent continental strategy of the South African government bears all the marks of a major policy orientation of the secret Afrikaner Broederbond: all the major actors in the South African government were members. It also bears the mark of the international interests headed by Rowland, castigated in Britain not long previously by former Prime Minister Edward Heath as 'the unacceptable face of capitalism'.

Early in July, de Villiers and van den Bergh met in Paris with Mark Chona, special political assistant to Kaunda, and a major figure in the subsequent relations between the two states. Chona then made several visits to meet Vorster in Cape Town to fix this indelicate 'special relationship'. In this way Lonrho provided the 'bridge' (ibid, p 137) to the subsequent Vorster/Kaunda détente that prepared the way for the first South African military invasion of Angola in October 1975. Following a meeting between the Zambian and South African foreign ministers in New York in September 1974, a secret document known as the détente 'scenario' was agreed between Chona, de Villiers and van den Bergh, typed at State House in Lusaka on 8 October, and endorsed by Vorster and Kaunda. This document was the prototype of all subsequent negotiations over Namibia, and expresses the essence of the current [1990] negotiating process over South Africa.[6]

Entitled 'Towards the Summit: An Approach to Peaceful Change in Southern Africa', the document noted that a military solution to problems in southern Africa was 'futile', and that the South African government had called for a meeting between Vorster and Kaunda.[7] The document looked to the release of Zimbabwean detainees and political prisoners, as well as the lifting of the ban on ZAPU (headed by Joshua Nkomo) and ZANU, then headed by the Rev. Ndabaningi Sithole. Leaders from both parties had been in detention in Rhodesia since 1964. The détente document envisaged circumstances in which 'the current armed struggle will be replaced by a new spirit of co-operation and racial harmony…' Zambia 'and friends' would 'use their influence to ensure that ZANU and ZAPU desist from armed struggle and engage in the mechanics for finding a political solution in Rhodesia.' A similar clause relating to South Africa covered 'ANC or other insurgent activities.' In addition Zambia 'and friends' undertook to persuade SWAPO 'to declare themselves a party not committed to violence provided the SAG [South African Government] allows their registration as a political party and allows them to function freely as such' — a minimal concession, since SWAPO was already technically legal within Namibia, despite unrelenting harassment. Point six of the section on Namibia reads: 'SWAPO to desist from armed struggle under conditions in paragraph 5 above.' Martin and Johnson continue:

> SWAPO were not consulted about this commitment being made on their behalf by Zambia and soon thereafter they received a letter from the Zambian government signed by the Minister of State for Defence, General Kingsley Chinkui, ordering them to stop fighting from Zambia. (pp. 138–42)

This order from the Zambian military, expressing the interests of the South African and Zambian regimes, cast the die for the subsequent cycle of purges in SWAPO. Already in September the foreign press corps in Zambia learnt that the government was intercepting international arms deliveries to SWAPO, and reported that it had prohibited all SWAPO military activities from Zambian soil. Nujoma and the Zambian foreign minister, Rupiah Banda (another leading figure involved with the South Africans), publicly denied the reports, despite or rather because of their being true. However, the South African press published the story, together with statements welcoming Zambia's action by General van den Bergh and Jannie de Wet, the Commissioner 'for Indigenous People' in Namibia. Again and again, the diplomatic talents of Nujoma extended to a crude denial of a sordid reality. According to de Villiers, the aim of the détente exercise was 'to sell Mr Vorster to Africa as a moderate and reasonable person'. Indeed he was 'sold'. Within weeks of the drafting of the document, in speeches 'carefully orchestrated as part of the détente 'scenario' (Martin and Johnson, 1981), Vorster spoke of 'bringing and giving order' to close neighbours in Africa, while Kaunda — recently author of a book on humanism — described Vorster's speech as 'the voice of reason for which Africa and the world have waited for many years' (Ibid, pp. 142–44). The siren voice of South African reason and order was to sing through a wasteland. Less than two years later, the regime of this 'moderate and reasonable' person had brought about the massacre of school students in Soweto, and Angola had been laid open, not to permanent revolution, but to permanent warfare. A recent study of modern Africa reports:

> No one can calculate how many billions of dollars Angola has lost in a decade of war nor how many civilians have died. But the effect is clear. The country has returned to the same sort of barter economy the Portuguese found centuries ago. Instead of slaves for trinkets, it is coffee for food. Since so many roads are cut, and so few airplanes fly, communication with the interior is hardly better than it was before colonialism. (Rosenblum and Williamson, p 189)

The genesis of these conditions was at the same time the genesis of the SWAPO spy-drama, the worst of which was acted out in southern Angola between 1984 and 1989.

ENTER KISSINGER, STAGE RIGHT

By October 1974, Kaunda had become particularly disillusioned in the MPLA, then preparing to make its grand bid for power in Angola. According to Bridgland, Reuters correspondent in Lusaka at the time, there had been a 'rapid rundown' in the MPLA's fight against the Portuguese during the early 1970s, as well as 'bitter and bloody strife between its factions on Zambian soil,' including a particularly hideous set of executions of dissidents in August (Bridgland, p 110). As the cycle of violence intensified within Angola, and as the tide of Soviet arms and Cuban troops flowing to the MPLA escalated to fresh heights, Kaunda switched Zambian support from the MPLA to UNITA. By August 1975, Savimbi had the use of a jet on loan from Lonrho, together with British pilots, 'provided by Kaunda's close friend, Tiny Rowland', for his military and political forays around the sub-continent (ibid, p 127): a matter not unconnected with the pivotal place of Lonrho in the détente 'scenario'.

James Callaghan, the British Labour Party foreign secretary, was informed in August 1974, by Chona and Zambia's then foreign minister, Vernon Mwaanga, of Kaunda's approach to Vorster (Martin and Johnson, 1981, p 137). In December, he sent his political adviser, Tom McNally, to Lusaka to 'find out just how far détente had gone' (ibid, p 193). At the end of the year he made a personal visit to southern Africa, and had talks with Kaunda and Vorster. Then, in the spring of 1975, during a visit to Washington, Callaghan sought active support for the Vorster/Kaunda détente from the US Secretary of State, Henry Kissinger (ibid, p. 233). About the same time, on 19 and 20 April, Kaunda visited Washington and was received by President Ford. According to Bridgland,

> While public attention was drawn by a White House speech of Kaunda's, criticising American policy in South Africa, Namibia and Rhodesia, privately he was warning Ford and Henry Kissinger of Soviet intentions in Angola and encouraging them to react effectively and give assistance to UNITA and the FNLA. (p 120)

This discrepancy between 'public' and 'private' was to mark the whole of the détente exercise, including direct military support by the Zambian government for the joint South African/United States military operation against the MPLA in 1975–76. In addition, systematic deceit by the principal SWAPO leaders against their own members — starting from Nujoma at the pinnacle — was printed into the fabric of the organization.

THE STORM IN ZAMBIA

Lusaka was a focal base of intervention of the world bourgeois countries in the civil war in Angola. Between July and December 1975, Brand Fourie, the top civil servant in the South African foreign ministry, made more than twenty clandestine trips to Zambia to see Kaunda. The US ambassador to Zambia, Jean Witkowski, according to Bridgland, bustled around Kaunda's presidential office suite at State House 'as if she owned it. She clearly had been at home there for some time' (p 157). A frequent visitor to Lusaka over this period, in his Lonrho jet, was Savimbi. Stockwell comments:

> The South Africans had some encouragement to go into Angola. Savimbi invited them, after conferring with Mobutu [of Zaire], Kaunda, Felix Houphouët-Boigny of the Ivory Coast, and Leopold Senghor of Senegal, all of whom favoured a moderate, pro-West government in Angola. (p 186)

The initial advance of the South African military into Angola, as it raced towards Luanda in October and November 1975 from its seat in northern Namibia, took place under the guise of being unspecified white mercenaries fighting for UNITA. According to a document issued in December 1975 as UNITA's Official Position on the war, South African troops first entered southern Angola the previous July. A permanent patrol was established on the Angolan side of the Kunene river in August, and a major force of 800–1,000 troops was in place in September (Legum, 1976b, p 36). Given the preceding history of the détente process and the full-scale invasion of Angola that immediately followed, it is not hard to imagine the content of the meeting between Vorster and Kaunda on 26 August on the White Train on a disused railway bridge above the Victoria Falls. This was the meeting called for the previous October in the secret document drawn up by van den Bergh, de Villiers and Chona at State House in Lusaka.

It is not true that this meeting was only a 'new exercise in futility', as Martin and Johnson assert (p 216), or that Vorster and Kaunda acted merely as 'umpire' to the — actually futile — meeting between Ian Smith and the Zimbabwe nationalist leaders, Nkomo, Sithole and Muzorewa (Legum, 1976a, p 23). Shipanga is almost certainly correct: the main event on this theatrical occasion was the separate and secret discussions between Kaunda (accompanied by Chona and his new foreign minister, Rupiah Banda) and Vorster (with van den Bergh and foreign minister Hilgard Muller), in which the 'main topic' could only have been the coming South African invasion of Angola. Shipanga states that officials of the UN Commission for Namibia later reported South African troops moving by truck and air through western Zambia into eastern Angola. Further, the meeting of Vorster and Kaunda could only have 'reinforced their common commitment to put the lid on SWAPO' (Armstrong, p 118).

The relation of the SWAPO fighters to this convergence with UNITA and the South Africans could only have been explosive. In effect, they were now required by the Zambian state to collaborate with the armed forces of the regime they were fighting to overthrow. The equivocal relation of the SWAPO leaders to the basic military dynamic of the organization they had founded now came into conflict with the idealism of the fighters of PLAN and the militants of the SYL in Zambia. With no internal democracy and the refusal of SWAPO leaders to call a national congress, all the elements were in place for rebellion. According to Shipanga,

> Discontent was rising everywhere in SWAPO, but it first manifested itself among the guerrillas and some of their commanders. From 1974 the commanders were travelling more than three hundred miles from the front in

south-western Zambia, where the country borders briefly on Namibia at the eastern end of the Caprivi Strip, to my home in Lusaka to complain of neglect by Nujoma and Nanyemba. (Armstrong, p 100)

SWAPO had in fact been coopted into the 'scenario', and it was resistance to this by the mass of militants in Zambia — together with a few individuals at leadership level, such as Shipanga and Solomon Mifima, a fellow founder of SWAPO and fellow executive member — which produced the misnamed 'Shipanga affair.' It was in truth the affair of SWAPO.

The first fruits of the Vorster/Kaunda détente had appeared in December 1974, when ZANU loyalists in Lusaka were attacked by a group of the guerrilla fighters from the front in Mozambique, led by a senior commander, Thomas Nhari. Martin and Johnson indicate that Nhari had been in touch with Rhodesian military and intelligence since September, 'about the same time as Zambian and South African officials were meeting in New York' (p 159). ZANU survived the revolt, with about sixty deaths from both sides. Then, on 18 March 1975, in one of the seminal events of the détente period, the principal ZANU leader not in detention, Herbert Chitepo — an adamant opponent of the détente politics of the Zambian government — was assassinated outside his house in Lusaka. Nyerere, who at this time also strongly supported détente, had angrily described Chitepo as a 'black Napoleon' because of his insistence on continuing the military struggle (Martin and Johnson, 1981, p 155). By this time Vorster and Kaunda were 'in daily contact through their secret envoys' (*Observer*, 9 March 1975). A week after Chitepo's murder, ZANU leaders meeting in Rhodesia decided to move their base of military operations from Zambia, sending Mugabe and Edgar Tekere secretly out of Rhodesia to a Frelimo camp in Mozambique to begin preparations. This was a military necessity. The day after Chitepo's funeral, the Zambian government had begun mass arrests of ZANU members. Soon over a thousand fighters from ZANU' s military wing were held at Mboroma camp at Kabwe, north of Lusaka: they were not released until nine months later. Rhodesian government and military officials were 'delighted' (*Star*, Johannesburg, 22 March 1975).

In mid-April 1975, top military leaders of ZANU based in Mozambique were lured into Zambia by the government, arrested by Zambian police, tortured, presented with falsified confessions and brought to trial a year later, in the week before Kissinger arrived in Lusaka. In October 1976 the case was thrown out of court, with the judge concluding that one of the accused had been the 'victim of unfair and improper conduct of the part of the police authorities' (Martin and Johnson, 1981, p 181). The judge, afterwards labelled 'anti-Zambian' by Kaunda, further asked the director of public prosecutions to begin proceedings against the police. (Nothing was done.) Thus during the crucial period of the Vorster–Kaunda–CIA détente covering the South African invasion of Angola, a crippled ZANU ceased to be a threat either to the white regime in Rhodesia or to Kaunda's regime in Zambia.

Unable to admit the truth about its own pivotal role in the line-up of world imperialism in Angola — referred to by Stockwell, the CIA task force director, as 'our war against the MPLA' (p 155) — the Zambian government had no other resort except repression and falsification. It faced three potentially dangerous sources of resistance. Firstly, there were substantial bodies of highly politicized, armed and trained fighters on Zambian soil not directly amenable to Zambian *raison d'état*. These were above all the guerrillas of ZANU, then operating out of south-eastern Zambia through Mozambique into eastern Zimbabwe, and the guerrillas of SWAPO, operating out of south-western Zambia into Namibia and penetrating into southern Angola.

The Zambian state's attempt to suborn the military forces of ZANU, and to subordinate it to the détente 'scenario', is described in detail by Martin and Johnson. They reveal the extent of Zambian repression of the ZANU fighters, which was not different to that inflicted on SWAPO shortly afterwards. What differed was the response to it of the top nationalist leadership and the leading guerrilla commanders. Whereas in SWAPO the result was systematic destruction of the most anti-imperialist cadres, in ZANU the outcome was the 'emergence of a strong, radicalized and relatively autonomous' military leadership, which for over a year 'virtually ran the situation on the ground' in Zimbabwe (*Big Flame*, p 10), compelling major concessions for a period by ZANU political leaders to the guerrillas.

Secondly, the Kaunda regime faced rebellion from within its own armed forces. From Bridgland's investigations, it appears that in late January 1976 — after the Clark Amendment in the US Senate had banned all covert US aid to UNITA and the FNLA, and at the very moment when the South African military had begun to withdraw — the Zambian Air Force was ordered to bomb the one important centre on the Benguela Railway inside Angola then not held by UNITA and the South Africans, at Teixeira de Sousa on the border with Zaire. The attack failed. Ordered from State House to return to the attack, the pilots refused, supported by their Air Commodore. Seven men then died in a gunfight in the militarized area of Lusaka Airport. Zambian student leaders secretly described the affair at the time as a 'small mutiny' (Bridgland, p 188).

Thirdly, the Zambian government's collaboration with South Africa, the United States and Britain — which through MI6 and agents of the electronics firm Racal placed long-range radio transmitters for UNITA in Angola and

Lusaka (Bridgland, p 167) — now produced an anti-imperialist rebellious climate within Zambia among the students. In meetings, leaflets and demonstrations, the student union at the University of Zambia in Lusaka condemned the government's support for UNITA, challenging the rule of the weak Zambian bourgeoisie and its monopoly of politics. The students gave voice to the most threatening crisis to date in the existence of the Zambian state, and it reacted with violence. On 28 January 1976, Kaunda declared a state of emergency, attacking an unnamed 'socialist imperialist power.' Students and lecturers were arrested, riot police sent to close the university (which was daubed with pro-MPLA slogans) and the students sent home. The Angolan war had compelled the students' union to 'charge the Zambian ruling clique, headed by Dr Kaunda, "our beloved President", with criminal treachery' (Bridgland, p 180).

BETWEEN IMPERIALISM AND REVOLT

The totality of antagonisms in Zambia, sharply heightened by the war in Angola and the détente scenario of Vorster and Kaunda, became concentrated within SWAPO during 1975. With the Zambian regime as active protagonist, the pressure bearing downward from the major bourgeois states coincided with a countervailing force pressing upward on the SWAPO leaders.

In late 1971/early 1972, Namibia was shaken by the most important labour struggle in the country's history: the strike of the Ovambo contract workers, who, as Soggot writes, demanded 'freedom to travel, to work where they liked, to live where they liked, and to work where the pay was highest' — basic demands against a system of labour control more severe than any existing in South Africa at the time.[8] This was the first salvo of the working class in its series of strikes in southern Africa during the 1970s, resulting in the organization of workers in combative trade unions: a phenomenon that was to change the balance of forces in southern Africa. Then, in April 1974, the officers' coup in Lisbon brought down the Caetano dictatorship, ensuring the emergence of black-ruled states on the borders of South Africa and Namibia, headed by organizations which had undermined Portuguese colonial rule through armed insurgency.

The new working class militancy, followed by the collapse of Portuguese colonialism, radicalized young people in South Africa, especially high school and university students, and acted as a mighty stimulus towards the Soweto revolt of June 1976. The effect was felt even more immediately in Namibia, with student campaigns that were the precursors to the events in Soweto. Both in its labour and its student struggles, Namibia lit the fuse to a mass of combustible material that was later to explode in South Africa. The interconnection between the two fields of struggle, at once so alike and so unlike, will prove a fruitful field of study for future historians. In a chapter headed 'The Young Prophets', Soggot records that the year 1973 'ushered in a startling efflorescence of SWAPO and SWAPO Youth League (SYL) activity' (p 76). Formed in the 1960s, the SYL had been roused by the Ovambo workers' strike to act on its own, independently of its parent body, during the second half of 1972:

> The way the Youth Leaguers went about their work was particularly memorable: they presented their listeners with a remarkable melange of prophecy and challenge. Though not given to the mystical belief that freedom would fall from heaven, many members were gripped by the certainty that 1974 was to be the definitive year of freedom in Namibia... [With] a mixture of interpenetrating fact and optimism, fantasy and political pragmatism, many SYL leaders came to believe and to put out the idea that 1974 was the final year of struggle. (p 77)

Soggot does not refer to the SWAPO crisis in Zambia in 1974–76; but he perceives its source within Namibia itself, indicating that the campaign of the SYL, with its 'promises of imminent messiah-like liberation', gave rise to a 'tactical tension between SWAPO and the Youth League...' (pp. 77–8). This tension within Namibia was reflected in rebellion abroad. Swept forward by the activism of the SYL, large numbers of youth, especially high school students, from a very broad ethnic spectrum, organised resistance within their home communities against the South African regime. They suffered repression and fled abroad to join SWAPO's military wing. Shipanga, in Lusaka at this time, recalls his astonishment as 'one group after another arrived. There must have been about six thousand newcomers between 1974 and 1975' (Armstrong, p 98).

Eager for combat, highly principled, courageous, intensely democratic, the young militants demanded intensification of the war with all the self-confidence of youth, just when the Vorster/Kaunda agreement required that SWAPO be curbed. As one activist in the SYL during that period in Namibia recalls: 'We felt that we had our own destiny in our own hands. Despite South African power and oppression, we felt that we could push it all through.'[9]

In a memorandum to the SWAPO leadership drawn up at the SYL's headquarters in Lusaka on 26 February 1975, the Youth Leaguers in Zambia expressed their 'fear' over the relationship between themselves and 'the comrades who have been here before us', noting 'a gap between us... a result of mistrust or suspicion'. Whenever they asked about something, the memorandum continued, we are accused of being.

1. Reactionaries
2. destroyers of the Party
3. and that we are fighting for power

— *Swapo: The 1976 Anti-Corruption Rebellion*, p 2.

The psychology of the SWAPO leaders against their internal critics is summed up here. This political mind-set, more than anything else, produced the purges of 1984–89. Against this ingrained suspicion, the SYL demanded full internal democracy within their organization. Their standpoint was emphatic and eloquent: 'we deserve every right to ask where we do not understand and to contribute wherever necessary.' These young militants had not left Namibia to exchange South African repression for an equivalent regime in SWAPO. 'We strongly repeat that our right to ask or criticize must not be denied or ignored…The call that "all members are free to challenge" must be put in practice.' Specifically, the SYL demanded information about SWAPO's constitution following its amendment and review at the Tanga congress more than five years previously, as well as requiring information about 'what form of government SWAPO shall establish in Namibia'.

The letter noted that there were times when members in SWAPO camps in Zambia did not have food, some were without clothes and there were severe problems with transport, while at the same time party cars were 'used as individual properties' by leaders. 'Leaders must be good examples,' demanded the SYL, noting that at almost every meeting up to that time the reverse had been the case, leading to 'a spirit of fear among the members towards our leaders'. These were telling demands to place on the leaders of any nationalist movement, ringing with the intemperate spirit of Paris in 1789 — and 1968! This rebuke from the SWAPO youth led to a meeting on 4 March 1975 at Libala in Lusaka between six members of the SWAPO's executive committee (EXCO) and 15 members of the SYL, the 'first of its kind', according to the leader of the SYL delegation, Ms Netumbo Nandi. Nujoma and Moses Garoeb, the administrative secretary, were absent, but among those present were: Shipanga, Mishake Muyongo (SWAPO vice-president, later to play a venal role in the arrest of SWAPO critics, only to leave the organization with his own accusations of tribalism and regionalism in 1980), Peter Sheehama (Muyongo's assistant in the 1976 repressions, now Minister of Security), Nanyemba as secretary for defence, and Peter Mueshihange, now Minister of Defence, whom Shipanga accuses in his book of 'working rackets' in Lusaka with Nujoma and Nanyemba at that time. Shipanga is specific in his charges:

> Nanyemba was very shrewd. He had little formal education, but he was clever. He lived liked a warlord, womanizing and spending money freely. He had many business interests: he was in partnership with Nujoma and Mueshihange in two nightclubs in Lusaka — the *Kilimanjaro* nightclub and the *Lagodara*.
>
> One of Nanyemba's tricks was to order supplies from the biggest chemist shop in Lusaka and to get one of our supporting governments or groups to settle the bill. Next day the goods were on sale in the Second Class Market [the Asian shopping precinct] . . . Nanyemba simply pocketed the proceeds. All this was well known in Lusaka, and there were even jokes about how blankets given by Swedish anti-apartheid groups were making the leaders of SWAPO rich. (Armstrong, p 101)

Charges of corruption were prominent in the criticism of the SWAPO leadership by the youth. At the Libala meeting, the SYL members expressed their 'burning desire to know the constitution of the Party'. A member of the EXCO (no doubt Shipanga) confessed that 'the drafting committee did not meet. *Nothing Is Drafted*.' The minutes continue: 'One member of the EXCO stressed that it is high time that SWAPO should be in possession of the constitution.' It then emerged that the Central Committee had never met since it had assumed office, and that its term of office of five years had expired (so also, therefore, had that of the executive committee). The tone of the meeting was heated. As the minutes report, 'anything short of the immediate calling of the [four months overdue] Congress was not acceptable, one youth shouted'. Severe criticism was made by the SYL of the absence of an acting treasurer-general or an independent auditor. If this was not remedied, the Youth could not rule out 'the suspicion of corruption and misappropriation of funds' (*Swapo: The Anti-Corruption Rebellion*, pp. 4–6).

What cheek! These young upstarts had dared interrupt their elders and betters, the future property-owners of Namibia-in-exile, in their act of primitive accumulation. As the cauldron of civil war in Angola now began to boil over, the young militants of the SYL began an intense struggle against the would-be bourgeoisie of SWAPO before it had even come into being. To the leaders of SWAPO this was more than just a threat, it was an outrage striking against their whole *raison d'être*. It was precisely an audit, financial or political, to which they could not submit.[10]

By the end of 1975, with the South African invasion of Angola in full spate, nothing had materialized from the March meeting of the SYL and the EXCO. On 10 December the SYL in Lusaka issued a follow-up memorandum to the EXCO, reiterating its demand for a congress, accusing the leadership of preventing a congress from being convened, and asserting that its mandate had expired (as it had, a full year previously). The SYL now also cited general corruption, indiscriminate 'round-ups', 'threats', 'oppression' and 'ruthless intimidation.'

Four months later, on 21 April 1976, the Zambian army and police made a pre-dawn raid in Lusaka, arresting 13 Namibians, six of them leaders of SWAPO, including the secretary-general of the SYL and three EXCO members: Shipanga, Mifima and Immanuel Engombe. The South African military had begun its withdrawal from central Angola in January, Savimbi had begun his retreat to southern Angola in February, the tortured ZANU military leaders appeared in court on the same day as the SWAPO arrests and Kissinger arrived in Lusaka six days later (27 April). These arrests without charge or trial of the most influential SWAPO critics secured the political environment for the détente talks in Lusaka between Kissinger and Kaunda.

The six SWAPO leaders were detained in Camp, where ZANU members had until recently been kept (*Swapo: The Anti-Corruption Rebellion*, p 7). By this time the bulk of the ZANU fighters, detained in Zambia since March 1975 following the murder of Chitepo, had been released and had left for Mozambique. The imprisoned ZANU commanders had smuggled a letter from their Zambian prison shortly before the SWAPO arrests, addressed to the front-line presidents, the Organisation of African Unity (OAU) and the UN secretary-general, stating that the Zambian government was 'itself a suspect' in the murder of Chitepo. They were convinced, now more than ever, that it was because of

> the resolute stand against détente and Nkomo which Chitepo and us took, that Comrade Chitepo was killed and we are being processed for our legalized murder. (Martin and Johnson , 1981, p 189)

By now, Robert Mugabe had been provisionally chosen as leader of ZANU by camp officers in prison in Zambia, in place of the more pliable Sithole. The ZANU detainees took this decision after Sithole — secretly chosen by Vorster and Kaunda to govern in a future Zimbabwe, along with Nkomo and Bishop Muzorewa — failed to condemn the killing of thirteen ZANU members by the Zambian army in Mboroma detention camp on 11 September 1975. Sithole's silence on the killing of his own party members by Kaunda's regime, acting for its détente partners, settled his future. Politically, he was finished as leader of ZANU. The lesson was not lost on the leaders of SWAPO. When the Zambian army killed four SWAPO members at the same camp nearly a year later, on 5 August 1976, Nujoma and the SWAPO leaders around him preserved their positions by enforcing a permanent state of siege within the organisation.

Sithole disappeared from view; Nujoma became father of the nation.

In a statement known as the Mgagao Declaration, 'one of the most important documents' of the nationalist struggle in Zimbabwe (Martin and Johnson, 1981, p 200), the jailed ZANU fighters declared Zambia to be 'hostile enemy territory' and called for the OAU Liberation Committee and the governments of Mozambique and Tanzania to evacuate them to a 'safer' country so that they could continue the armed struggle. ZANU's central committee, meeting in Salisbury a week after Chitepo's murder, had already sent Mugabe and Edgar Tekere secretly to Mozambique at the end of March 1975 to prepare for resumption of military activity.

Later, in London, Mugabe stated on the BBC Africa Service on 21 January 1976 that:

> President Kaunda has been the principal factor in slowing down our revolution. He has arrested our men, locked them up, and within his prisons and restriction areas there have been cases of poisoning, and there's also been murders.
> *Interviewer*: By who?
> *Mugabe*: By his men. By Kaunda's army.
> (Martin and Johnson, 1981, p 210)

On the same day, in another interview, Mugabe asserted that the détente exercise had 'caused the death of our Comrade Chairman Chitepo'. Assisted by the presidents of Tanzania, Botswana and also Mozambique (the Frelimo leader, Samora Machel), Kaunda aimed to 'throttle us and throttle us completely.' Chitepo had been murdered 'through or by direct participation of the Zambian government.' The Zambian government had turned out to be 'an enemy of our revolution' (*Revolutionary Zimbabwe*, No. 3, pp. 1–5). As Mugabe pointed out in a speech in London on 30 January, the détente exercise had in fact been 'hatched in the cities of Washington and London' (ibid, p 29): it was to these powers that Kaunda was responding.

Mugabe gave expression here to a very general opinion within ZANU. Within weeks of Chitepo's assassination, an official ZANU publication produced in Sweden accused the Smith regime of having carried out the murder 'with the connivance and complicity of Kaunda', so as to further the 'horse and rider, master-slave détente in Southern Africa' (*Zimbabwe Chimurenga*, March 1975).

From the subsequent detailed investigation of the assassination by Martin and Johnson, Zambian state connivance with Chitepo's killers is not proven but is not excluded. The writers identify the actual killer as Hugh 'Chuck' Hind, a former member of the British Special Air Service (SAS), who had been recruited in Britain in 1967 by Watchguard, a private security firm run by the founder of the SAS, Col David Stirling, as one of a small team of instructors of the Zambian Police Paramilitary Unit and Kaunda's presidential bodyguard. Possibly still while working with Kaunda's bodyguard in Zambia, Hind was recruited to the Rhodesian security body, the Central Intelligence Organisation (CIO), for which he did secret agent jobs on call on a retainer basis after he had gone to live in South Africa. As Martin and Johnson remark, one of Hind's 'very considerable' assets was 'his contacts with the Zambian police and paramilitary from his days as a Watchguard instructor...' (1985, p 52). Hind had no problem flying out of Zambia shortly after Chitepo's murder, later returned 'frequently' to Zambia and was killed in a car crash there on 'one of the missions to Zambia' in January 1977 (pp. 85, 86). It remains possible that Chitepo's assassination was a joint Rhodesian–Zambian state operation, as ZANU radicals suspected at the time.

A year later the Zambian state apparatus was turned on SWAPO. Shortly after the arrests of Shipanga and his colleagues in April 1976, two of the six escaped and secretly told diplomats and the foreign press in Lusaka what had happened. Unlike Mugabe and the ZANU commanders, however, the top SWAPO leaders had actively connived at the Zambian arrests. Shipanga reports that Theo-Ben Gurirab (subsequently Minister of Foreign Affairs in Namibia) visited his house suspiciously late a few hours before the arrests began, and two other SWAPO leaders — Muyongo and Sheehama — publicly supervised their detention. 'Muyongo was in a transport of delight. In his red sports car he drove ahead of the convoy hooting the horn' (Armstrong, pp. 109–10). Shipanga reports having been told earlier that Muyongo, Nanyemba, Ben Gurirab and Dr Libertine Amathila (now Minister of Health) had said they were 'going to arrest me and my group', and that at another meeting before their detention, Sheehama, Amathila and John ya Otto (now secretary of the National Union of Namibian Workers) had 'sentenced us all to death' (ibid, pp. 108, 132). Given the history of arrests and executions within SWAPO, these are matters that require investigation, especially since three of the six people mentioned by Shipanga became government ministers.

The arrest of Shipanga and his colleagues followed a further sharpening of the political struggle within SWAPO, similar to the struggle within ZANU. After the abortive meeting between the SYL and the SWAPO executive in March 1975, the focus of opposition to détente had moved to a still more potent force: the SWAPO military wing, concentrated in Zambia's Western Province. These troops were in camps intermediate between Zambia and areas controlled by UNITA, and within striking distance of the eastern prong of the South African army's thrust into Angola. With the South African invasion of Angola, it became both a political and a military necessity to neutralize them. Together Nujoma and the Zambian army ensured this.

SWAPO'S SECRET WAR

The South African army had moved in strength into southern Angola in September 1975, a month after the beginning of fighting between UNITA and the MPLA.[11] By mid-November a South African motorized column had arrived at Huambo (formerly Nova Lisboa) and Bie (formerly Silva Porto) on the Benguela Railway, half way to Luanda. Under 'enormous pressure emanating from Washington', according to R.W. Johnson, writing not long afterwards, the South African army attempted to hold its forward position on the coastal route to Luanda despite superior MPLA and Cuban forces (p 155).

Some time after this, units of the SWAPO military were ordered into battle in Angola on the same side as UNITA and the South African army, against the MPLA and its Cuban allies. This crucial, hidden episode in the history of SWAPO was the subject of a letter written on 13 March 1976 by members of the SWAPO military wing based in Zambia in Western Province. Addressed to Nujoma as president, the letter of the SWAPO fighters implicated the top leadership. According to the letter, Nujoma had taken responsibility for the Angolan front and Nanyemba for the Zambian front. The then chief of intelligence of SWAPO, Jackson Kakwambi, had himself 'led our fighters to fight alongside the Boers against the MPLA'. Although it was Kakwambi who had given this order to the fighters, it is unthinkable that as chief of intelligence he would have taken such a perilous political step without a policy decision at the highest level of SWAPO. The subsequent purge of SWAPO members who opposed collaboration with the South African army rules out any other interpretation. One can only infer that Nujoma, Nanyemba, Sheehama, Mueshihange and others, under pressure from the Zambian military and from Kaunda himself, ordered this action.

The SWAPO fighters who sent this letter to Nujoma in March 1976 apparently still had no knowledge of the détente operation or the constraints it placed on SWAPO's military struggle against the South African regime. They supported the SYL demand for a national congress and a new constitution, repeated accusations of corruption, denounced the closing down of SYL offices and reported the following bizarre incident:

> **Captured Metal Boxes**
>
> The Investigation Committee has captured two metal boxes ... which were at a certain Island approximately 1000 metres from enemy [presumably South African] bases in Angola. It was guarded by a special group paid by Defence

> Secretary comrade Peter Nanyemba. These guards receive special treatment. On the day when the Investigating Committee captured these Metal Boxes, the Chief in Commander [sic] Awala told the Committee that these boxes contain Party Secret Documents.
>
> (a) Why are the Party Secret Documents kept at the front-line while the headquarters is in Lusaka?
>
> (b) Why are these comrades [the guards] paid although they are Party members?
>
> — *Swapo: The Anti-Corruption Rebellion*, p 8.

The SWAPO fighters were near to mutiny, but on opposing grounds to those of the revolt led by Thomas Nhari in ZANU. They complained that their commanders had given their weapons to UNITA, leaving them without guns. Other weapons had been buried, while they had had to arm themselves with sticks. Some 150 SWAPO fighters had been sent into Angola 'without enough ammunition, weapons, no communication and no food, and their fate is unknown to this date'. Further, a certain Shikangala had been 'given a gun by Peter Mueshihange to kill the comrades who are against corruption'. They protested against public accusations that Shipanga (not yet arrested) was 'collaborating with the enemy.' Against the 'treacherous acts of the commanders,' in whom they had 'completely lost faith', they declared:

> WE REJECT:
>
> A. ANY MISSION ASSIGNED BY THEM,
>
> B. TO BE LED INTO BATTLE BY THEM.

This was, unwittingly, an act of defiance against the détente scenario itself. It could not go unpunished, nor did it.

In another letter, written the same day and addressed to the Liberation Committee of the OAU (which at this period also endorsed détente), the SWAPO military wing in Western Province declared that it had passed a motion of no confidence 'in the leadership of the whole party, and the commanders in particular'. Their arms had been intercepted by the Zambian authorities and their commanders had told them they were 'not allowed to operate from Zambian soil anymore'. They were resolved to go and fight, but not under the present leadership. First they had to reorganize the party through the holding of a congress. Concerning their own safety, they wrote:

> we have 900–1000 ready-trained soldiers without arms or any means of self-defence. We are expecting a surprise attack at any time. The enemy is always shelling in our vicinity. At night we observe flare-lights from the enemy side.

Effectively, they had been disarmed within distance of the South African army and its allies. Their own leaders had placed them in a situation in which they could be massacred at will. Out of desperation, they appealed to the OAU to provide transport to convey food to them at the front 'during the whole transitional period until the congress is held', as well as arms for each soldier and heavy guns for self-defence. This appeal from the expendable victims of détente, an appeal against a cynical act of betrayal, leaves a sickening impression: as also the whole of the subsequent spy-drama, which followed inexorably from the conduct of the SWAPO leaders at this time. The dedication and naivety of the SWAPO fighters had its complement in the duplicity both of the organization to which they belonged and of the OAU, to which they appealed — fruitlessly — against it.

On 23 April 1976, two days after the arrests of the dissident SWAPO leaders in Lusaka supervised by Muyongo and Sheehama, the disarmed fighters on the front again defied what they expected to be their imminent death, this time by execution. From Western Province, they issued 'The PLAN Fighters' Declaration', noting that some members of their committee had already been detained by SWAPO. SWAPO's Political Commissar had told them 'we are going to cut off your heads'.

The whole history of SWAPO, they declared, was 'a tragic one.' In the face of anticipated death, they made a specific statement of their ideals. They gave a detailed account of SWAPO's military collaboration with the South African/UNITA forces and — for the first time in these documents — issued a general declaration of their belief in a socialist future. 'We won't be silenced because of fear to be executed', they stated.

> To be silent means to betray our country. This is a noble task to us, for we believe that Namibia will only be free if these internal enemies are destroyed. We sacrifice to die in order to open and smooth the way to the next generation. To close one's eyes to these evil things means not only to betray Namibia, but also to betray Africa as a whole. Some people may prove us wrong today but history will prove us right. (p 12)

They considered the Angolan civil war to be 'a tragedy to Africa'. Indeed it was, and is, except so far as it served at the cost of immense suffering to wear down (but not defeat) the South African military. Once again, the PLAN fighters expressed their revulsion at being 'forced by reactionary commanders to fight alongside the boers against the MPLA'. They had illusions in the socialist character of the MPLA, whose troops they regarded as 'not only our African brothers, but . . . allies in pursuing socialism . . . our comrades in arms against colonialism, imperialism and foreign domination from the African soil'. While naive in taking the politics of the MPLA at its face value, the declaration called emphatically if simplistically for socialism, against which they contrasted the corruption and property interests of the SWAPO leaders. They had information from reliable sources, they wrote, that there were

> people in the SWAPO leadership who are having farms, hotels, shops and bank accounts, that is why they are less interested in the liberation struggle. When we demand the National Congress where a clear, socialist line be drawn, they consider us enemies, this is because we believe that socialism is a better society. We are against exploitation of man by man and condemn in the strongest terms the exploitation of our mineral resources by foreigners. This is one of the reasons why they don't want the Congress to be held, because they know that in a socialist Namibia there will be no room for private owned shops, hotels etc. (p 13)

The declaration gives extensive details of SWAPO battles against the MPLA in central Angola: at Munyango, Kangumbe, Luso and Serpa Pinto. These appear to have been railway battles, in keeping with the interest not only of UNITA but of the Kaunda regime and its patron, Lonrho. As Bridgland reports, Kaunda had 'stressed to Savimbi the importance of reopening the Benguela Railway' (p 187). The same interest was doubtless stressed, no less forcefully, to the leaders of SWAPO, dependent then on Zambia for their military bases. Luso, Kangumbe and Munyango are station-towns running east to west along the railway. Keeping these open for Zambian (and Zairean) colliery traffic under a UNITA administration was the main concern of the Kaunda regime.

Further west along the line of the Benguela Railway, UNITA had major bases at Huambo and Bie during the period of the South African advance. It was from Huambo that UNITA had declared a Social Democratic Republic on independence day (11 November), at the same time as the MPLA declared the People's Republic in Luanda. Serpa Pinto was the eastern terminal of a shorter, more southerly east-west railway line meeting the Atlantic at Moçâmedes. It would appear that SWAPO troops were committed to battle in early February during the MPLA/Cuban counter-offensive which dislodged the South African army, and with it UNITA, from the Benguela Railway, from Huambo and Bie, and from central Angola. Their role would then have been to help protect the South African army and its UNITA clients in retreat, when they were most vulnerable. It was a complete reversal of the military goal for which the PLAN fighters had left Namibia to join SWAPO.

In each case, the SWAPO commanders in these battles against the MPLA are named: Kakwambi, Nakade, Intamba, Haulyondjaba and Embashu. Details are given about three separate incidents in which UNITA was given truck-loads of SWAPO arms, while SWAPO fighters were in one case left only with sticks.

When they demanded weapons, they were told 'SWAPO is UNITA and UNITA is SWAPO'. In another incident, PLAN fighters say they were 'defending the MPLA flag at Ruyana and Mivungu in a major engagement involving trucks, helicopters and reconnaissance planes, against 'the boers, Shipenda rebels and foreign mercenaries'.[12] The civil war in Angola, which was also a war of the super-powers and thus also an ideological war, had become a civil war within SWAPO, with its troops committed simultaneously on both sides: by coercion on the side of UNITA, voluntarily on the side of the MPLA. It was a critical moment for the SWAPO leadership. Under these conditions, write the PLAN fighters, the SWAPO commanders 'began to hate us' and made a separate base for 'loyal' forces. 'They began to call us rebels and a splitting faction within SWAPO with Andreas Shipanga as president.' At this point the declaration becomes unclear. It emerges — without details — that between fighting in Angola and their subsequent suppression, the PLAN fighters mutinied.[13] They arrested two commanders (Kafita and Ushona), whom they accused of burying arms in the ground. Ten days before Shipanga's arrest, on 11 April, a delegation of 15 PLAN fighters from the rebel camp went to the 'loyal' camp at Shatotua to present their case to 150 fighters and trainees, under the command of a SWAPO officer, Namara, and under the overall control of a Zambian lieutenant with his own troops. The PLAN delegation was overpowered by SWAPO loyalists, seriously beaten up, tied up for a night and a day and compelled to release the 'two corrupted commanders' in return for their own temporary freedom. According to the PLAN fighters, the Zambian troops saved their lives but did not intervene when they were tied up. When they wrote their declaration 12 days later, they expected the firing squad.

Mass round-ups by the Zambian army were already under way, clearly with the agreement of SWAPO leaders, when the declaration by the PLAN fighters was written. By June 1976, well over a thousand dissidents were in the Zambian army's detention camps (*Swapo: The Anti-Corruption Rebellion*, p 16). Nujoma and the exile leadership responded to the threat to their authority by the method of the witch-hunt, with Shipanga cast in the role of Satan.

At the same time two other means were employed by the leaders against their members: a party commission of inquiry, which was not to inquire but exonerate, and the long-delayed SWAPO congress, which was not to express the interest of the membership but to thwart it. In the report of the party commission of inquiry submitted to Nujoma in June 1976 there was no mention of SWAPO's part in the détente process, and only rudimentary references to corruption: wisely for the commissioners.[14]

Shortly before this the SWAPO congress, convening at long last in Walvis

Bay at the end of May, condemned those who had most ardently called for it — then in detention in Zambia — as South African government spies. The participation of the exiled leaders in the Vorster détente strategy, alongside the South African army, together with their corruption, was concealed from the members within Namibia. Only with the detention of a major part of the exile membership could the leaders have safely convened the congress, and then only by staging this fraudulent token of democracy as far away as possible from those who knew what had happened. Nujoma was re-elected president. As the editor of the anti-corruption document wryly observes:

> In telephonic contact with Lusaka, the internal leadership distributed pamphlets describing how the youth were 'misled' by Andreas Shipanga, the arch villain. At public meetings, house-gatherings, and in private conversations an account was given of Shipanga, the Pied Piper of Windhoek, leading two thousand well-trained guerrillas and Youth members against minor problems in the movement. He 'plotted' against the life of Nujoma, et cetera, et cetera. (p 16)

In the same month, leaders of the Youth League arriving from Europe were taken straight from Lusaka Airport to detention. In effect, they were lured by the Zambian state and by SWAPO leaders into a trap — a phenomenon that appeared again in the SWAPO spy-drama in Angola in the 1980s.[15] With the PLAN fighters and the SYL imprisoned in Zambia, the Walvis Bay congress subverted the substance of the demand for democracy by conceding its appearance. It had a strange and horrifying sequel. For many who played a prominent role in organizing this corruption of democracy, or who slandered the Youth League in the interests of the clique around Nujoma, there followed a tragic fate.

Tauno Hatuikulipi, later a member of the Central Committee and the military council, died in a SWAPO prison in Angola in 1984, accused of being a South African government spy. In the 1970s he had been the director of the Christian Centre in Windhoek, a forerunner of the Council of Churches of Namibia which functioned practically as the religious arm of SWAPO. His death was not announced for six months, and it was then alleged that he had died by swallowing poison.[16] Another member of the Central Committee, Lucas Stephanus, was killed by SWAPO in Lusaka the same year, and his body never found.[17] Eric Biwa, also on the Central Committee and now a representative of the Patriotic Unity Movement (PUM) in the assembly in Windhoek, was deported from Cuba to Angola by plane in 1984 with one leg in a plaster cast, detained on arrival and kept for five years in pits in the ground. Benedictus Boois, also on the Central Committee, suffered the same fate. The vice-secretary of the Walvis Bay congress, Othniel Kaakunga, subsequently a member of the

SWAPO Politburo, went into exile and was then tortured and detained for three years, two of them in solitary confinement. Of these, Hatuikulipi, Stephanus, Biwa and Boois had scornfully dismissed a group of SWAPO members, led by Hermanus Beukes, who approached them in Namibia in August 1976, concerned about rumours of impending executions of dissidents (*Swapo: The 1976 Anti-Corruption Rebellion*, p 16).

Having helped to strangle the demand for democracy raised by the '74 Youth League, these internal leaders were caught in the noose they had helped to weave. The accusation 'South African spy' which they had pinned on the SYL and the PLAN fighters in the 1970s came to haunt them in the 1980s. At the same time, the PLAN security apparatus necessarily took on the character of witch-finder general, the grand inquisitor for whom even the slightest sign of mental independence was threatening.

In this it was assisted by its *alter ego*, the South African army. Not long after the May congress, perhaps aiming to inflame internal strife within SWAPO and discomfit the opponents of the now discredited détente strategy, South African forces attacked two camps of SWAPO 'loyalists' in western Zambia on 11 July, killing 24 guerrillas and wounding 45. That, more than anything, wrote *finis* at the bottom of the détente scenario. One of these camps, Shatotua, was the base at which Nujoma's loyalists had captured and nearly killed the members of the PLAN fighters' committee exactly three months earlier, on 11 April. Despite Shipanga having been in detention at this time for 82 days, Katjavivi continues to report — without investigation or even further comment — that 'SWAPO attributes this attack to Shipanga's followers and holds him responsible' (p 107).

By the time of the Shatotua attack, the SWAPO leaders were rapidly adapting to the changed turn of events. They had committed their troops to the losing party in the Angolan war, and had compromised themselves through their association with the South African army: policy blunders which could only be covered over by suppression of the most principled of their members, systematic falsification of the truth and vilification of any critic. It still remained necessary to adapt to the winning side. This Nujoma and his cohorts did with alacrity. Nujoma's alliance with Savimbi had begun in the mid-1960s, when, as Bridgland reports, SWAPO enabled the first trained UNITA fighters to traverse Tanzania and Zambia in order to reach Angola, and when Nujoma provided Savimbi with a Soviet Tokarev pistol (pp. 69–71). Now, with the cry *vae victis* [woe to the vanquished!] in the air, Nujoma threw in his lot with the conqueror, abandoning SWAPO soldiers in UNITA-held regions to their fate. Former SWAPO members say these fighters were killed by UNITA.

Despite continued fighting, the result of the Angolan war in its first phase was clear. By December 1985, the US Congress decided to end all aid to UNITA and the FNLA. As Shipanga explains, from that time

> the Vorster–Kaunda–Ford plan for Angola, with Nujoma in tow, was doomed. Nujoma began detaching himself from the Pretoria–Lusaka–Washington coalition, and by March 1976 he was spending a lot of time in Luanda negotiating with the MPLA and the Russians....' (Armstrong, p 131)

Already in December 1975 he was visiting Cuba and the USSR (*Black Review*, 1975–1976, p 215), and in July 1976 — following an enlarged central committee meeting near Lusaka — SWAPO played the Brezhnev card with a new political programme cut to the changed political situation, adapted specially to its need for bases in southern Angola. It pledged to unite all Namibian people 'particularly the working class, the peasantry and progressive intellectuals' into a vanguard party 'capable of safeguarding national independence and of building a classless, non-exploitative society based on the ideals and principles of scientific socialism' (Katjavivi, pp. 108–9). In the same tones might Mafia Godfathers seek the solace of Mother Church. Having played one side in the cold war system in Angola, Nujoma now reversed his alliances to play the other. Stalinization of SWAPO advanced apace, leading to the crimes of the 1980s.

Only the grisly final act of the Vorster–Kaunda–Nujoma détente required now to be completed. In a press statement on 5 August 1976, Nujoma publicly threatened all the 'dissidents' with death by firing squad, adding the graceless lines quoted at the head of this article: 'The agents of the South African regime and imperialists have been rooted out of our movement, and the Central Committee carried out a systematic purge of all the traitors'. (quoted in Armstrong, p 133)

By this time, in addition to the thousand SWAPO fighters at Mboroma camp at Kabwe, north of Lusaka, a further six hundred returning from training in the Soviet Union had been immediately arrested and also locked up there. On 5 August 1976, the same day that Nujoma made his brutish remark about the firing squad, the starving unarmed guerrilla fighters tried to break out of Mboroma to march in protest to Lusaka. The Zambian army opened fire, killing four and seriously wounding another thirteen. It was a replica of the killing of thirteen ZANU fighters at Mboroma by the Zambian army the previous year. Shipanga reports:

> In documents that they smuggled out of Mboroma, the fighters' complaints were familiar. They demanded a Congress. They objected to corruption in the leadership. They objected to the transfer of SWAPO arms to 'UNITA

> reactionaries'. They wanted the OAU to provide them with trucks so that they could be transported from Zambia to Angola to begin fighting again in Namibia.
>
> Eventually many of them were transferred to Angola, but several went before SWAPO firing squads as soon as they arrived. Many were also kept back in Zambia. There has been very little news of them since, although several are known to have died in detention over the years. (pp. 133–34)

Angola now became the killing ground for the SWAPO leadership, in mockery of the PLAN fighters' illusions about the socialist character of the MPLA for which they had been ready to give their lives. The SWAPO leaders, who directed their troops to fight against the MPLA on the side of the South African army, were now given a free hand by the MPLA to murder on Angolan soil the Namibian fighters who had demanded to fight with the MPLA, against the South Africans and in opposition to the SWAPO leaders. Swapo in Angola became a mincing machine for any member with critical opinions.

Shipanga, whose application for habeas corpus was an embarrassment to the Zambian state, was secretly hustled across the border with his colleagues to prison in Tanzania, where there was no habeas corpus. On 4 March 1978 South African troops slaughtered hundreds of Namibian civilians in a refugee camp at Kassinga in southern Angola. Again, as in the Shatotua killings, Shipanga was accused by SWAPO in radio and press reports of having personally led the South African troops into Kassinga. Despite the fact that Shipanga had been a guest of the Zambian and Tanzanian prison systems for nearly two years at the time of the massacre, and was only released on 25 May 1978, the slander stuck. The SWAPO leaders were diligent students of Goebbels' doctrine of the Big Lie. Shipanga reports that when he eventually returned to Namibia after his release from prison — to commence a political career that actually did involve collaboration with the South African authorities, which he had denounced before — he met 'terrible hostility' from the black population because of his alleged complicity in the massacre at Kassinga (p 142).

The psychopathology of SWAPO in exile lies in its double life as a nationalist movement: as rebel against the South African regime, and as accomplice of that regime against its own members. Discussing his recent novel, *Chicago Loop*, which deals with murder, the writer Paul Theroux has spoken of the fascination of people leading a double life, since here the writer can 'explore the public and private life and the contradictions between them and also the way in which they mesh together' (*W.H. Smith Bookcase*, Easter 1990). SWAPO concentrates within itself the contradictions of the whole genus of nationalist movements which came to power in Africa since 1957, and also of those international agencies, organizations and individuals which support them. In the relation between the apparent rationality of its aims and its psychotic inner life, its totalitarian internal regime and its proclaimed goal of liberation, the needs it purported to address and the self-interest of its leaders, SWAPO provides a laboratory for study of the inadequacy of the existing politics in Africa. It is a form of politics that requires to be submitted to criticism, as a barrier to a genuine emancipation.

As an organization living a lie, SWAPO could only be hyper-sensitive to the opinion of any honest person, or even the gentlest of critics. From this stems its guilty paranoia, its morbid suspiciousness, the stuff of which in governments historic crimes are made. With its para-statal authority — first in Zambia, then in Angola — SWAPO was camouflaged not only by terror and secrecy but by the whole spectrum of late 20th century official society, including states (both bourgeois and stalinist), churches, the United Nations secretariat, the liberal media, Labour and stalinist parties, well-meaning individuals of all kinds and the majority of the 'trotskyist' left. Its true history tells us as much about these agencies as about itself.

Common purpose between the South African regime and SWAPO, as much as their antagonism, acted to produce a common methodology of rule by terror. Its sources are international as well as local. In this way, through the civilizing agencies of the great powers — the USA and the USSR — as well as their medium and lesser acolytes, a process of barbarism was cultivated in southern Africa, now reigning in Windhoek with all the panoply of state. The investigation of Namibia's modern history has barely begun. It has the texture of one of the bloodier of Shakespeare's dramas. That is sufficient for the liberal and socialist luminaries of the universe to find in Namibia the pretext for their suppressed religious zeal.

NOTES

1. Quoted in Armstrong, p 133.
2. According to Shipanga, the Club's name was taken from the Chinese title of a booklet with texts on guerrilla warfare by Mao Zedong and Che Guevara.
3. Nanyemba died in southern Angola in 1983, reportedly in a car crash, after serious disputes between SWAPO's military leadership and the security apparatus.
4. In May this year, following the stalinist collapse in eastern Europe which was its model, Kaunda broached the idea that one-party rule in Zambia come to an end. The problem in relation to many African countries is that forthright representatives of capitalism, such as the British Conservative MP, Neil Hamilton, a 'long-standing Thatcherite radical', are often factually correct, while the left and the reformist centre glamorize despotism.

Concerning Zambia, Hamilton writes: 'All candidates for parliament must belong to his (Kaunda's) United National Independence Party and support the incumbent president. Trade unions also have to be extensions of the UNIP regime; even then, most strikes are banned.

'All national newspapers, radio and television networks are state-controlled. The courts are subject to the president's decree powers and the police have automatic rights to search the individual and his property without a warrant. There is a permanent state of emergency under which the president can order detention without trial of any alleged opponent to the regime' (*Independent*, 5 May 1990). What Hamilton and his kind omit to mention is how serviceable this is to imperialism, that of his country in particular, as the détente operation showed. As for the left and the reformists, most would be outraged — correctly — if the same conditions appeared, say, in Britain. As apologists for despotism, they operate a double standard in relation to Africa, with an actually racist content. The essence of their outlook is that blacks are not fit for anything better.

Author's note, 2009: The role of the Namibia Support Committee in London, which made no response to a letter about SWAPO's purges sent to it by the Committee of Parents in Windhoek in late 1985, deserves particular research.

5. This book provides an understanding of the politics of the sub-continent during the 1970s. Martin covered the Zimbabwe struggle at the time for the *Observer*, Johnson for the Canadian Broadcasting Corporation.
6. Bledowska and Bloch write: 'Bizarrely, Van den Bergh believed that he could torture blacks at home in South Africa but then act as a conciliator for détente with other black African states' (p 89). Van den Bergh not only believed this, he practised it. For two years at least (1974–76), he did reconcile torture and détente. As author and administrator of Vorster's torture system, inflicted systematically on SWAPO members (among them the subsequent Minister of Mines and Energy, Toivo ya Toivo), he succeeded through Kaunda in drawing Nujoma and Nanyemba into Vorster's military strategy. Van den Bergh was the spider at the centre of the web in the SWAPO spy-drama.
7. There is a fascinating but unexplained reference in a table listing meetings in 1974–75 that needs further research. Anglin and Shaw, table 7.1 (p 274), indicates that between 21 and 25 October 1974, a meeting took place in Lusaka between Presidents Kaunda, Nyerere, Machel, and Mobutu together with Chitepo of ZANU and J.Z. Moyo of ZAPU (both later assassinated), as well as the South Africans Oppenheimer and Luyt. This presumably refers to the leading capitalists Harry Oppenheimer and Louis Luyt. If so, it would indicate that direct capitalist involvement in the détente process went far beyond Lonrho. This meeting took place two weeks after the détente 'scenario' had been typed at State House.
8. Soggot acquired first-hand knowledge for this superbly written factual history as senior counsel in trials of SWAPO members in Namibia. People whom he helped save from prison and even from the gallows, such as Victor Nkandi, later died in SWAPO's prisons in Angola. Among those he defended in court against the South African regime was the most prominent leader of the contract workers' strike, Johannes Nangutuuala, whose brother Frans was murdered in Angola after resigning from SWAPO — allegedly by a prominent member of the present government in Namibia (personal communication from Windhoek, February 1990).
9. Interview with Hewat Beukes, London, 8 April 1990. Editor of the pamphlet on the *1976 Anti-Corruption Rebellion*, Beukes is a son of Hermanus Beukes. His older brother

Hans, who had been a member of SWAPO's National Committee in the early 1960s, fled from Lusaka after the 1976 arrests, and his sister Martha Ford — a member of SWAPO's Politburo, and secretary of its Women's Council — was later forced out of SWAPO. Hewat Beukes and his wife Erica were active in the SWAPO Youth League inside Namibia in the 1970s and became leading members of the Workers' Revolutionary Party of Namibia,

10. My thanks to FS for these comments.
11. Oleg Ignatyev, *Pravda* correspondent in Angola, asserts that South African troops crossed the border into Angola to take command of the Calueque dam on the Cunene river on 8 August: in his view 'the beginning of direct South African aggression against Angola' (p 137). Stockwell says the advance into Angola began in the second week of September (pp. 163–4). Johnson gives the date of the initial South African military advance into Angola as 14 July, part of a series of events that 'bear all the hallmarks of Pretoria–Washington coordination' (pp. 144, 147). Marcum indicates that South African troops first crossed into Angola in June. About this time, when military collaboration was being prepared with the South African regime, Savimbi made statements distancing himself from SWAPO (Marcum, p 268). Marcum cites a report in *Die Transvaler* (Johannesburg) in May 1975 on the break-up of the UNITA–SWAPO alliance (note 233, p 441). Reality was more complex.
12. Daniel Chipenda, the former MPLA leader and military commander, subsequently fought alongside UNITA and the South African army. Mivungu is possibly Mavinga, a south-easterly town near the Zambian border.
13. Eight years later, between January and May 1984, the 'overwhelming majority' of ANC military cadres in Angola mutinied against oppressive conditions in Umkhonto weSizwe after fighting against UNITA alongside the MPLA in western Angola (see Bandile Ketelo et al, 'A Miscarriage of Democracy', *Searchlight South Africa* No. 5 — Chapter 2 in this book). The outbreak of mutiny in the ANC military wing, following the mutiny in PLAN in 1976, can only have played a part in setting loose the SWAPO spy-drama of the 1980s.
14. Similarly, there is nothing concerning SWAPO's participation alongside the South Africans in the Angolan war, or of charges of corruption against the main leaders, in the 'official' history by Katjavivi (1988), formerly SWAPO representative in Western Europe and now a deputy in the National Assembly. This contrasts with a factual presentation of the allegations of the SWAPO militants by R.W. Johnson in 1977, only a year after the mutiny. As he notes, since late 1975:

> even the external (guerrilla) wing of SWAPO had been racked by a major split. A large section of the leadership had launched a bitter attack against Nujoma for refusing to call a party congress ... Among the allegations they wished to ventilate at such a congress were their claims that the leadership had connived in Zambian support of UNITA; that arms meant for SWAPO had been diverted by Kaunda to UNITA; that SWAPO forces had actually been ordered to fight alongside UNITA and the invading South African columns in Angola.... (p 254)

Relying apparently on some of the same documents published in Namibia in 1987 by the 'Independent Group,' Johnson's merit as a historian — writing shortly after the events he was recording — was that he took these documents seriously. He was in no doubt of Nujoma's venality as a political leader, reporting Nujoma's threat to punish the dissidents by firing squad. How is one to characterize the subsequent historians who neglect this episode, and Johnson's book? (The author became aware of this passage in Johnson's book only after publication of the first half of this article).

15. Rudolf Kisting, a member of the SYL in Namibia in the 1970s, enjoyed a meal with Nujoma in Harare in the 1980s after returning from study (and marriage) in the Soviet Union. Nujoma urged Kisting to give his services to SWAPO in Angola. This was Kisting's intention in any case. He then flew to Luanda in the company of one of Nujoma's bodyguards, who had been present at the meal, and was arrested by SWAPO security very shortly afterwards. After torture and years in the pits in southern Angola, he was released last year along with other recipients of President Nujoma's hospitality (communication from Kisting's sister, Dr Sophie Kisting, who was present at the meal). The same fate befell Kavee Hambira, then working for the SWAPO radio programme in Luanda. 'In May 1984 I was told by Mr Hidipo Hamutenya that I was to fulfil an assignment for approximately one week in Lubango. I flew from Luanda to Lubango. When I arrived at the airport the chief of security of SWAPO, Solomon Hawala, met me and he immediately arrested me'. (affidavit submitted to the supreme court in Windhoek, 15 September 1989, published in Basson and Motinga, p 176) Hamutenya is a member of the SWAPO Politburo and is now Minister for Information and Broadcasting in government. Hawala has been appointed head of the Namibian army. After torture on a daily basis for ten days and imprisonment in the pits for five years during which time he states Hawala and Hamutenya personally forced detainees to make false confessions on video, Hambira was released in May 1989.
16. Herbstein and Evenson transmit a crucial error of historical fact, which serves to besmirch people such as Hatuikulipi. They write of 'SWAPO's ally MPLA' at the time of the 1971–72 contract labourers' strike in Namibia (p 21). This is incorrect. SWAPO at that time was allied not with the MPLA, which then had minimal influence in southern Angola, but with UNITA: an alliance which SWAPO retained until 1976 when UNITA, with its CIA and South African backers, lost the war (in its first phase).

    This error obscures the nature of SWAPO's relation to UNITA and to the South African army, during the war in Angola in 1975–6. This prevents an undertanding of the evolution of the spy-drama and allows the authors to write of 'the network' in relation to SWAPO's prison victims, as if Hatuikulipi and others were in fact spies (p 168). There is no word in this book on SWAPO's *de facto* convergence with the South African military in Angola in 1975–76.

    Though they deal of necessity with the war in Angola, Herbstein and Evenson do not refer to Marcum 's basic two-volume study, *The Angolan Revolution* (1969, 1978). There they would have read that 'As late as 26 September 1975, the MPLA reported that it confronted hostile SWAPO soldiers in southern Angola' (Marcum, 1978, note 277, p 444).
17. Communication from Othniel Kaakunga, Windhoek, 23 February 1990.

BIBLIOGRAPHY

1. Abrahams, Kenneth (1989), Interview in November, published by *AKOM* Berlin (typescript).
2. Amnesty International (1990), 'Namibia. The Human Rights Situation at Independence', August.
3. Angin, Douglas, and Timothy Shaw (1979), *Zambia's Foreign Policy: Studies in Diplomacy and Dependence*, Westview Press, Colorado.

4. Armstrong, Sue (1989), *In Search of Freedom: The Andreas Shipanga Story As Told to Sue Armstrong*, Ashanti, Gibraltar.
5. Astrow, Andre (1983), *Zimbabwe: A Revolution That Lost Its Way?*, Zed.
6. Basson, Nico, and Ben Motinga [eds.] (1989), *Call Them Spies: A Documentary Account of the Namibian Spy Drama*, African Communication Projects, Windhoek/-Johannesburg.
7. Big Flame, Southern Africa Group (1980), 'Zimbabwe: How Much of a Victory for ZANU and ZAPU?', Conference on Zimbabwe, University of Leeds, June.
8. Bledowska, Celina, and Jonathan Bloch (1987), KGB/CIA: *Intelligence and Counter-Intelligence Operations*, Bison.
9. Bridgland, Fred (1986), *Jonas Savimbi: A Key to Africa*, Mainstream, Edinburgh.
10. Cliffe, Lionel (1980), 'Towards an Evaluation of the Zimbabwe Nationalist Movement', Annual Conference, Political Studies Association of the United Kingdom, University of Exeter.
11. Davidson, Basil (1975), *In the Eye of the Storm: Angola's People*, Penguin.
12. —Joe Slovo and Anthony R. Wilkinson (1976), *Southern Africa: The New Politics of Revolution*, Pelican.
13. Ex-SWAPO Detainees (1989), 'A Report to the Namibian People. Historical account of the SWAPO spy-drama', Windhoek.
14. Helbig, Helga and Ludwig Helbig (1990), 'SWAPO's Violations of Human Rights. An Argument', Akafrik, Munster, May.
15. Herbstein, Denis, and John Evenson (1989), *The Devils are Among Us: The War for Namibia*, Zed.
16. Hodges, Tony (1976), 'How the MPLA Won in Angola', in Legum and Hodges.
17. Ignatyev, Oleg (1977), *Secret Weapon in Africa*, Progress, Moscow.
18. Independent Group, The (1987), *Swapo. The 1976 Anti-Corruption Rebellion: A Fully Documented History*, Windhoek.
19. Johnson, R.W. (1978), *How Long Will South Africa Survive?*, Macmillan.
20. Katjavivi, Peter H. (1988), *A History of Resistance in Namibia*, UNESCO/James Currey.
21. Legum, Colin (1976a), *Vorster's Gamble for Africa: How the Search for Peace Failed*, Rex Collings.
22. — and Tony Hodges (1976), *After Angola: The War over Southern Africa*, Rex Collings.
23. — (1976b), 'A Study of Foreign Intervention in Angola', in Legum and Hodges.
24. Marcum, John (1978), *The Angolan Revolution*, Volume 2: Exile Politics and Guerrilla Warfare (1962–1976), MIT, Cambridge, Mass.
25. Martin, David, and Phyllis Johnson (1981), *The Struggle for Zimbabwe: The Chimurenga War*, Faber and Faber.

26. —(1985), *The Chitepo Assassination*, Zimbabwe Publishing House, Harare.

27. Mercer, Dennis (1989), *Breaking Contract. The Story of Vinnia Ndadi*, IDAF.

28. Political Consultative Council of Ex-SWAPO Detainees [PCC] (1989), 'Murdered by SWAPO', Windhoek.

29. Rambally, Asha [ed.] (1977), *Black Review* 1975–1976, Black Community Programmes, Lovedale, South Africa.

30. Ranger, Terence (1980), 'Politicians and Soldiers: The Re-emergence of the Zimbabwe African National Union', Conference on Zimbabwe, University of Leeds.

31. Rosenblum, Mort, and Doug Williamson (1987), *Squandering Eden: Africa at the Edge*, Bodley Head.

32. Soggot, David (1986), *Namibia: The Violent Heritage*, Rex Collings.

33. Stockwell, John (1978), *In Search of Enemies*: A CIA story, W.W. Norton, New York.

34. ZANU (1975), *Zimbabwe Chimurenga*, Vol. 2, No. 3, Stockholm, March.

35. Zimbabwe Solidarity Front (1976), *Revolutionary Zimbabwe*, No. 3, London.

PRESS

Independent, *Guardian*, *Observer*, *Independent on Sunday*, *Economist* (Britain), The *Star* (Johannesburg).

Author's note, 2009: This article was discussed in a subsequent academic study by Colin Leys and John Saul, *Namibia's Liberation Struggle: The Two-edged Sword* (James Currey, London/Ohio University Press, 1995). The authors, both lecturers at universities in Canada, describe SWAPO's purges of the 1980s as the work of 'a Stalinoid monster' and a 'one-party state in the making,' executed by 'hardline securocrats' ... with their cruel arrogance and their Stalinist mind-sets.' (pp. 56, 57) What they described as 'SWAPO's diplomatic accomplishments' had the effect of masking the 'suppression of democratic politics inside SWAPO'. (pp. 3, 5) In an independent contribution in this book, Philip Steenkamp (also a university lecturer in Canada) wrote: 'Solidarity organizations, driven by liberal guilt, were similarly [like the churches — PT] ineffectual: their fixation on the evil of apartheid blinded them to the terror within SWAPO.' (p 106)

14 *The 'Totalitarian Temptation' in Zimbabwe**

Zanu-PF's rule is founded, as Stalin's was, on the ordinary human emotion of resentment

The decision of the states of the Southern African Development Community to endorse the dictatorship of Robert Mugabe in Zimbabwe under the fiction of a re-run election was anticipated in an analysis of totalitarianism by the English philosopher Roger Scruton.

In an essay, 'The Totalitarian Temptation', delivered in an address in 2003 to a conference on totalitarianism organised by the University of Cracow in Poland (a country that knew both Hitler's and Stalin's boot), Professor Scruton considered the origin of totalitarianism to lie in the ordinary human emotion of resentment. Totalitarianism he considers to be present when there is the 'absence of any fundamental constraint on the central authority.' It is a form of government that 'does not respect or acknowledge the distinction between civil society and the State.... Nothing limits the power of the State in the way that might be limited by a representative legislature or a system of judge-made, or judge-discovered, law.'

Following the model pioneered in Russia by Lenin and Trotsky and perfected by Stalin, its form is as follows: 'Society was controlled by the State, the State was controlled by the party, and the party was controlled from the top by the leadership.' This conception fits the reign of ZANU-PF as led by Mugabe in Zimbabwe.

This party leadership defines itself by its particular ideology. This ideology is 'not a truth-seeking device but a power-seeking device.' It is 'a power-directed system of thought'. Scruton suggests that 'the interests advanced by totalitarian ideology are those of an aspiring elite'. What is important, according to Scruton's analysis, following Nietzsche, is that totalitarian ideologies — like the race and class ideology of ZANU-PF — are 'ways to recruit resentment',

*This first appeared on the `www.politicsweb.co.za` website, 14 April 2008.

or as Nietzsche put it, using a French word, *ressentiment*. This is a 'virulent and implacable state of mind, that precedes the injury complained of'.

Resentment occurs in all societies, but what is unique about totalitarian ideologies is that they 'rationalize resentment, and also unite the resentful around a common cause. Totalitarian systems arise when the resentful, having seized power, proceed to abolish the institutions that have conferred power on others: institutions like law, property and religion which create hierarchies, authorities and privileges, and which enable individuals to assert sovereignty over their own lives... Once institutions of law, property and religion are destroyed — and their destruction is the normal result of totalitarian government — resentment takes up its place immovably, as the ruling principle of the State.'

That is the case in Zimbabwe, with the endorsement of the Southern African Development Community (SADC). Once in power, 'the resentful are inclined to dispense with mediating institutions, and erect a system of pure power relations, in which individual sovereignty is extinguished by central control. They may do this in the name of equality, meaning thereby to dispossess the rich and the privileged. Or they may do it in the name of racial purity, meaning thereby to dispossess the aliens who have stolen their birthright. One thing is certain, however, which is that there will be target groups.' In Zimbabwe, the totalitarian project exercises its right to rule through a combination of the two forms, the appeal to equality and to race (and, more specifically, but implicitly, to tribe). It unites both the Stalin (hostility to privilege) and the Hitler (hostility to race) forms. As such, it is 'directed collectively against groups, conceived as collectively offensive and bearing a collective guilt'.

As Scruton argues, this project is 'not conducted from below by the people, but from above, in the name of the people, by an aspiring elite'. Totalitarian ideologies, very widely endorsed in southern Africa, as the decision of the SADC shows, 'legitimize the resentments of an elite, while recruiting the resentment of those needed to support the elite in its pursuit of hitherto inaccessible advantages. The elite derives its identity from repudiating the old order. And it casts itself in a pastoral role, as leader and teacher of the people', as if it were a 'priestly caste'. The elite then 'justifies its seizure of power by referring to its solidarity with those who have been unjustly excluded'.

The leader of such a totalitarian project, according to Scruton, is frequently an embittered and isolated person, who seeks 'some opportunity to take revenge on the world that has denied him his due'. Such people are 'fired by a negative energy, and are never at ease unless bent on the task of destruction'. When such a person achieves power, he will 'compensate for his isolation by establishing, in the place of friendship, a military command, with himself at the head of it. He will demand absolute loyalty and obedience, in return for a share in the reward. And he will admit no one into his circle who is not animated by resentment, which is the only emotion that he has learned to trust'. Such a characterisation suits Mugabe.

The political project of this leader 'will not be to gain a share of power within existing structures, but to gain total power, so as to abolish the structures themselves. He will set himself against all forms of mediation, compromise and debate, and against the legal and moral norms which give a voice to the dissenter and sovereignty to the ordinary unresentful person. He will set about destroying the enemy, whom he will conceive in collective terms, as the class, group or race that hitherto controlled the world and which must now be controlled. And all institutions that grant protection to that class or a voice in the political process will be targets for his destructive rage.'

At this point Scruton very precisely identifies the sham and scam that the electoral process has revealed itself to be in Zimbabwe, as a typical feature of the totalitarian regime. He writes that the inevitable result of the seizure of power in this project will be the 'establishment of a militarized core to the State — whether in the form of a party, a committee or simply an army which does not bother to disguise its military purpose. This core will have absolute power and will operate outside the law. This law will itself be replaced by a Potemkin version that can be invoked whenever it is necessary to remind the people of their subordinate position.'

In citing this 'Potemkin version' of law, Scruton refers to the supposed tricky practice of Prince Grigori Aleksandrovich Potemkin when acting as chief minister to Empress Catherine the Great of Russia, who held absolute power in the late 18th century. The Russian peasantry lived in abysmal poverty and shabbiness. Empress Catherine wanted however to believe that everything was for the best under her enlightened government. Potemkin was alleged to have squared the circle by having fake, cardboard villages erected along the route the Empress travelled on her tour of the Crimea. Constitution, law and elections in Zimbabwe are a Potemkin village. By implication they are also actually or potentially so throughout the states of the SADC, South Africa included, their leaders having so crassly endorsed Mugabe's Potemkin-type electoral scam.

As Scruton writes, under the totalitarian regime this 'Potemkin law' will be a 'prominent and omnipresent feature of society, constantly invoked and paraded, in order to imbue all acts of the ruling party with an unassailable air of legitimacy. The 'revolutionary vanguard' will be more prodigal of legal forms and official stamps than any of the regimes that it displaces.... In this way the new order will be both utterly lawless and entirely concealed by law.' In this way, as Scruton quotes the former President of the Czech Republic, Václav Havel, the people oppressed under the totalitarian regime are required to 'live within the lie'.

Scruton gives also a telling characterisation of the Mugabe type. He notes the pathological character of the resentments carried by the great leader in the totalitarian project, people who 'have an exaggerated sense of their own entitlements, and a diminutive capacity to observe them... Their resentments are not concrete responses to momentary rebuffs but accumulating rejections of the system in which they have failed to advance.' Intellectuals, it seems, are 'particularly prone to this generalized resentment.... Hence we should not be surprised to find intellectuals in the forefront of radical movements, or to discover that they are more disposed than ordinary mortals to adopt theories and ideologies that have nothing to recommend them apart from the power that they promise.'

This fits Mugabe to the tip of his little moustache.

[Roger Scruton's essay, 'The Totalitarian Temptation' is in Roger Scruton, *A Political Philosophy* (Continuum, London and New York, 2006. pp. 146–160)]

About the author

Paul Trewhela was born in Johannesburg, South Africa, in 1941.

His parents were active in cultural life in Johannesburg.

In the early 1950s they received a bequest for his education from Morris Isaacson, a family friend who provided funds for establishing the Morris Isaacson High School in Central Western Jabavu, Soweto, the second school to join the school students in Soweto demonstrating against Bantu Education on 16th June 1976.

Paul Trewhela attended the Ridge School, Johannesburg (1952–54) and Michaelhouse in KwaZulu-Natal (1955–58), which in June 2008 presented him with the St Michael medal for service to his fellows 'of an exceptional and selfless nature.'

He studied for a BA degree in English and Political Science at Rhodes University, Grahamstown, Eastern Cape (1959–61), where he became active in student politics following the massacre at Sharpeville in March 1960.

In 1960 and 1961 he was elected a non-voting member of the executive of the National Union of South African Students (NUSAS) as representative for the Eastern Province. This took him to Fort Hare University College in Alice for secret night-time meetings on the campus with student members of the African National Congress.

Trewhela was sacked from his first job as a trainee reporter with *The Star* newspaper, Johannesburg, which began in January 1962, following arrest and trial on two occasions in Cape Town while on a journalists' training course after he had become a member of the Congress of Democrats (COD), the white section of the still racially segmented Congress Alliance. He was arrested in the course of protests by COD against provision for detention without trial (and torture) under the General Law Amendment Act of 1963 (the 'Sabotage Act' or '90-day Act').

He was then given employment as a reporter on the *Rand Daily Mail* in Johannesburg by its courageous editor, Laurence Gandar, one of the great editors internationally at that time. A year later he was employed in Johannesburg as Africa Editor on a news magazine, *News/Check*.

Over the same time he was recruited as a member of the illegal South African Communist Party by Joe Slovo, later the SACP general secretary.

He began underground journalism for the SACP, the ANC and their military wing, Umkhonto weSizwe, under the direction of Ruth First, who was later assassinated by South African state security agents in Maputo, Mozambique, in 1982. A leaflet written by Trewhela at Ruth First's request was published and distributed by Umkhonto weSizwe in May 1963, a month before the raid on its underground headquarters at Liliesleaf Farm at Rivonia, Johannesburg, which resulted in the Rivonia Trial.

After Ruth First's release from detention and departure for exile, he continued underground journalistic work for Umkhonto weSizwe under the direction of Hilda Bernstein, whose husband, Rusty, was one of the accused in the Rivonia Trial. This was as editor of *Freedom Fighter*, the underground journal of Umkhonto weSizwe. *Freedom Fighter* survived four issues before arrests finished it off.

Arrested by the security police during mass raids in July 1964, Trewhela was held in solitary confinement for 53 days and subjected to two periods of interrogation by means of standing torture at Compol (Commissioner of Police) Buildings in Pretoria, one lasting for three days and nights..

He was then charged with membership of the Communist Party in a large trial which began in November 1964, in which the number one accused was Bram Fischer QC, the chairman of the SACP, who had led the defence in the Rivonia Trial. Fischer absconded from the trial in order to attempt to re-organise the shattered underground structures, but was sentenced to life imprisonment when later re-arrested.

Following eight months on remand with trial colleagues in The Fort prison, Johannesburg, Trewhela served two years in Pretoria Local and Central Prisons, at one stage sharing a cell with Fischer. A disagreement with Fischer concerning his right to talk freely with a political prisoner in bad grace with the Communist Party led to Trewhela resigning from the party while in prison, a matter concluded in discussions with Joe Slovo and Ruth First in London on his arrival there in exile in June 1967.

Later that year, while a post-graduate student at the University of Sussex, Trewhela left the ANC Youth and Students Section in London together with Moeletsi Mbeki, the younger brother of the subsequent South African President, Thabo Mbeki, and the subsequent Arts and Culture Minister, Dr Zweledinga Pallo Jordan. Together they opposed the Soviet invasion of Czechoslovakia in August 1968: the invasion was endorsed by the SACP and the ANC.

The following year Trewhela began work as a schoolteacher, mainly in state schools in England. As a trotskyist opponent of the stalinist form of regime in the Soviet Union, to which the SACP was committed, the break-up of his South African political connections led him to leave Britain for Ireland in 1974 for nine years, an experience he regarded as one of 'exile from the exile'.

On returning to Britain with his family in 1983, he formed a close friendship in London with a former prison colleague, Dr Baruch Hirson, following completion of Hirson's nine-year sentence for leadership of a non-Communist sabotage organisation, the National Committee for Liberation (later called the African Resistance Movement). Having transformed himself while in prison from a physicist into a historian, Hirson was the premier trotskyist political activist and thinker in South Africa.

Hirson and Trewhela together founded a banned exile journal, *Searchlight South Africa*, produced by desktop publishing from a front room in Hirson's London home between 1988 and 1995. With the great bulk of its material written by themselves, *Searchlight South Africa* was unrivalled during the transition period from apartheid for its independence of spirit, the quality of its research and the character of its writing over the transition period from apartheid. Prohibited from commercial distribution in South Africa, it had severe problems in securing funding and in reaching a wider readership, however. Its work on the ANC and SWAPO is discussed more fully in the Introduction.

From 1993, Trewhela placed more than 30 obituaries of South African political figures in the *Independent*, London. Occasional articles by him appeared also in journals such as the *Sunday Times* (Johannesburg) and the *New York Review of Books*.

From 2007 he began contributing numerous articles to the South Africa-focused website, Ever-fasternews.com (now available as an archive), edited by Stanley Uys and James Myburgh, and to Politicsweb.co.za, edited by James Myburgh in Johannesburg. These articles cover the watershed in South African political life following the ending of apartheid, marked by the deposition of Thabo Mbeki as President and the accession of Jacob Zuma.

In 2006, Paul Trewhela and Florence Duncan were married in Aylesbury, Britain. Flo Duncan had been a co-defendant in the SACP trial of 1964/65, and had served two years in Barberton women's prison. He has five children from a previous marriage.

Paul Trewhela is a painter. He has exhibited in group and solo exhibitions in Britain.

Index

In compiling the Index, an attempt has been made wherever possible to align real names to Umkhonto weSizwe 'travelling names' or *nommes de guerre*, using the ANC submissions to the TRC. The travelling name is given after the real name, in square brackets containing the letters 'MK'. A number of terms have been omitted for lack of space.